Thinking Faith

Anthony J Kelly CSsR

Scholars Collection

1. *Opening the Scripture*, 2014, Antony Campbell SJ

2. *Amplifying that Still Small Voice*, 2015, Frank Brennan SJ

3. *Gospel Interpretation and Christian Life*, 2017, Francis J Moloney SDB

4. *The Natural World and God: Theological Explorations*, 2017, Denis Edward

Thinking Faith:
Moods, Methods, and Mystery:

Selected Essays

Anthony J Kelly CSsR

Adelaide

Text copyright © 2017 remains with Anthony J Kelly for all papers in this collection. All rights reserved. Except for any fair dealing permitted under the Copyright Act, no part of this book may be reproduced by any means without prior permission. Inquiries should be made to the publisher.

Unless noted otherwise, the Scripture quotations contained herein are from the New Revised Standard Version of the Bible, and the Revised Standard Version of the Bible copyright © 1989, and are used by permission. All rights reserved.

Layout, in Minion Pro 11, by Extel Solutions, India.

Published by:

An imprint of the ATF Press Publishing
Group owned by ATF (Australia) Ltd.
PO Box 504
Hindmarsh, SA 5007
ABN 90 116 359 963
www.atfpress.com
Making a lasting impact

Dedicated to friends

and

colleagues over many years,

Brendan Byrne, SJ,

and

Francis J Moloney, SDB

Men of Wisdom

Servants of the Word

Witnesses to the Light

Table of Contents

Acknowledgments	ix
Preface	xi
Introduction	xiii
1. The Incarnation and Human Sensibility	1
The Pope's Day of Peace, ASSISI 27 OCTOBER 1986	16
2. Making the Resurrection Intelligible—Or Intelligence 'Resurrectional'?	17
Beginning Again	47
3. Exploration into God	49
Letter to the Hebrews (Hb 12:18–24)	66
4. Christ, Risen and Ascended, and Interfaith Dialogue	69
John The Baptist	84
5. Creator and Father Almighty	85
Bede	113
6. Trinitarian Connections: Inside Knowledge	115
Brother Anthony	140
7. By Way Of Negation: Biblical and Philosophical Perspectives	141
Strange Universe	163

8. The Exegete and The Theologian: Is Collaboration Possible? ... 165

    Derrida at Monash For KH ... 176

9. Refreshing Experience: The Christ-Event As Fact, Classic and Phenomenon ... 177

    Lost Art ... 196

10. Mary, Icon of Trinitarian Love ... 197

    Messiah ... 224

11. Faith Seeking Fantasy: Tolkien on Fairy-Stories ... 225

    Ron ... 245

12. 'Come Holy Spirit, Renew The Face of the Earth!' Invocation: Holy Space and Crying Need ... 247

    Monastique ... 266

    Transfiguration ... 267

Indices

    Index of Names ... 269

    Index of Biblical References ... 273

Acknowledgments

Some of this material has been previously published in other books or journals, at least in an original version. I am grateful to the editors concerned.

'The Incarnation and Human Sensibility', in Robin Horner, David Kirchhoffer, Patrick McArdle (eds), *Being Human: Groundwork for a Theological Anthropology for 21st Century*. (Melbourne: Mosaic Press, 2013), 145–160.

'Making the Resurrection Reasonable—or Reason "Resurrectional"?' in J Bloechl (ed), *Christianity and Secular Reason. Classical Themes and Modern Developments* (Notre Dame, IN: University of Notre Dame Press, 2012), 187–216

'Exploration into God' [not previously published]

'Christ, Risen and Ascended—and Interfaith Dialogue', in *AEJT* 20/12 (June 2013): 180–184.

'Creator and Father Almighty' [not previously published]

'Trinitarian Connections: Inside Knowledge' [not previously published]

'By Way of Negation: Biblical and Theological Perspectives', [not previously published]

'Beyond Locked Doors: The Breath of the Risen One', in Scott Cowdell, Chris Fleming and Joel Hodge (eds), *Violence, Desire and the Sacred: Girard's Mimetic Theory Across the Disciplines* (New York, NY: Continuum, 2012), 69–85.

'The Exegete and The Theologian: Is Collaboration Possible?', is revision of a longer version of 'Dimensions of Meaning: Theology and Exegesis', in Rekha M Chennattu and Mary M Coloe (eds), *Transcending Boundaries. Contemporary Readings of the New Testament*. (Rome: LAS, 2005), 41–56.

'Refreshing Experience: The Christ-Event as Fact, Classic, and Phenomenon', in *Irish Theological Quarterly*, 77/4, November 2012: 336–348.

'Mary and the Creed: Icon of Trinitarian Love', is an extensive reworking of an article from the *Irish Theological Quarterly*, 69 (2004): 17–30.

'Faith Seeking Fantasy: Tolkien on Fairy Stories', in *Pacifica*, 15 (June 2002): 190–208

'Come, Holy Spirit: Renew the Face of the Earth' [given on an ecumenical occasion]

Preface

I first encountered Tony Kelly back in the early 1970s when I was a senior seminarian and he a young theologian recently returned from study overseas and assigned to teach us Christology at Catholic Theological College in Melbourne. Little did either of us know then how closely our lives would interweave through the years.

Tony and I worked together closely through the time he was President of Yarra Theological Union and I the Master of Catholic Theological College. We had a shared vision of what was possible for theological education in Melbourne and beyond. That vision never quite came to pass but the friendship was sealed, and that was achievement enough. Tony was one of my chaplains when I was ordained bishop years later, and he lived with me for a time in Archbishop's House in Canberra when we both ended up there. To me he has been teacher, mentor, friend, adviser and much else to boot.

But Tony has been many things to many people through the years: priest, theologian, preacher, teacher, poet and even painter. He has always been a prismatic presence—turn him one way and you see one thing, turn him the other and you see something else. In that, he is not unlike the founder of the Redemptorist congregation to which he belongs, St Alphonsus Liguori who was himself a man of many parts: pastor, moral theologian, hymnographer and much else. Something of the saint's DNA has emerged in Tony Kelly, as the essays contained in this volume make clear.

The title of this collection, 'Thinking Faith', suggests the intellectual rigor and the quality of belief that have always characterised Tony's work. The sub-title, 'Moods, Methods and Mystery', suggests the more poetic, even lyric impulse which has also marked his writing. In fact, the combination of argument and poetry as voices of faith lies at the heart of what Tony has offered not only in the essays published here but throughout his long publishing life.

In his writing, teaching and especially his supervising of research, Tony has been an outstanding figure in the academy, but he has also been very much a man of the Church. This was perhaps clearest in the years when he was a member of the International Theological Commission, where his service became more global. It is not always easy to hold academy and Church together; but few have done it as gracefully and successfully as Tony Kelly.

Perhaps the last and best thing that might be said of this prismatic figure is that he is a human being. As I have grown older, I have come to see that the art of being truly human is the most difficult of all to learn. It takes a lifetime, and these essays trace key elements of Tony's own long journey into the humanity from which his work comes and to which it returns. They suggest what it means to be in the world but not of it.

Tony has often mused about the future of theology in Australia, and rightly so as the scene here continues to change in ways we scarcely imagined years ago. One thing is certain: theology in Australia in the future will be different from what it has been in the past. It will not perhaps produce figures quite like Tony Kelly. But what is equally certain is that, in the midst of all the flux, theology in the future will have to learn from what Tony Kelly has taught and seek to embody in new ways the great legacy of wisdom to which this collection attests.

Archbishop of Brisbane
16 June 2017

The Most Reverend Mark Coleridge
GPO Box 282, Brisbane Qld 4001 Australia
Telephone +61 7 3324 3324 archbishop@bne.catholic.net.au

Introduction

The title of this collection of essays is *Thinking Faith: Methods, and Mystery*, and it might need a word of explanation. The aim is to suggest something of what is involved in 'thinking faith', while indicating examples of my modest contribution over all these years. Given the exuberant data of faith, beliefs, doctrines and tradition, the task of the theologian is always to reflect on what is so richly given, and to communicate in the most telling fashion its meaning. There are certainly *moods* that colour the way we think, even though theological writing must show an intellectual concentration of some kind. That is quite compatible with a great variety of approaches, sometimes more hopeful, sometimes more sober, defensive and argumentative. But whatever the mood, our theological efforts must always be focused on the inexpressible richness of what the faith has revealed. I hope, then, that the reader will notice the variety of moods and mentalities animating these essays.

But there is also the question of *methods*. The strange thing about a particular theological method or style of thought is that it is seldom an explicit series of procedures. It is something more spontaneous and formed through the practices of many years. Quite clearly, in this collection of writings a number of methods is implied. The metaphysical and contemplative approach of St Thomas Aquinas is always present, at least beneath the surface, as is Bernard Lonergan's theological method as a framework for collaborative creativity—as outlined in his *Method in Theology*. Lonergan's framework has been of immense value to me over the years, especially in its analysis of the human consciousness implied in all our knowing and willing and doing. Likewise, his presentation of the gift of grace as the transformation of that consciousness has been singularly illuminating. There are course other methods and in more recent years, I have learnt a great deal from continental phenomenology, mainly in the writings of Jean-Luc Marion, Claude Romano, and Kevin Hart. Kevin has been a friend of many years, and is now resident in America. I remain amazed at his extraordinary poetic achievement and his critical contributions to great swathes of modern theological, philosophical, and literary thought.

Whatever the mood, whatever the method, the *mystery* remains—of God, Christ, and who we are in that light. To this degree, theology is a way of thinking *within* mystery, not outside it. In this respect, doing theology is humbling for us theologians when confronted with the limited span of our knowledge—and our poor capacities to express it. There always remain infinite expanses of what is not yet given us to see, so to leave theologians, inarticulate, in splendid defeat. And yet so much has been given, even in the most routine life of the Church, in its Scriptures its sacraments, and in the luminous witness of the many who have gone before us, and live now in the light.

One of the essays in this collection is called 'By Way of Negation'. It draws attention to the darkness that surrounds the knowledge of faith and the theologies it inspires. That blessed darkness will never allow us to think that we can, in any way, encapsulate the mystery of God in human meaning, try as we may, and even as we must. Anything I might say about theology would be quite defective if it left out an essential awareness of the mystery in which we live and move and have our being.

But it is one thing to talk about the title of this collection, and another to make a few remarks about the origins and influences that have formed the writer. Many years ago, I grew up in the shadow of the Redemptorist Monastery in Mayfield, Newcastle. That happy circumstance resulted in me joining that religious order and in being set on the road to assimilate, ever more deeply, the Redemptorist motto, *Copiosa apud eum redemptio*, ('with him there is plentiful redemption'). Being a Redemptorist meant belonging to an international congregation with its increasing contacts in the many countries of Asia, Europe, America and Africa. Such a form of belonging was a strange blend of the local and the international. In terms of the local, I think it gave me the beginnings of an ecological consciousness in the years I spent at St Clement's College, Galong, NSW, followed by the novitiate set in the bush wonderland around Pennant Hills outside of Sydney, and then, Wongarra, on the Great Ocean Road, during the long summers of my student years. Then, in the seven year course of studies in Ballarat at the House of Studies of our order, I was exposed to a number of remarkable teachers, eminent among whom was Kevin O'Shea, CSsR, my first and greatest teacher in theology. Of course this was a time when the Church was building up to the Second Vatican Council, and that made it difficult to fix a date for our ordination by the local bishop. Eventually, that happened and on 30 June 1963, I was ordained by Bishop O'Collins in Ballarat—on the very day that Pope Paul VI was crowned (the last papal coronation). I like to think that somehow I shared in the wisdom of that great Pope, and perhaps even something of his modest infallibility! It is hard to recapture the sense of excitement and novelty that Vatican II brought into the Church. As it turned out, during my time in Rome, the organisation of one of the daily Council masses had been assigned to the Redemptorists, with the result that I found myself reading the gospel to the assembled council fathers. After that, I struggled shamefully in my efforts to put a mitre on the missionary bishop who was presiding—quite a disruption for that good man who, no doubt, was feeling honoured to celebrate Mass in St Peter's on that day in the presence of his fellow bishops.

In the meantime, I studied for my doctorate at the Anselmianum—in those days quite a centre for theology, under the direction of Benedictines from all parts of Europe and the Americas. My thesis director was a young Swiss Benedictine, Dom Magnus Löhrer, who with wisdom and patience navigated the shoals of having me as his first doctoral student. Within a few years I was doing postdoctoral studies at St Michael's College University in Toronto, at a time when the richness of its faculty was truly extraordinary. Thereafter most of my teaching life was passed in Melbourne's Yarra Theological Union in the Melbourne College of Divinity, and in 1980 I was made president there before going on a sabbatical to Paris. On my return, I continued to be president of that lively institution which was, from year to year, a miracle of improvisation. This was a time when theology was becoming more available option for the laity in the Church and for women in particular. I was always grateful for the energy and inspiration deriving from Yarra Theological Union!

Eventually, after a sabbatical at Boston College, I moved to Australian Catholic University as the Professor of Theology in 1999, and have been there, one way or another, ever since. These university years gave me the opportunity for a greater productivity in my theological career: there followed many books and articles, some of which appear in this collection.

Over the years, I lived for more or less extended lengths of time in different countries in Europe, Asia and in North America. Owing to the strong involvement of the Redemptorists, in the Philippines and in Malaysia-Singapore, I became aware of cultures and Church struggles that were far from my experience in Australia, or even in Europe. The career of a theologian these days is inevitably marked by international experience, which can serve as a broadening of the mind, along with an increased sensitivity to other cultures and peoples. I have often wondered how my privileged situation was in contrast to the experience of the great theologians who thought and worked and prayed in the cauldron of war in Europe in generations past. It seems to me that the theologians of today, at least in the English-speaking world, have had a more peaceful existence, and perhaps a more international one; though I cannot but think that our distance, historically and geographically, from situations of violence, dramatic conflict, persecution and the horror of war, has left us with a somewhat bland mentality compared to our colleagues suffering behind the Iron Curtain and even in South America.

I realise that to be a theologian is to serve the faith in a given situation and in dialogue with a given culture, so that a certain patience and acceptance is of the essence. At different times, I made considerable effort to identify the religious situation here in Australia, as in my *A New Imagining: Toward and Australian Spirituality*.[1] After all, in contrast to Europe, here Christmas is in summer and Easter in autumn, while the South wind blows cold. A comparatively brief history of European settlement stands against the backdrop is 40,000 year history of indigenous presence in this land. This is beginning to be far more deeply understood and appreciated today—with considerable effect on the theological approach to the present and past reality of the Aboriginal peoples. Today's theologians are beginning to understand more deeply the significance of how these original inhabitants dwelt in this land with song and dance and that exuberant and

---

1. Tony [Anthony J] Kelly, *A New Imaging: Toward and Australian Spirituality* (Melbourne: Collins Dove, 1990).

distinctive symbolic world of the 'Dreaming'. A renewed appreciation of the Aboriginal presence on this continent serves as a model in many ways for the Christian encounter with other faiths and religions in other parts of the world today.

A further influence on my theological career was my appointment to the International Theological Commission (ITC), from 2004 to 2014. Admittedly, its great days were beginning to pass. Under the chairmanship of the then Cardinal Joseph Ratzinger, the ITC continued as a deliberative body and produced some influential documents. But times changed, Cardinal Ratzinger became Pope Benedict XVI, and while the theological membership of the commission was increasingly inclusive and international, the time of the great European theologians had passed. Still, the annual meetings of the commission provided an opportunity to meet colleagues from other countries and cultures, and even a succession of popes during that time, not to mention the great variety of visitors who passed through Casa Santa Marta—members of other commissions, visiting cardinals and bishops, and public figures: on one occasion that meant having breakfast with Henry Kissinger!

The dozen or so articles in this collection are interspersed with some of my poems, written over the years and published in various forms. Adding the poems was an editorial suggestion. It was thought to be a good idea, but that remains to be seen. It is true that sometimes, to my annoyance, readers considered that my theological writings were 'poetic'. That may be so, but my intention all along was to give the most worthy expression to the theological topics being considered. Perhaps I gave the impression that my way of writing was not sufficiently academic and too imaginative. I must plead guilty—even while recognising that ordered, expository prose is the usual mode of theological discourse and the most helpful.

Then again, the connection between poetry and theology is a complex subject. Some of the poems suggest as much, expressing 'a strange confiding gift/flowing with a more elements,/and welling up from where forgotten things/are felt, and spell, in a giving too deep to be one's own/existence, if only for the moment,/ irresistibly ecstatic' (*Address for a Special Occasion*). There is some grace in simply waiting for something to be given: '. . . to write freely/not knowing what you have to say,/but being written in a way . . . /Lowercase inspiration you might call it . . .' So that, 'the times being as they are,/to wait, pencil poised, or fingering a keyboard,/listening . . .' (*Beginning Again*). Or, with John the Baptist, realising that 'it's different now:/reality is so climactically appalling' (*John the Baptist*).

Karl Rahner has written movingly on poetry as a kind of training and sensitising of the mind for faith.[2] More to the point, if theology is to be based firmly on experience, then that experience can often be evoked only in a more imaginative and phenomenological manner before the exercises of analysis and critical thought can occur. Here, I am much influenced by my good friend and colleague, Claude Romano, a noted phenomenologist now teaching at the Sorbonne. His recent book *At the Heart of Reason*, is an extended treatment of how to intelligence is earthed, as it were, in a totality of experience that precedes and founds all intellectual activities.

A couple of years ago, friends, colleagues and former doctoral students presented me with a celebratory volume (commonly called a *Festschrift*). It was edited by two eminent theologians, Neil Ormerod and Robert Gascoigne, and entitled *Priest, Poet, and Theologian: essays in honour of Anthony Kelly CSsR*.[3] I am most grateful for the way the various writers contributed different responses to my work, while expressing any number of ways in which it could be extended into new areas. For me to read those fourteen essays was very instructive, and suggested a rich collegial context shaped by the eminent and generous scholars involved. Of particular relevance is an essay by Meredith Secomb, entitled, 'Speaking from experience: A Theologian in the Presence of the Revealed God'. Not only did this essay incorporate the title of my original doctoral thesis completed in the late '60s, but also it suggested how that thesis was destined to remain ever unfinished in the years ahead. My concern of not wanting to be too abstract and academic, but to serve more immediately the life of the Church and its communities of faith, had its own outcome. It is now clearer, to myself and others, as to how I was understanding theology in the course of my academic career. It entailed a constant insistence on experience, however indefinable that might be. That insistence may have resulted simply from the fact that I am a Redemptorist, and, therefore, marked by the spirit of St Alfonso, 'the most Neapolitan

---

2. Karl Rahner, 'Poetry and the Christian', *Theological Investigations IV* (Baltimore: Helicon, 1966), 357–367.
3. *Priest, Poet, and Theologian: Essays in Honour of Anthony Kelly CSsR*, edited by Neil Ormerod and Robert Gascoigne (Melbourne: Mosaic Press 2013).

of the saints and the saintly of Neapolitans', as they say. His practical orientation in every area in which he worked (moral theology, devotional writing, meditations and pastoral communications of all kinds, hymns, music and painting)—all contributed eventually to his being declared a Doctor of the Church in 1900.

On the other hand, there is a more academic reason for this insistence on experience: theological and philosophical methods have advanced. That is now a widespread insistence on giving much greater weight to the singular character of experience in contrast to promoting any kind of finished system expressing itself in more abstract concepts and refined definitions. In this respect, a phenomenological and experiential emphasis does not replace metaphysical reflection, but grounds and sustains it. One can note also that an experiential emphasis evident in the towering achievements of such theologians as Karl Rahner, Bernard Lonergan, and in the critical expositions of the life of faith in the writings of Blessed John Henry Newman. Some of the essays making up this collection bear explicitly on the experiential substrate out of which we think and in which we communicate. See, for instance. the essays, 'Making the resurrection intelligible—or intelligence resurrectional?', And, more explicitly, 'Refreshing experience: the Christ-event as Fact Classic and Phenomenon'. Each of the essays making up this collection grapples, one way or another, with the question of how to think within experience, and in the manner in which experience might be enriched and gain critical assurance. Consider for example the Marian experience in the life of the Church, or the continuing efforts to clarify what we mean by 'natural law'.

I must mention, albeit in passing, what a privilege and resource it has been for me over these long years to have worked in the company of remarkable scriptural colleagues such as Frank Moloney, SDB, and Brendan Byrne, SJ. Their erudition and love for the Scriptures offered sure guidance and inspiration at a time when biblical studies were in a state of transition and somewhat removed from theology.

I conclude in the hope that something of the various moods that animate theology and the variety of methods that are used will be clarified, along with the depths of mystery from which theology begins and to which it returns. I know, however, that theology can appear peripheral to busy people in the Church and more so, to those outside it. Nonetheless, there is some consolation in being involved in the things that truly matter and in contributing to the way these deep matters might be best understood and spoken of—if not for now, then for some future generation. The basic objection to faith is that it is too good to be true; and it is amongst the more humble services of theology to remind oneself and others that 'the too good to be true', is true! There lies our hope.

In what follows, each the of twelve essays will be followed by a poem—without implying too great an association in terms of subject matter. I am grateful to Hilary Regan and ATF Press for suggesting this format.

Address for a Special Occasion

How the bishop gamely tried
to tickle the plump sense of occasion
into a little wriggle of transcendence!
-- to take a step beyond
the mundane of the heat, summer frocks,
smart suits, and rows of polished cars
beyond where family values are secure,
spouses faithful, children obedient,
motherhood a treasure, and even fathers
have a special role –
to that other region . . .
In the religious perspective
the vanishing point
makes all meaning shrink:
old bird-words are no longer winged;
no more abiding the open air
they roost moulting,
pecking seed from the preacher's hand.
Some wild amazing thing has flown away:
once reachable in a bound of hope or praise,
or in the dart of love or pang of guilt.
Piety lives here now
as a drugged bird of paradise,
smuggled in, and revived,
allowed to live decoratively,
at least as a specimen
in the ecology of a cage.
Customs check the contraband
when importing exotic fauna
is against the law:
the safer option is taxidermy . . .
But jokes get by –
ironic resonance
with what we barely know,
as everything comes tumbling down,
and nothing sure can stand
against the earthquake tilt from nowhere.
For all I know, tears may be

*a surer path, a strange confiding gift
flowing with more elements,
and welling up from where forgotten things
are felt, and spell,
in a giving too deep to be one's own,
existence, if only for the moment,
irresistibly ecstatic.*

The Incarnation and Human Sensibility

From whatever perspective, the Incarnation is the singular constitutive event for Christian identity, 'for in him the whole fullness of the deity dwells bodily' (Col 2:9; see Jn 1:14). This implies neither negation nor diminishment of the human but rather shows forth its potential under the power of God. As a culminating event in divine self-communication, it has a transformative effect on Christian consciousness and its awareness of God, the self, and the world.

In what follows, I wish to explore the reality of the Incarnation as a source of distinctive Christian sensibilities. This exploration will be presented under the following five headings:

1. Humanity—the Open Question;
2. Creation and the Incarnation of the Word;
3. The Word Embodied in the World;
4. The Body-Language of the New Testament
5. The Analogical Language of Body

Humanity—The Open Question

Humanity is a question to itself.[1] The dynamics and structures implied in who we are and what we experience allow for no one simple response: nature and person, male and female, body and soul, individual and community, society and culture, cosmos and history, God

---

1. For a classic treatment on the theme of the questioning character of human existence, see Eric Voegelin, *Order and History IV: The Ecumenic Age* (Baton Rouge: Louisiania State University Press, 1974), especially 316–330.

and the universe—these are just some of the dualities encountered by anyone disposed to look for answers—above all, in the domain of theology. Alert to the polarities inherent in any discussion of the human, the great saint of East and West, Maximus the Confessor, speaks of the human being as 'the laboratory in which everything is concentrated and itself naturally mediates between the extremities of each division, having been drawn into everything in a good and fitting way through its development'.[2]

An essential cultural task for theology is to provoke an uninhibited conversation on the meaning of our shared humanity. The current revulsion against the flat, quantitative, purely economic description of society, so favoured in modern politics, demands a larger frame of reference. More deeply still, the increasing robotisation of human language is a cause for irritation if not for alarm. Terms such as stimulus and response, conditioning, input and output, turned on and switched off, being burned out or blowing fuses, individual magnetism and the right chemistry, being programmed or brain-washed or hardwired, developmental cycles or stages, projecting the right image, software and hardware, and so on, figure in a current vocabulary. There is the obvious danger of linguistically reducing the total range of consciousness to the model of the machine, the computer, the camera, and chemical, physical or electrical interaction. A total explanation of human consciousness is ever elusive—as instanced in Richard Tallis' vigorous, informed debunking of the idea that neuroscience can offer a complete explanation of what makes us human in his book *Aping Mankind: Neuromania and Darwinitis, and the Misrepresentation of Humanity*.[3] His work is all the more persuasive since the author is both a materialist and an atheist!

Whatever the range of language and the variety of perspectives it provokes, the Incarnation is the necessarily focal meaning of the Christian understanding of humanity. In Christ, the world's path to God and God's way into the world are embodied: 'the Word became flesh and lived amongst us, and we have seen his glory' (Jn 1:14). Though the Word is uttered into the human history, it does not stop

---

2. Maximus Confessor, *Difficulty* 41:1305B. See Andrew Louth, *Maximus The Confessor* (London: Routledge, 1996), 19–33. I follow Louth's translation. See also, Lars Thunberg, *Man and the Cosmos. The Vision of St Maximus The Confessor* (New York: St Vladimirs's Seminary Press, 1985), 132–137.
3. Richard Tallis, *Aping Mankind: Neuromania and Darwinitis, and the Misrepresentation of Humanity* (Durham: Acumen, 2011).

the human conversation, but provokes it to further questioning: '... what we will be has not yet been revealed' (1 Jn 3:2). In this respect, the first words of the Word in John's Gospel are instructive. They are in the form of a question: Jesus turns to the two disciples of the Baptist following him, to ask, 'What are you looking for?' (Jn 1:38).

The Incarnation is God's personal entry into human history. That must mean being part of the cosmic process of emergence and evolution, a divine affirmation of all the variety of agencies involved in the genesis of life, humanity and the emergent world. In the world of God's creation and incarnation, nature possesses its own dynamism working in the complex interactions of atoms and molecules, DNA and molecules, cells, neurons, organs, organisms, bodies, bondings, populations, eco-systems and the biosphere of this planet. Because God's infinite creative Act is involved in each of these activities, because the creative process is initiated and finalised 'in Christ' (*cf* Col 1:15–20), a higher integration is entailed at each step in the process of emergence. Without such successive integrations, there could be no higher self-realisation in the emergence of the human, and in the awareness of human minds and hearts made open to the Word made flesh in this terrestrial milieu.

Whilst the Incarnation is an ultimate point of integration, being human is to be involved in complexity. Levels of living and non-living things exist below and before human consciousness. These levels of hierarchically related to one another, not as closed, but as open systems.[4] Whilst each level has its own laws and schemes of recurrence, there are instances of randomness, openness, even of 'chaos', as entropy is dissipated, and possibilities of higher realisation occur. Each level looks beyond itself to something more. Sub-atomic particles assemble themselves into the elements of the periodic table. Chemical elements come together into increasingly complex compounds as in the structure of enzymes and acids within the living cell. Cells come together in all the variety of plant and animal life. Cellular structures, in turn, are subsumed into the astonishing emergence of the brains of the human beings, just as they participate in the ecological biosphere in the food we eat, the air we breathe, the water we drink, the wine of our celebrations.[5]

---

4. Ian G Barbour, *When Science Meets Religion: Enemies, Strangers or Partners?* (New York: HarperCollins, 2000), 90–118.
5. See Arthur Peacocke, *God and the New Biology* (London: JM Dent and Sons, 1986), 120–127.

All this is far from a world of fixed and static natures whether these are imagined as more or less blended—or as adversarially juxtaposed. What emerges is a kind of participatory interlinking of all levels of reality in the makeup of our humanity.[6] But a distinctively human consciousness has a universal range: indeed, from a cosmic point of view, the universe has become conscious of itself in the human body, mind and heart. As a result, the emergent and evolutionary dynamics of reality inevitably affect faith's understanding of the Incarnation.

The Word and Creation

A contemporary theology of the Incarnation must develop in a world immeasurably more vast, intricate, and disenchanted, compared to what previous generations could have imagined. As a result, the classic New Testament perspective of the prologue of John's Gospel, for instance, can be interpreted at a new depth and breadth, given its sense of the universe of God's creation centred in the Word made flesh.[7]

> In the beginning was the Word, and the Word was with God, and the Word was God. He was in the beginning with God. All things came into being through him, and without him not one thing came into being (Jn 1:1–3).

For John, the divine *Logos* is all-creative and inclusive: 'all things' came into existence through him, and depend on him, in some causal sense, in their origins, just as all meaning and intelligibility derive from God's self-meaning in the *Logos*. The verses which follow suggest the quality of human consciousness as 'light' and 'life' derived from the Word:

---

6. See Rupert Sheldrake, *The Rebirth of Nature: The Rebirth of Nature: The Greening of Science and God*, (New York: Bantam Books, 1991), 100–108, for another, but associated vocabulary: *holons* as successively 'nested hierarchies'. At each level, the *holons* are wholes containing parts which are themselves wholes containing lower-level parts, and so on.
7. For a fuller theological consideration of the prologue, see John Macquarrie, *Jesus Christ in Modern Thought* (London: SCM, 1990), 105–122. Macquarrie's own translation of this passage, especially his use of 'meaning' for *Logos* is particularly imaginative. For a fuller discussion, see Anthony J Kelly and Francis F Moloney, *Experiencing God in the Gospel of John* (Mahwah, NJ: Paulist, 2003), 29–60.

> All things were made through him, and without him, nothing was made. What took place in him was life, and the life was the light of humankind. The light shines in darkness, and the darkness has not overcome it (Jn 1:3–5).

In the vocabulary of faith, the meaning of 'God' begins from, and returns to, this Word who is 'with God' in the beginning. Nonetheless, the Word is not an abstract principle, but 'he', *this one* (Jn 1:3–4, 10–11). An actual addressable subject is implied, one whose original identity will unfold only in the conversational world of human subjects. The people he meets, confronts and calls will know him as 'you', and all the ages of history refer to him as 'he', Jesus of Nazareth.

'All things were made through him' (Jn 1:3a): despite the differences existing among all created things, and despite their difference, even alienation, from God, the *Logos* is the genetic and unifying principle of the universe. The diversity of creation is a 'uni-verse' because of its origin and coherence in the Word. All of creation is a field of divine communication, being 'Word-ed' into being. This is the fundamental 'logic' of the Gospel: nothing has meaning outside the divine *Logos*. Nothing and no one stands, in its own right, outside the primordial Word.[8]

The *Logos*, by reason of the incarnation and the mission of the Son, creates a *dialogical* space in which Jesus will enter into conversation with all the range of *dramatis personae* involved in the dramatic unfolding of the Gospel narrative. Addressed by this Word, they will evince acceptance, incomprehension, hesitation, doubt, questioning or rejection, or any combination of such attitudes. The Word, dwelling among us (Jn 1:14b), thus opens a unique field of communication. Indeed, the 'God-ward' (*pros ton theon*) status of Word in the first verse of the prologue presumes a certain dialogical dimension within the divine mystery itself.

The extremes, on the one hand, of enclosing God and creation within the sameness of human experience, and, on the other, the sense of an unbridgeable gulf permitting no communication between God and the world, are met with what is always implicit in the Johannine vision. In the light of the incarnation, the ultimate meaning

---

8. Aquinas, *STh* 1, 34, 3: 'Because God understands both himself and all things in one act, the single divine Word is expressive, not only of the Father, but also of all creatures.'

of God and the radical meaning of the universe—and of ourselves within it—are ultimately intelligible only in reference to the incarnate *Logos*. The knowledge of faith is, therefore, in the deepest sense, 'ana-*logical*', governed and proportioned in accord with the concrete singularity of the One who has chosen to share the flesh of this world and to live 'among us'.

Since *he* is the Word both of God, and of the universe of all that exists because of him, a new way of speaking about God is set in motion. The classic themes of Word, being, life and light common to all ancient philosophies and religions are subsumed into a new mode of meaning. God is not known by a further refinement or extension of notions inherent in human traditions. All such are given a new twist by being tied to the singular and the personal—'earthed', as were, in the story of the man, Jesus Christ. Divine revelation entails an encounter with the Word made flesh, and with the story he tells and embodies. God is thus 'ana- *logically*' knowable as the One revealed in the expressiveness and resonance of this Word.

In contrast to an exclusive understanding of the Word as an englobing cosmic presence, the focus is shifted to an event within creation and its history. Where before all things came to be in the Word, now the Word comes to be within that universe.[9] The singular advent of the Word as the source and form of true life has occurred. This life is evidenced in the new consciousness made possible by what has happened: 'and the life was the light of humankind' (Jn 1:4). The Word, therefore, throws light on who God is, on what the world of creation is, and on the promise inherent in human destiny.

We pass now to the expanding cosmic horizon in which the Word is made flesh.

---

9. For this interpretation of 1:3b-4, see FJ Moloney, *Belief in the Word: Reading John 1-4* (Minneapolis: Fortress Press, 1993), 30-34. For a magisterial overview of the Word's coming to be within the becoming and evolving universe, see Karl Rahner, 'Christology within an Evolutionary View of the Word', in *Theological Investigations* V, translated by Karl-H Kruger (Baltimore: Helicon, 1966), 157-192. Rahner's article can be read as a particularly effective transposition in an evolutionary world-view implied in Aquinas' words: 'The mission of divine person can be taken as implying, from one point of view, a procession of origin from the sender; and from another perspective, a new way of being in what is other. Thus the Son is said to be sent by the Father into the world, in that he begins to be in the world in the visibility of the flesh he has taken to himself' (*Summa Theol*, 1, 43, 1).

Humanity Within the World

The universe envisaged in traditional theological doctrines was inevitably limited to a worldview of a fixed, hierarchical order. But that way of looking at the world has changed. There are dimensions of time and space, and relationships between mass and energy that were previously unimaginable. The world of our present understanding is a process, unfolding through billions of years in increasing differentiation of physical, chemical and biological forms. There are successive levels of organisation, from the quantum behaviour of particles to the formation of increasingly complex molecules to the emergence of life, from the protozoa to the millions of species we now classify. The path of emerging differentiation heads to the phenomenon of the human, and its consciousness of the universe as a vast interrelated whole.

The emergence of the human is connected to its capacity to register meaning beyond sense impressions, to respond to value beyond instinctual attractions, and, with the progressive awakening of consciousness, to transcend the enclosure of a habitat into an ever-growing sense of a world and the universe in which we live. In that respect, there is a distinctiveness of the human which, however much it shares a genetic inheritance with other animals, must be respected—and defended. After all, there have been no reports so far of a pod of whales holding a conference on the declining quality of plankton; or of leopards gathering to plan a cosmetic makeover in order to change their spots; or of dolphins who, after meeting in prayer, have decided to assert the rights of fish. We have no information of on lemmings exploring less wasteful organisational procedures, or of the higher apes writing monographs on the meaning of life . . . Any developments in such a direction have so far escaped detection. As a result, questions of meaning and value, of a universal sense of the totality and of our responsibility within it, seem to be left to the human.

Even though we *are* animal with the animals, it belongs only to the human among this planet's life-forms to experience the capacity for reflective intelligence and global responsibility. With all other animals, the human being breathes the air of this planet; but human consciousness inhales the atmosphere of another realm—that of spirit which exceeds the generative capacities of matter, and intimates the presence of ever-active, infinite source of intelligence and goodness.

From Aristotle on, previous generations spoke of the human as the 'rational animal' (*zoon logikon* in Greek, *animal rationale* in

Latin). This was the classic description of the human as the biophysical life-form that can reflect on itself, and even reflect on its own reflecting, in an intelligence that is, in principle, open to everything. Evolutionary biology has taken as its particular focus the biophysical or 'animal' feature of human emergence. In this respect, we have new understanding of the process in which human existence has emerged. It amounts to a rediscovery of the basic animality of the human—so that it is not as though a human being is somehow circling the globe looking for a temporary physical habitation. The human animal shares with all other animals a common emergence and structure in a biophysical world, with needs, emotions, and the instincts to bond, reproduce, care for young and so forth.

Yet there remains the 'rational' aspect—that strange capacity in the human for thought and freedom. There is the capacity for reflective openness to everything—from the genetic makeup of our bodies and the brain's trillion neurons, to the phenomenon of consciousness itself—and all its manifestations in faith, science, philosophy, art. How, then, does the Incarnation fit into such a scheme? The paradox remains: the world is created in the Word; but that Word has entered the world, and dwelt amongst us in the 'flesh' of an evolving and unfolding cosmos. The Word, embodied in Jesus Christ, is personally and cosmically related to everything and everyone in the universe: the Incarnation is not an isolated event.

The Body-Language of the New Testament

The Christian community lives the presence of Christ *performatively*, that is, through the mediations of liturgy and preaching, in its missionary outreach and dialogical encounters, in its serving Christ in the neighbor, and in loving him even in the enemy. In this respect, the Church is the historically embodied mediation of Christ. Its paradigmatic moment occurs in celebration of the Eucharist as the sensible, sacramental, and relational setting of the Body of Christ. Eighteen hundred years ago, Irenaeus of Lyons had to deal with Gnosticism, the heady 'new age' spirituality of his day. He laid down a basic rule for every age of the church: 'Our way of thinking is attuned to the Eucharist; and the Eucharist in turn confirms our way of thinking.'[10]

---

10. Irenaeus, *Adv haereses* 4.18.5; PG 7.1.1028.

Thus, the Eucharist is the basic criterion of incarnational sensibility and imagination. It is not simply a memorial intent on recapturing the past, nor an extrapolation of the present into an unknown future. It is rather an embodied instant, in which both past and future are brought to an intense focal realism.

The Church is the Body of Christ in more than a metaphorical sense. There is a realism of the Church's union with the crucified and Risen One whose body is the organ of God's communication in the world. In the words of Augustine,

> If, therefore, you want to understand the body of Christ, listen to the Apostle telling the faithful, 'but you are the body of Christ and its members' (1 Cor 12:27). So if you who are the body of Christ and its members, it is your own mystery that has been placed on the Lord's table; what you are receiving is your own mystery. You say *Amen* to what you are, and when you say that, you affirm what you are. You hear, 'the Body of Christ,' and you reply, 'Amen!' Be, then, a member of the body of Christ in order to make that *Amen* true.[11]

The Church, in this realist sense, is the 'live performance' of incarnational faith as it celebrates the Eucharist.[12] As the Eucharist forms the Church and the Church performs the Eucharist, a unique 'body language' is implied though this can hardly be appreciated if a reductively materialist understanding of the body is in possession. For the body is more than what someone 'has' in a transient way, that is, as a physical organism and a delimited object in time and space.

---

11. See Augustine, *Sermo* 272; PL 38.1247; my translation of *Corpus ergo Christi si vis intellegere, Apostolum audi dicentem fidelibus: Vos autem estis corpus Christi, et membra. Si ergo vos estis corpus Christi et membra, mysterium vestrum in mensa Dominica positum est: mysterium vestrum accipitis. Ad id quod estis, Amen respondetis, et respondendo subscribitis. Audis enim, Corpus Christi; et respondes, Amen. Esto membrum corporis Christi, ut verum sit Amen.*

   For a less literal translation, see Augustine, *Sermons (230–272B) on the Liturgical Seasons, The Works of Saint Augustine: A Translation for the 21st Century*, pt 3, vol 7, translated by Edmund Hill; edited by John E Rotelle (New York: New City, 1993) 300.

12. A valuable reference here is Kevin J Vanhoozer, *The Drama of Doctrine: A Canonical Linguistic Approach to Christian Theology* (Louisville: Westminster John Knox, 2005) with its emphasis on the performative character of Christian faith.

The human phenomenon of the body implies a personal 'somebody' organically immersed in a field of communication and relationships with others. The experienced reality of this 'somebody' throws light on the 'body language' in which Christian faith expresses its distinctively incarnate intentionality.[13] At the very least, that would mean acknowledging that the incarnate Word has not been 'ex-carnated' by being raised and assumed into heaven. Though he is indeed 'out of sight' as far as his physical, historical presence among us as Jesus of Nazareth is concerned, he is not so lost in the clouds of heaven as to be removed from the all human communication, to be dematerialised into some other realm. It is, then, not as though he has become disembodied. Rather, it is better to confess that we human beings are not yet fully embodied in the Body of Christ. From this point of view, the resurrection-ascension of Christ is an expanding bodily event, in accord with God's continuing incarnational action in the world, involving ever more persons as history unfolds.

Theological exploration does not call for the invention of some new form of celestial physics. Science will, we hope, continue to astound us with its explorations. The humble task of theology, however, is to elaborate first of all what pertains to the phenomenality of the primal Christian event—the formation of the Body of Christ, Head and members.

While a reflective faith must continue to build connections with philosophical and scientific world views, it cannot do so without a heightened receptivity to the data of faith. Before theology can be 'faith seeking understanding', its necessary first step is to be attentive, not only to what has been given to understand, but also to the way it has been given—as gift—and so, to the source and goal of such giving.[14] There is much to be learned from the generalised phenomenology of revelation: what appears as the given, must be allowed to be registered on its own terms—that is, as a gift—before hurrying to press it into

---

13. In the labour of *distinguer pour unir*, many distinctions need to be made that cannot be treated here—between body and soul, matter and spirit, person and community, the one and the many, the church and the world, etc. these are some of the distinctions necessary for a full exploration of what the Body of Christ means.
14. See Anthony J Kelly, *The Resurrection Effect: Transforming Christian Life and Thought* (Maryknoll, NY: Orbis), 15–23, 24–43.

other frames of reference.¹⁵ The phenomenality—or mode of givenness—of the total Christ event can be blocked by a narrowly empiricist point of view. It tends to take 'my body' as something I 'have', as one among many physical bodies. Rather, the body as a field of intentionality informed by consciousness-shaping relationships must be the focus of attention.¹⁶ The human body is, of course, a physical and physiological object. It is both legitimate and indeed desirable that it be treated as such, and its unique complexity explored, as with the stupendous neural complexity of the human brain. But the consideration of *somebody* only in this way, detached from personal and interpersonal consciousness, is to relegate it to an alien state.

But things appear differently when the body is appreciated as the 'saturated phenomenon' of a personal *somebody*. It is disclosed through a special sense of immediacy and un-objectifiable intimacy in regard to oneself and others. At this point, there is value in distinguishing the 'body-subject' from the 'body-object'.¹⁷ The body-subject is not merely something I possess, but is rather the field of my communication with the other. This body or 'flesh' intimately constitutes the subject's being in the world. It implies possibilities of intimate self-giving and self-disclosure, as is eminently the case in erotic or maternal love. In this sense, the 'flesh', the whole realm of incarnate consciousness, is a field of mutual indwelling, of being with, and for, the other, and of conscious interactions within a zone of incarnated relationships.¹⁸ In the eros and generativity of love, one's bodily being is re-experienced in, with, through and for the 'flesh' of the other.¹⁹ Thus, the body of my conscious being is affected by the encompassing phenomenon of the other and the world it embodies, and, in turn, affects it. It is at once an elemental bonding with the world, an imme-

---

15. Rolf Kühn, 'Phänomenologische Leibbegriff und christologische Inkarnation', in Münchener theologische Zeitschrift 59 (2008): 239–55.
16. Anthony J Godzieba, 'Knowing Differently: Incarnation, Imagination, and the Body', in *Louvain Studies* 32 (2007): 361–382.
17. See Louis-Marie Chauvet, *Symbol and Sacrament: A Sacramental Reinterpretation of Christian Existence*, translated by Patrick Madigan, SJ, and Madeleine Beaumont (Collegeville: Liturgical, 1995), especially 146–55.
18. Jean-Luc Marion, *Le phénomène érotique: Six meditations* (Paris: Grasset, 2003), 170.
19. Marion, *Le phénomène* érotique, 185. John Paul II's treatment of this point is necessarily more general but still with a strong phenomenological emphasis. See John Paul II, *The Theology of the Body: Human Love in the Divine Plan*, foreword John S Grabowski (Boston: Pauline, 1997), *Theology of the Body*, 42–63.

diate exposure to it, a multi-leveled participation in it, and a primal communication within it.[20]

By exploiting this notion bodiliness and this experience of embodiment, we begin to have an analogical sense of the bodily resurrection and ascension of Christ as inaugurating a new expansion of the incarnation and, consequently, a new way of relating to Christ. What the bodily dimension of this might entail, and what a connatural sensibility to it might mean, are dimensions of both being and consciousness that resist adequate expression. The dimensions of time and place as understood in former cosmologies and implicit in much of Christian tradition, are long surpassed. But that is not to say that they have been replaced by completely clear ideas. Even the meaning of energy and its various manifestations and material concretions are not areas of clear definition.[21] If this is the case, one is tempted to ask, would it not be better to bequeath the body to science? The theologian would be better advised to leave behind bodily and material concerns to order to concentrate on the spiritual self and its transcendence over matter. Though the incarnation is the original defining event, should not faith be now concentrated in the gift of the Spirit in a less physical way?

The Analogical Language of Body

Our point throughout this brief reflection, however, is that Christian theology—especially in its Christological and anthropological specialisations—must continue its proper task—which is, in this instance, to suggest the effect of the Incarnation on our sense of humanity, in its own terms, and within its own field of meaning. Theology can nonetheless explore analogical connections with other notions of body—anthropological, phenomenological, scientific, aesthetic, etc—that arise in other disciplines and styles of thought. In this respect, Christian body-language can call on a wide variety of analogies, old and new, to develop its meaning. In line with vision of Maximus the Confessor, yet alert to the findings of modern cosmology, Teilhard de Chardin perceptively remarked,

---

20. Jean-Luc Marion, *In Excess: Studies of Saturated Phenomena*, translated by Robyn Horner and Vincent Barraud (New York: Fordham University, 2002) 100; *Le phénomène érotique* 170, 180–81.
21. See *The Ghost in the Atom: A Discussion of the Mysteries of Quantum Physics*, edited by PC W Davies and JR Brown (New York: Cambridge University, 1993), 26. For further remarks, see James P Mackey, *The Scientist and the Theologian: On the Origins and Ends of Creation* (Dublin: Columba, 2007), 192–95.

> My own body is not these or those cells which belong exclusively to me. It is what, in these cells and in the rest of the world, feels my influence and reacts against me. *My* matter is not a *part* of the universe that I possess *totaliter*. It is the totality of the universe that I possess *partialiter*.[22]

With his christocentric perspective, Teilhard insists, 'Christ must be kept as large as creation and remains its Head. No matter how large we discover the world to be, the figure of Jesus, risen from the dead, must embrace it in its entirety.'[23]

Further, we cannot ignore the fact that today we are all participants, however disoriented on occasion, in the amazing development of the 'cyberspace body' of our humanity. The pulse of electronic energies are extending not only our senses, but also our consciousness as a body-subject. The body is in some measure being re-formed through the experience of new kinds of communication and a sense of 'being in contact' with others to a hitherto unimaginable degree. As writers such as Teilhard de Chardin and Walter Ong noted decades ago, such developments cannot be left unrelated to the event of the incarnation of the Word as it continues to expand throughout history.[24] Our understanding of the Word becoming flesh is extended not only to the evolutionary and ecological world, but also to the electronic or cyberspace dimensions of the world of communication.

We can ask, then, to what degree these developments contribute to our understanding of the expanding event of the Incarnation and the formation of the Body of Christ? If the spirit of human inventiveness and creativity has so transformed our embodied existence, how will the Holy Spirit, having already raised the Crucified One from the tomb and animated the Body of Christ, penetrate and transform all creation? In the present context, the there are multiple relationships to be explored—between the Body of Christ and the humanity of the risen Lord, and to the living reality of the Church celebrating

---

22. Pierre Teilhard de Chardin, *Science and Christ*, translated by René Hague (London: Collins, 1965), 13.
23. Cited in Christopher Mooney, SJ, *Teilhard de Chardin and the Mystery of Christ* (London: Collins, 1966), 136. While I have been arguing for the unique realism of the Church as the Body of Christ, I am not thereby conceiving of the whole universe as his body, even though he is 'head', etc., of all creation. I am leaving open the question of what that universal and cosmic headship entails.
24. See, for example, Walter J Ong, *Orality and Literacy: The Technologizing of the Word*, second edition (New York: Routledge, 2002).

the Eucharist as the sacrament of his Body and Blood. The different aspects or realizations of Christ's Body are so interwoven, that one has a sense of a God-given corporeal field of incarnational communication, in contrast to the isolation of discrete entities.

Conclusion

The drift of our argument moves toward the one point, namely, the Incarnation as an expanding event in the economy of God's self-communication. It must affect the Christian sense of humanity and of the universe overall. Christ is still the incarnate Word, and Christian self-understanding recognises that, to profess faith in Christ, is to be members of his paschal Body. No uncritical univocity is implied such that would result in any kind of physical monophysitism or, more accurately, 'monosomatism', in understanding how the incarnate reality of Christ is related to this present bodily existence. Nor, on the other hand, is the Body of Christ reducible to a vague sense of a metaphorical or symbolic 'mystical body'. Something more vital, more material, and specifically incarnational, is involved–and this is not to be dissolved in a general consideration of the Holy Spirit (see Jn 16:7, 12–15). The rapid advances of science have led to a radically changed sense of matter, time, and space have undoubtedly affected the sensibilities of faith in the Word incarnate in this material universe. And this is especially so when such faith remains tethered to bypassed cosmological conceptions. If that is the case, the Christian sense of the Body of Christ loses its assurance as a cosmic and historical reality, and veers toward a new kind of docetism. It is then defenceless against the soul-less body of materialistic modernity, and, for that matter, unable to deal with the bodiless soul of a rootless postmodernity.

When the life of faith is understood as an actual participation in the Body of Christ, there are realist consequences. There is in Catholic tradition a sense of intense physicality in the understanding of the real presence of Christ in the Eucharist. It must be admitted, however, that this does not always inspire a larger body-consciousness flowing from the Eucharist into every aspect of Christian life. This 'summit' and 'font'[25] of the life of the Church can, indeed, provoke

---

25. Vatican II, The Constitution on the Sacred Liturgy *Sacrosanctum concilium* no. 10, http://www.vatican.va/archive/hist_councils/ii_vatican_council/documents/vat-ii_const_19631204_sacrosanctum-concilium_en.html (accessed July 26, 2010).

ecological responsibility, an openness to the cosmic dimensions of faith, and inspire solidarity with the suffering, and, in the context of a nuptial mass, express a redemptive affirmation of sexuality. But to what degree do such developments of faith find their motivation in the incarnational action of God, ever in the process of forming the Body of Christ? It is almost as though the real presence of the Body of Christ, head and members, has been tabernacled in an interiority that has lost a sense of corporate and incarnate relationships. The reality of the one expansive Body of Christ slips out of the clear intentionality of faith. Of course, the doctrine of the incarnation continues to inspire a grand vision of human culture, but its assimilation is somewhat anorexic when it comes to bodily expressiveness in prayer, artistic imagination, community relations, and moral conduct. While there is no need to fabricate some new ideology of body, there is need to recover a sense of participating in the Body of Christ in the cosmic and communitarian dimensions of the new creation. An extreme individualistic interiority works against the graced materiality and vitality of participation in the living Body of the Lord.

Many further questions need be faced if we are to appreciate the expanding character of the incarnation. It might be that a satisfactory answer will be beyond the epistemic capabilities and imagination of our age. There is no doubt a sense of the Body of Christ reserved to those most fully transformed into him. For the rest of us, it means remaining alert to the point of convergence of many aspects of faith: the risen Lord already fills the universe, and through the Eucharist forms the Body of the church as the dwelling place of God.[26]

Clearly, the incarnation is a doctrine of faith. But its reality is not only a cognitively objective datum. It inspires feelings and shapes sensibilities as it informs Christian consciousness, underpins relationships and inspires action. It is, therefore, constitutive of human identity and subjectivity. The Word made flesh affects the sense of self and the depth and range of its participation in the world as a whole, as the Body of Christ grows.

---

26. As Mary L Coloe argues in her *Dwelling in the Household of God: Johannine Eschatology and Spirituality* (Collegeville, MN: Liturgical Press, 2007), points out, it is not a matter merely of future existence in a divine realm, but also of God dwelling with us in the world, in the great household of faith (see also 1 Pt 3:21f; Acts 3:21).

The Pope's Day of Peace, ASSISI

They met for peace that day,
far from my own heart's foreboding,
in the city of the Poverello --
to pray, these holy ones,
in a conspiracy of faiths and ways,
bright spirits, in hope that darkness
need not be our doom:
the TV showed them almost as boys playing,
as they set the white doves free --
distracted to a smiling fluster
from the solemnity of ceremony
in the elusive practicality
of in opening cages,
and letting startled birds
flutter off . . .
to what fate?
White doves in grey landscape,
whirling up and off
defying the gravity of the occasion,
into certain danger:
a fleeting gesture to decorate
the perilous land of the heart:
No more cages, only wings,
and the hawks of winter waiting . . .
what of the prayers?
Flying doves, falling leaves,
old men smiling,
attempting greater goodness,
a hour of good behaviour,
even for the religious,
with some guns stopped,
and the missiles waiting for another day;
though no pause, I think,
in the great factories of death;
and the world as my own heart felt.
Still, withal, the imagination
just a little bit disarmed
by possibilities of mercy . . .

Making the Resurrection Intelligible—
Or Intelligence 'Resurrectional'?[1]

Christ's rising from the dead is an irreplaceable 'given in the consciousness of Christian faith: 'No Christianity without the resurrection of Jesus. As Jesus is the single great 'presupposition' of Christianity, so also is the resurrection of Jesus.'[2] In the same vein, Pheme Perkins considered that the resurrection is 'the condition for the emergence of Christian speech itself'.[3] Without this event there would be no New Testament. Only the light of the resurrection can prevent the life, teaching and death of Jesus from being lost in the largely irrecoverable particularities of the past. But because the resurrection is central to faith's perception of the saving action of God, it inspires the experience of its universal significance and continuing effect in every age. But theological reflection on this topic is not without its problems. Let me indicate some of them.

Theology's Problems in 'Placing' The Resurrection

As a foundational event, the resurrection is so embedded in Christian tradition as to never having required 'definition' in the way that the mysteries of the incarnation and the Trinity eventually demanded doctrinal clarification. Though doctrinally undefined, the resurrection of the crucified Jesus is the indefinable factor in every aspect of

---

1. For a fuller treatment of this topic, see Anthony J Kelly, *The Resurrection Effect: Transforming Christian Life and Thought* (Maryknoll, NY: Orbis, 2008).
2. James Dunn, *Christianity in the Making*, Volume 1: *Jesus Remembered* (Grand Rapids, Michegan: Eerdmans, 2003), 826.
3. Pheme Perkins, *Resurrection: New Testament Witness and Contemporary Reflection* (Garden City, NY: Doubleday, 1984), 18.

christological, trinitarian, ecclesial, sacramental and eschatological theology. Still, there is also a certain sense of defeat. The resurrection, however focal, however pervasive its effect on the whole of Christian life and experience, however much it animates an eschatological hope, often in fact leaves theology tongue-tied. The singular event of Christ's rising from the dead a certain embarrassment and diffidence compared to the assurance in which the supposedly meatier themes of Christian life and practice are treated. Perhaps it is inevitable that the resurrection must represent for theology, not only a peculiar difficulty, but also something of a frustration or even failure. It is true that the dominant focus of theology from the third century has been on the incarnation. But unless Christ had been raised, there would be no theology of the incarnation—and no 'merry Christmas' in popular greeting. However much one may ascribe to a thoroughly incarnational theology in the tradition of Chalcedon, one cannot but notice that this classic Christological definition does not so much as mention the resurrection in its lapidary phrasing. It may well have established the basic grammar for all subsequent Christology, but it would have provided no answer and provoked no questions if Jesus had not risen from the tomb.

FX Durrwell's *The Resurrection* appeared fifty years ago in its original French edition.[4] It stands out as a brave attempt to recall theology to its focal point. Yet it came, and went, possibly because it was lost in the no-man's land of 'biblical theology'—too biblical for theology, and too theological for the exegetical styles that were then developing. It lacked the critical hermeneutical categories to have a lasting effect. To a lesser extent, this is the case with NT Wright's monumental study.[5] He embarks on what is termed a 'ground clearing task', with the aim of directing his readers back to 'a phenomenon so striking and remarkable that it demands a serious and well-grounded historical explanation'.[6] Note, however, how Wright quickly moves from this 'striking and remarkable phenomenon' to offering a 'serious and well-grounded historical explanation', with an explicitly apologetic intent. We may ask whether more attention should be given to the phenom-

---

4. F-X Durrwell, *The Resurrection* (London: Sheed and Ward, 1960).
5. NT Wright, *The Resurrection of the Son of God* (Minneapolis: Fortress Press, 2003).
6. *The Resurrection of Jesus. John Dominic Crossan and NT Wright in Dialogue*, edited by Robert B Stewart (Minneapolis: Fortress Press, 2006), 18.

enon itself. A renewed attention to what is most obvious, most taken for granted, is surely a humble but often overlooked function of a theology. Yet the taken-for-granted 'obviousness' of faith in the resurrection is also what has made it most vulnerable to a strange neglect. Karl Rahner lamented, decades ago, the dwindling theology of the resurrection.[7] Before him, Durrwell expressed a similar concern, 'Not so long ago theologians used to study the Redemption without mentioning the Resurrection at all'.[8] Theology seems to observe a strange silence here. It is not only the women in Mark's Gospel who 'said nothing for they were afraid' (Mk 16:8) when it comes to speaking of what made all the difference. We can sympathise with the quandary of the Roman governor, Porcius Festus, concerning 'a certain Jesus, who had died, but whom Paul asserted to be alive. Since I was at a loss how to investigate these questions, I asked whether he wished to go to Jerusalem, and be tried there on these charges' (Acts 25:19). Festus is not the only voice of common sense finding itself 'at a loss' when it comes to the resurrection, and therefore willing to refer it to the adjudication of higher authorities.[9]

However many centuries have passed since then, the puzzlement continues, and the stakes are still as high. Festus found that Paul was asserting the crucified Jesus 'to be alive'. How this is so continues to provoke many a question for pagan governor and Christian believer alike. Still, Paul was intimately convinced of the reality that had been revealed to him, understanding it to be central to the tradition he both knew and handed on. In addressing a situation of confusion in Christian community of Corinth, he expressed a provocative logic: 'if Christ has not been raised, your faith is futile, and you are still in your sins' (1 Cor 15:17). Paul presumes a knowledge of the life, death and words of Jesus, and even includes a saying of Jesus not recorded in the Gospels (Acts 20:35). However, the resurrection of the crucified One is for him the decisive event. Later theology inherits both Paul's conviction, but also his frustration in trying to communicate what it was based on. After all, if theology is to speak of the resurrection to its contemporaries in any age, it must face the problem of appearing oddly mythological in a world where the dead do not rise. Paul

---

7. Karl Rahner, 'Dogmatic Questions on Easter', in *Theological Investigations IV*, translated by Kevin Smyth (Baltimore MD: Helicon Press, 1966), 121–133.
8. Durrwell, *The Resurrection*, xxiii.
9. For a fuller treatment of these points, see Kelly, *The Resurrection Effect*, 1–23.

knew this back then, and theology knows it now. The apostle earned the mockery of the Areopagus after his attempt to tell his learned audience of 'the good news about Jesus and the resurrection' (Acts 17:18). If the cross is a stumbling block to the Jews and foolishness to the Gentiles (1 Cor 1:23)—to say nothing of its subversive impact on Roman imperial claims—the resurrection makes it more so.

Then, as regards the Church, it is inevitably preoccupied in defending its freedom to exist and conduct its mission, especially today in non-Christian or post-Christian societies. More positively in terms of other-directedness, it assumes the role of being the guardian of ethical values and the promoter of human dignity. Such concerns are urgent, and, in some usually unrecognised and unreflective way, flow from faith in the resurrection of the betrayed, condemned, tortured and crucified Jesus. To what degree is the assurance of authentic ecclesial identity to be found only in the resurrection? How does the effect of the resurrection permeate every aspect of the Church's communal life and mission?

When we turn to Christian ethics, the situation is somewhat alarming.[10] Paul's speaks of the new creation and conformity to Christ crucified and risen, and John elaborates on 'the life that has been revealed' (1 Jn 1:2). In contrast, moral theology is most occupied with speaking of the 'natural law' of a world in which the resurrection has made little difference. Likewise, in treatises on the sacraments, though sophisticated and helpful connections are made with the anthropology of ritual, symbols and signs, reference to the resurrection can be muted. Here, I have in mind two recent works of sacramentality in which the resurrection is barely mentioned![11] I would not for a moment indulge in an arrogant dismissal of such excellent works–especially since one of these authors has written a book on the resurrection[12]—but they do illustrate the problem: the

---

10. Brian V Johnstone, CSsR, 'Transformation Ethics: The Moral Implications of the Resurrection', in *The Resurrection. An Interdisciplinary Symposium on the Resurrection of Jesus* edited by Stephen T Davis, Daniel Kendall, SJ, and Gerald O'Collins, SJ (New York: Oxford University Press, 1997), 339–360.
11. Kenan Osborne, OFM, *Christian Sacraments in a Postmodern World: A Theology for the Third Millennium* (Mahwah, NJ: Paulist, 1999); David N Power, *Sacrament: The Language of God's Giving* (New York: Crossroads, 1999).
12. Kenan Osborne, OFM, *The Resurrection of Jesus: New Considerations for its Theological Interpretation* (New York: Paulist Press, 1997).

resurrection is simply taken for granted, and not *as* granted, the culmination and the focus of a gift given from beyond this world but having its transformative effect within it.

Furthermore, it must be recognised that there is always the temptation to reduce the resurrection to faith's experience of the Spirit. The crucified Jesus does not rise himself, but faith in some sense rises as empowered to leap into a new spiritual assurance. Though all agree that a refreshed theology of Spirit is long overdue, it can never be a substitute for the resurrection-event. In the horizon of faith, the resurrection is given as an in-breaking event as distinguishable from the gift of the Spirit, even though faith is discerning two, interrelated, distinct events in the *economia* of salvation. For example, in the resurrection of the crucified One, the transforming power of the Spirit is climactically manifested, and overflows from the risen Christ into the lives of all believers.

We can sum up the situation as something like this: if theology concentrates on the incarnation, the defining character of the resurrection is too easily presumed. If it highlights the risen Christ's gift of the Spirit to the Church in history, the resurrection of Jesus is easily relegated to an increasingly elusive past. If theology addresses the responsibilities of compassionate involvement in the liberation of communities and peoples from dehumanising political and economic oppression, the resurrection of Jesus appears as all-but a distraction from the future that is still to be realised for in a suffering humanity. Even von Balthasar's dramatic treatment of the Paschal Mystery seems to have been exhausted its creativity in a rather operatic treatment of Holy Saturday—to the neglect of the resurrection.[13] Then, in the sphere of interfaith dialogue, when theology searches for points of contact with the great spiritualities of the world, the resurrection so intensifies the particularity of Christ, that it might be best left unmentioned. Perhaps it might be given the status of an addendum to be considered later, but, in the business of dialogue, it has no productive significance in its own right, neither as inspiring a

---

13. As will be clear, I depend on von Balthasar in many other places and instances, where the resurrection is given its due. It is just that he seems to lose all sense of proportion when it comes to Holy Saturday. For a vigorous critique of von Balthasar's Holy Saturday theology, see Alyssa H Pitstick, *Light in Darkness: The Traditional Catholic Doctrine of Christ's Descent into Hell and the Theological Opinion of Hans Urs von Balthasar* (Grand Rapids: Eerdmans, 2005).

mood, nor as forming the horizon in which dialogue might be initiated and conducted. The resurrection is certainly not to be used as the knock-down argument to justify Christian imperialism, or, for that matter, as an obstacle to dialogue impossible. On the other hand, when Christians engage in reverent dialogue with people of other faiths or spiritualities, the transparency of such engagements is rather compromised if the resurrection of the crucified victim pertains to sensitive domain of topics that cannot be mentioned—or deemed irrelevant to the consideration of what is most important. How, then, does theology keep its focus on the resurrection?

The problem is intensified in the experience of moral impotence and the resultant humbling frustration. So much of life is so clearly undecided; so much sacrifice goes unrewarded; so many of the once strongly flowing currents of renewal end up in the arid sands of no effect. A discouraging lack of direction and positive result favours an individualistic self-serving culture of being 'law unto oneself', no matter how the suffering other or the common good might suffer. The profound existential significance of the biblical description of sin as *harmartia* and *anomia* begin to resonate loudly in our cultural consciousness. There is a twisted, self-referential, directionless impotence in the air we breathe. The unmasking of any one evil allows others to take its place—dishonesty, vengeance, violence, and in the end, further hopelessness. The true grip of evil contrasts to an anodyne listing of sins and impotent figure of a kindly divine judge who forgives our often amusing and banal naughtiness. But the closer we come to the luminous centre of the Christ 'who takes away the sin of the world', the more the driven, grotesque absurdity of the human situation stands out—as what he saving us from. We must wonder whether the event that represents Christ's victory over death and the evils we have caused or suffered is little appreciated because our hope has dwindled in a groaning world of fear, boredom and absurdity.

A More Phenomenological Approach

How, then, does the resurrection point the way forward. Part of the answer consists in cultivating a more phenomenological awareness and with its to refine our sense of the originality of Christian faith. Theology can thus recover its original freshness, and overcome the threat of boredom and stagnation. It will mean not taking the resurrection-event *for* granted, but *as* granted, as it was originally given into consciousness. The phenomenon must not be lost in abstract generalities, but be appreciated first of all on its own terms,[14] for the resurrection is not first of all a theoretical problem to be solved, but a gift to be lived. Newman catches the point:

> Instead of looking out of ourselves . . . throwing ourselves forward upon Him and waiting for Him, we sit at home bringing everything to ourselves . . . Nothing is considered to have an existence so far forth as our minds discern it . . . in a word, the idea of Mystery is discarded.[15]

A closer attention to experience of faith and the phenomenality of the resurrection event enables theology to reevaluate the place of the resurrection in Christian theological reflection. If this is lacking, any teaching on the resurrection look like an ice-sculptures needing the controlled atmosphere of a protective philosophical system set against the hot winds and the changing seasons of historical experience. Without phenomenological perception and vigilance, theology will be confined in the locked room of its own making: its floors and ceilings allow for a certain number of doors and windows—but all along, letting in the light and atmosphere of an eschatological event is at stake. Just as the risen Jesus entered the locked room to the surprise of his fearful disciples, a more phenomenological attentiveness can make any theological space more hospitable to light of Christ and the fresh air of his Spirit. The conclusion of John's Gospel remains a healthy reminder: the risen Jesus is not contained within the linear print of any book—or of all the books of the world (Jn 21:25). The phenomenon precedes and exceeds all efforts to express it. In a more contemporary vein, theology is not engaged in a video replay of the highlights of the game, passively assured of the outcome, once one's team was won. For beyond the play of images, there is the risk of openness to the 'given'. It is not a matter of reproducing impressions or trying to capture a dwindling after-effect, but of entering into an involvement with what causes everything to be seen anew.

---

14. Further elaborated in Kelly, *The Resurrection Effect*, ix–xiii, 24–43.
15. John Henry Newman, 'On the Introduction of Rationalistic Principles into Revealed Religion', in *Essays, Critical and Historical 1* (London: Longmans and Green, 1890), 34–35.

Aquinas understands that the radical darkness inherent in our knowledge of God remains, the dark knowledge of faith is illumined by 'many and more excellent effects' disclosed in the history of salvation:

> Although through the revelation of grace in this life we may not know the essence of God (*quid est*), and so are united to him as to one unknown, nonetheless we know God more fully in as much many and more excellent his effects disclose him to us; and, in so far as we attribute to him from divine revelation things that natural reason cannot attain, as that God is both one and three.[16]

We can specify the direction of his thinking here in regard to the 'more excellent effect' of the resurrection itself. The God who acts in the resurrection remains unknown, and, in a sense, more 'unknown' to the natural scope of reason limited to a world of death in which the resurrection is not a possibility. On the other hand, the event of the resurrection indicates a more a more intimate participation in the life of God through the personal and cosmic effects of Christ's rising from the tomb. Moreover, it offers possibilities of a further graced mode of knowing through the light that emanates from it. Amongst 'the more excellent effects', the resurrection has a focal status in that it illuminates the whole climactic movement of divine self-disclosure. Implicit in this outstanding effect, is that of the witness of the tradition to which the events of revelation give rise, above all the testimony of the chosen witnesses to whom the risen Christ has disclosed himself, as divine revelation is unfolded in history.

Attentiveness to the focal phenomenon of the resurrection will have a purgative effect on theology, expelling the waste material of misplaced rationalism that has long accumulated. It will be no unhealthy outcome if the resurrection is be allowed to shock theology to its foundations with the immeasurable, original 'excess' embodied in the risen Jesus. Thus, the silvering which backs the mirrors of theological perception is stripped away, so as to let the light of the 'given' shine through.

---

16. *STh* 1, q. 1, a. 13, objection 1.

What is required is a continuing conversion to the data, to what is 'given'. Again, Aquinas is instructive. We catch him reacting to the objection that his use of the psychological analogy amounts to an attempt to prove the mystery of the Trinity. He defends his procedure with the words, *posita trinitate, congruunt huiusmodi rationes*[17]—translatable as, 'once given the Trinity, an analogical manner of elucidating it is appropriate'. This, of course, raises the question of how the mystery of the Trinity is first 'given' or assumed or 'posited', and the sense of congruence or 'fittingness' in any form of theological thought. But while Thomas certainly takes as given the scriptural and doctrinal tradition, he also speaks of the quasi-experimental knowledge of the Trinity through the missions of the divine persons in the gift of grace.[18] There is a gift experienced before it is objectified or expressed in propositional form. As an indicator of his realist sense of faith, he writes, 'the act of the believer does not reach its end in the proposition, but in the revealed reality itself'.[19] The sense of 'fittingness' and analogical congruence in theological reasoning derives from a form of primary contact with the revealed realities.

Though St Thomas is no phenomenologist in the contemporary sense, he provides clues to a less propositional and more experiential approach to the data of revelation. Here, we limit our reflections to the primary datum, to what originally collapsed all categories, and left tongue-tied the original disciples who witnessed to it. Christ's rising from the tomb interrupts the linear format of our books and intrudes into the locked doors of all previous positions. Something else is at work, involving believers in a way that no video replay of highlights can satisfy. How might this decisive event be best approached?

A 'Turbulence' in The History of Reason

To heighten a sense of the phenomenality of the resurrection, we find a valuable resource in Eric Voegelin's treatment of Paul's experience of the risen Christ, as it is set out in his great unfinished *Order and History*.[20] He locates this kind of experience within the context of a

---

17. *STh* 1, q 32, a. 1, ad 2.
18. *STh* 1, q 43, a. 5, ad 2.
19. *STh* 2–2, q 2, a. 2, ad 1.
20. Eric Voegelin, *Order and History*, Volume 4: *The Ecumenic Age* (Baton Rouge, Louisiana: Louisiana State University Press, 1974), 239–271.

profound contemplation of the direction of human existence and the meaning of history itself. For him, history is the realm of existence in which the dynamism of the cosmic order becomes luminous in human consciousness.[21] It is imperative never to foreclose on the openness of 'being', nor lose its 'in-between' character—the *metaxy* in Voegelin's terms. The dynamism of metaxic consciousness finds expression in key 'symbolic' experiences. They keep history open to a transcendent, ever-indefinable order of being and life. As affected by the resurrection, Paul experiences a 'theophanic' event—in contrast to a purely human 'egophanic' projection. Here, Voegelin is concerned to reject any doctrinally rigid or superficial objectification of what occurs in the depths of existence. That would result in congealing the open-endedness of the quest, and reducing it to subjective or 'egophanic' limits of the self-projective ego. In contrast, participation in the transcendent order is a depth experience, never to be fully objectified in mundane and established categories. Yet, as an 'in between' movement, this radical experience is, of its nature, proleptic and provisional. In the in-between-ness of the enlargement of consciousness that occurs, categories such as subject and object, even human and divine, prove too dogmatically rigid and exclusive. What counts is the occurrence of the irreducible experience. It can be expressed only in the compact 'symbolic' terms determined by the experience itself so as to mediate the inspired movement through time and history.[22] From a luminous centre, Paul looks outward to the whole of reality transfigured by what has taken place.[23] His vision evidences a sense of passing from decay to transformation. It occurs beyond any mundane conception or calculation: 'If for this life only we have hoped in Christ, we are of all people most to be pitied' (1 Cor 15:19).

Paul's experience is profoundly vertiginous, for it leaves the apostle pushed to the limits of language and expression. Voegelin describes the giddying character of this experience in a key passage:

> In its experiential depth, a theophanic event is a turbulence in reality. The thinker who is engulfed by it must try to rise ... from the depth to the surface of exegesis. When he comes up he wonders whether the tale he tells is indeed the story of

---

21. Voegelin, *The Ecumenic Age*, 242.
22. Voegelin, *The Ecumenic Age*, 242–3.
23. Voegelin, *The Ecumenic Age*, 246.

> the turbulence or whether he has not slanted his account to one or other aspect of the complex event; and he will wonder rightly, because the outcome depends on the interaction of the divine presence and the human response in the depth, as well as the cultural context on the surface that will bias his exegesis toward what appears at the time the most important part of the truth newly discovered.[24]

The impact of revelation occasions a 'turbulence' in Paul's way of seeing the world. It remains always vulnerable to a pragmatic or ideological reduction. The experience occurs as an event in the depths of what is moving on so as to 'engulf' its addressee. But the way it the depth of the event is interpreted and communicated is inevitably conditioned by what is shaping the surface in terms of social and cultural concerns and structures. The temptation is so to shape the event that it will lead eventually to conceptual abstraction or pragmatic usefulness, and so be taken over by immediate needs and routine patterns of thought and expectation. On the other hand, if the irruptive and turbulent excess of the event is respected in its true measure, if those who witness to it and participate in it seek to communicate what has happened, its effect continues, by moving history forward and enlarging the sense of transcendent order of existence.[25] Attempts to define precisely what has taken place float on the surface of the experiential turbulence from which it has emerged. It is ever in danger of being lost in superficial concerns. The eventful 'mutation'—a term borrowed from evolutionary science and increasingly favoured in recent writings (for example, Wright, Crossan, Hurtado, Byrne and Martelet)—can be missed. A theophanic experience can be reduced to 'egophanic' projections of either a dogmatic or pragmatic type. The egologically or self-referentially structured consciousness becomes closed in on itself and loses the dynamic 'metaxy' of its depth-experience. In that occurs, the theophanic character of the Pauline vision of the risen Christ is prevented from affecting the constitutive meaning in history. The advance of insight is frustrated.[26] As a result, the egophanic revolt of modernity disallows the breakthrough that has taken place, and floods consciousness with new forms of ideology

---

24. Voegelin, *The Ecumenic Age*, 252–3.
25. Voegelin, *The Ecumenic Age*, 253.
26. Voegelin, *The Ecumenic Age*, 255.

and Gnostic totalitarianism.[27] Voegelin sees a symptom of this is the modern concentration on the 'historicity of Christ' which reduces the 'symbolic' character of the event to the world of academic abstract generalisation and rational control. This mind-set of the historical analysis which has become incapable of appreciating the true direction of history, has been irremediably infected by centuries of separating symbols from experience. As a result, the experience is missed, and new mystical possibilities are not pursued.[28] Under the dead hand of analysis, abstraction and control, existence atrophies, and the vacuum of forgetfulness is filled by egophanic ideologies of power. The radically world-forming event is interpreted on the surface-level of rational analysis in terms of cause and effect. The revelatory 'given' thus loses its originating uniqueness. The glory on the face of Christ is only a mirror image of ourselves.

Admittedly, Voegelin's account of the revelatory impact of the risen Christ on Paul cannot pretend to be a comprehensive account of the full scope of Christian experience—in all its historical, liturgical, mystical, doctrinal, moral and theological dimensions. He attention is more focused on the Christ-symbol than the historical person of Jesus—which is, in fact, far removed from Paul's approach. Moreover, for Voegelin, key Christian doctrines are dogmatic distortions. He falls short, therefore, of an adequate appreciation of the historic objectivity of revelatory events in which the incarnation of the Word, the realism of faith and its differentiated sacramental and doctrinal expressions each have their part to play.[29]

---

27. Voegelin, *The Ecumenic Age*, 260–266.
28. Voegelin, *The Ecumenic Age*, 265–266.
29. It would be a productive exercise to contrast Voegelin's approach with that of Alain Badiou in his *Saint Paul: The Foundation of Univeralism*, translated by Ray Brassier (Stanford, CA: Stanford University Press, 2003). Badiou, holding the chair of philosophy at the Ecole Normale Supérieure in Paris, considers historical Jesus as largely a fable, and the resurrection a mythological objectification of something else, namely, the subject as a universal singularity. What interests Badiou is not Christian faith, let alone the Christian Church, but the subjectivity of Paul's creative and provocative universalism calling into question all the dull sameness of the world based on distinctions between Jew and Greek, slave and free, male and female. Paul is to this extent our contemporary, witnessing to a new subjectivity, a new way of being human unencumbered by objectifying limitations of particular and oppressive modes of belonging based on social, cultural or religious divisions.

Nonetheless, Vogelin's analysis of the experience of the Risen Christ is informative in at least five ways: (1) The Pauline vision of the risen Christ constitutes a decisive event in the openness of history towards its consummation; (2) It communicates a quality of self-transcending consciousness, opening its horizons to the radically new; (3) It eludes all articulation, so that any social or cultural effort to put a meaning on it can easily end in forgetting the novelty of experience; (4) The turbulent fertility of Paul's visionary experience, though never fully objectifiable, comes to expression in different contexts; (5) The egological character of modernity, both because of its ideology and pragmatism, works against an appreciation of the singular originality of the Christian phenomenon. Each of these five points underscores the need of a refreshed phenomenological approach to what Paul witnesses to in such a personal manner.[30] How, then, can Voegelin's approach be made more specific?

Aspects of a Theological Phenomenology of the Resurrection

Theology can begin to develop a more adequate sense of the resurrection by calling on the resources of phenomenology. Here, we are limiting ourselves mainly to the writings of Marion.[31] He makes his point in reference to five especially saturated phenomena: an event, a painting, the flesh, the face, and, in a way that tends to combine all four, revelation.[32] All five 'saturated' instances of phenomena have this in common, namely, a primordial self-imposing.[33] None of them is constituted by the subject, but each appears in its originality and arresting power. Thus, the subject comes to itself in a new consciousness only through self-imposing otherness of the phenomena concerned.

---

30. For further perspective on Paul, see Kelly, *The Resurrection Effect*, 79–100.
31. In some ways, as his critics point out, this emphasis on the sheer self-givingness of the phenomena is so extreme, so one-sided, that the conscious subject seems to have no role at all, in responding to and interpreting what is being given. But need subject and object be so adversarially opposed? I do not think so, as we shall later explain later in reference to the multiple dimensions of meaning the phenomenon provokes.
32. Jean Luc Marion, *Being Given: Toward a Phenomenology of Givenness*, translated by Jeffrey L Kosky (Stanford, CA: Stanford University Press, 2002), 234–6.
33. Marion, *Being Given*, 5.

Janicaud's has objected to an unwarranted intrusion of theological perspectives into phenomenological methods.³⁴ But that is not our problem. In fact, Marion conveniently poses a question:

> Could not theology, in virtue of its own demands, and solely in view of formulating them, suggest certain modifications of method and operations to phenomenology? . . . Could not theology's demands allow phenomenology to transgress its own limits, so as finally to attain the free possibility at which, from its origin, it claims to aim?³⁵

I think so. Theology can be only enriched by phenomenological attentiveness. And, in its turn, it can enrich the scope of phenomenology with possibilities deriving from the singularity of positive revelation.³⁶ Still, the general phenomenological principle stands. The saturated phenomenon shows itself by giving itself; and more intense and saturated manner in the case of theology.³⁷ Let us then apply some instances of Marion's (mainly) saturated phenomena to the resurrection.

The Resurrection as Revelation

For our theological purposes, it is best to start with the phenomenon of revelation,³⁸ and then offer a brief exposition of the phenomena of event, art, flesh and face. Philosophy's difficulties in dealing with religion, let alone divine revelation in history and the singularities it contains, are well known and understandable. Though metaphysical perspectives can accommodate mythic and symbolic expressions, the historic particular is off the page. The speculative impossibility of

---

34. Dominique Janicaud *et al*, translated by Bernard G Prusak, *Phenomenology and 'The Theological Turn': The French Debate*, (New York: Fordham University Press, 2000).
35. Marion, 'Le possible et la revelation', in *Eros and Eris: Contribution to a Hermeneutical Phenomenology: Liber Amicorum for Adriaan Peperzak*, edited by P van Tongeren, P Sars, C Bremmer and K Boey (Dordrecht: Kluwer Academic, 1992), 228.
36. Marion, 'Le possible et la revelation', 231; *Being Given*, 242.
37. Marion, *Being Given*, 367.
38. Marion, *Being Given*, 235–6.

anything being God-given is often entrenched in philosophical systems and the ideologies they support.[39] An idealist or empiricist system must have difficulty with the singular phenomenon purporting to be a self-revelation of a transcendent Other.[40] With some theological abandon, Marion focuses on Christ as the phenomenon saturating the whole of the New Testament and Christian life.[41] For Christ is given in a way that exceeds all expectations. He gives himself by way of an excess. The density and expansiveness of the resurrection of the crucified One outstrips quantitative assessment of any kind. Moreover, there is a qualitative intensity inherent in the Christ-event that makes its 'unbearable' (Jn 16:12). The resurrection appearances are a troubling irruption.[42] The whole frame of previous relationships is radically rearranged: the Word becomes flesh, and in that flesh, he is crucified, and raised from the dead and ascends to heaven.[43] A plurality of horizons converge and collide in the inexhaustible excess confronting any human expression of the event (*cf* Jn 21:25). The singularity of Christ's appearances overflows the expressive range of all the terms, genres, symbols, concepts, testimonies, and descriptions related to time and place and form.[44]

The self-revealing phenomenon is presented to faith, not to theoretic understanding. What is perceived in the excess of the given phenomenon leaves the believer tongue-tied. Because intelligence is at a loss to frame what has been received in faith into any conceptual system, it is a sense dazzled and rendered sightless:

> Standing before Christ in glory, in agony or resurrected, it is always words (and therefore concepts) that we lack in order to say what we see, in short to see that with which intuition floods our eyes . . . God does not measure out his intuitive manifestation stingily, as though he wanted to mask himself at the moment of showing himself. But we do not offer concepts capable of handling a gift without measure and, overwhelmed,

---

39. Marion, 'The Saturated Phenomenon', in *Philosophy Today*, 40 (1996): 103.
40. Marion, 'Le possible et la revelation', 232.
41. Marion, *Being Given*, 236.
42. Marion, *Being Given*, 238.
43. Marion, *Being Given*, 239.
44. Marion, *Being Given*, 240.

dazzled and submerged by his glory, we know longer see anything.[45]

Marion is making a point. Still, the event of revelation, with its form revealed on the face and in the flesh of the risen One, does not so stun and overwhelm contemplative intelligence that understanding necessarily atrophies. Insights, judgments, artistic expression and verbal forms, however limping in their respective contexts, can positively nourish and direct the contemplation of faith. An appropriately critical, realism is governed by the imperative to allow the Christian phenomenon to impose itself in its own evidence and on its own terms. For Christ is encountered as the revelation of a love and the source of life, at once within the world and beyond it. The excess of light goes beyond the capacities of meaning.[46] There is a play of appearance and disappearance, of presence and absence, of self-revelation and withdrawal.

Yet this saturated phenomenon *par excellence* continues to present itself through its manifold effect in the life and mission of the Church.[47] The self-disclosure Christ once enabled a privileged seeing on the part of chosen witnesses has passed into the tradition. Compared to their 'seeing', faith is the experience of 'not seeing', but 'believing'. To that degree, faith is an experience of non-experience. On the other hand, it is not a form of blindness, nor a directionless surrender to nothing or no one. The self-giving of the risen One saturate faith's other senses. Faith hearkens to the Word.[48] It breathes the Holy Spirit. It is strengthened by the testimony of privileged 'eye witnesses' and cumulative evidence of transformed lives. It sacramentally eats and drinks the 'real presence' of the One gives himself. It tastes in the savor of mystical wisdom. It enjoys the flickering illuminations of theology itself. Though all this, the self-giving phenomenon of Christ draws believers into its field, in the summoning to a conversion that is never fully attained. It amounts to a rebirth in a new world in which

---

45. Marion, 'They Recognised Him; and He Became Invisible to Them', in *Modern Theology* 18 (2002): 148.
46. Marion, 'They Recognised Him', 149.
47. Marion, 'They Recognised Him', 151–2.
48. For a theological phenomenonolgy of voice, see Sergio Gaburro, *La Voce della Rivelazione: Fenomenologia della Voce per una Teologia della Rivelazione* (Milano: Edizioni San Paolo, 2005).

praise, thanksgiving, communion, compassionate intercession, confident prayer and love for the dimensions of life.

With the resurrection in mind, we now turn to other kinds of saturated phenomena,[49] namely, the event, the aesthetic form, the flesh and the face.

The Resurrection as Event

In its singular and expanding impact, the phenomenon of an event is not circumscribed by any concept of reality or being in general. Needless to say, it bears little resemblance to the mass organisation of events for a limited purpose, for example, entertainment, or religious gatherings, political rallies and so forth. For an event in the saturated sense is inexpressible in its scope and implications. As unpredictable, it occurs outside any calculus of cause and effect. The origins and effect of such events can never be fully grasped, despite their expanding impact.[50] In its 'excess' and irrepeatable particularity, the event is beyond any metaphysical or cultural theory.[51] The tragedy of the First World War is still largely inexplicable in destructiveness. It overflowed the bounds of any horizon of rationality, then and now.[52] More positively, the historical emergence of Christianity, and, indeed, other world religions, each in its own way, are events of world-shaping proportions. Attempts to reduce such events to a particular cause, aim or purpose serve only to blind rationality to the overwhelmingly novel character of what has taken place. Claude Romano helpfully distinguishes a mere event from a far more significant happening.[53] A factually-recorded event is impersonal in its objectivity. It has no existential import. It is datable as a *fait accompli*—an inner-worldly empirical fact. In contrast, there is the event of another kind. It hap-

---

49. This account makes no pretense of giving a critical treatment of Marion's work in this area. I do, however, find in it a number of evocative starting points, taking us in the direction of the phenomenon of the resurrection. See also Brian D Robinette, *Grammars of the Resurrection: A Christian Theology of Presence and Absence* (New York; Crossroad, 2009), especially 71-77, 96-98.
50. Marion, *Being Given*, 140, 165, 172.
51. Marion, *Being Given*, 170-2.
52. Marion, *Being Given*, 201.
53. The phrase, 'Evential Hermeneutics', while truer to the French text, does not travel so well in English.

pens beyond all previous calculations and intimately involves those caught up in it. Its impact leads to world-changing decisions. In this kind of event, the world of one's previous life is reconfigured, and made newly meaningful and significant beyond prediction or calculation. Obvious examples would be, say, religious or moral conversion, a devastating grief or failure, or falling in love, the real history of a marriage, or even a deeply significant friendship . . . or even the breakthrough of a seminal insight into what had previously resisted understanding. Events of this kind give rise to a certain 'anarchy', as the fixed points of settled horizons are dramatically shifted. As a result, the full significance of the event in question can emerge only as the future unfolds.[54] Carried along in the event, the self is caught up in an incalculable existential venture, not as a passive recipient, but as an active participant, impelled to a new level of action. In this respect, it is not a matter of projecting new possibilities on an already established world, but of being involved in a new register of existence—within a world newly understood. Something has happened, breaking in previously settled world. A convenient example is one's own birth—or that of others. For each birth is an event that occurs as given from beyond, yet at the same time opens possibilities that are not predetermined against any settled horizon.[55]

The resurrection of the Crucified is pre-eminently such an event. By any showing, it is world-changing occurrence. It radically shifts the death-bound horizon of existence to open it to the promise of eternal life, already fulfilled in the act of God's raising Jesus from the tomb. The origin and outcome of the resurrection transcends the world of previous calculations—after all, Jesus was condemned, tortured and crucified, abandoned and betrayed by his followers, and rejected by his own people. Yet the Easter event 'saturates' the lives of Christian believers to affect their sense of the universe itself: 'if anyone is in Christ, there is a new creation: everything old has passed away; see, everything has become new' (2 Cor 5:17). This 'new creation' is presented in various ways as a new spiritual birth—the beginning of a life that looks to an eschatological fulfilment (1 Jn 3:2). The Christian

---

54. Claude Romano, *L'événement et le monde*. Épithée. Essais Philosophiques (Paris: Presses Universitaires de France, 1998), 60–69.
55. Romano, *L'événement et le monde*, 72–96.

caught up and carried forward in an adventure of life, to a degree unimaginable within the horizon of previous existence.[56]

The Resurrection as Aesthetic Form

The phenomenonality of art adds a further dimension. A great painting saturates our perceptions in an especially intense fashion. It cannot be merely a tasteful adornment to the décor of a room or a dwelling. Its aesthetic impact causes everything to be re-arranged in the living-space of mundane experience. If the art-work is regarded as an item of decoration, or as something owned and catalogued as property, it simply mirrors back one's own criteria of taste or status. A great work of art overflows any individual mode of appreciation because of its universal appeal. The painting dazzles the viewers' limited perceptions with a peculiar and inexhaustible excess, and so invites an endless contemplation that exceeds any flat manner of looking at an object.[57] Viewers, with their varying sensitivities and appreciative capacities, are drawn to behold what it frames and are thereby enabled to see the world in a fresh way. To this degree, a great painting possesses an iconic quality. It presents itself not so much as an arresting object within the routine scope of our vision, but is luminous with a light beyond the familiar.[58]

Theology is indebted to Hans Urs von Balthasar for attempting to restore an aesthetic dimension into the heart of faith. The first of his three volumes of *Herrlichkeit*, *The Glory of the Lord*, 'Seeing the Form', appeals to the aesthetic form of divine revelation itself. Before God's self-revelation is taken into various systematic expositions, it is first of all a glory, a beauty, possessing its own attractive force. It comes as a *Gestalt*, an irreducibly concrete, whole and complete form. Beholding this form does not stop short at the limits of vision as though we are simply dispassionately 'looking at' an object. It invites participation.

---

56. An *advenant* in Romano's vocabulary.
57. Marion, *Being Given*, 203.
58. Marion, *God Without Being: Hors-Texte*, translated by Thomas A Carlson (Chicago, IL: Chicago University Press, 1991), 9–14; *In Excess: Studies of Saturated Phenomena*, translated by Robyn Horner and Vincent Barraud (New York: Fordham University Press, 2002), 72.

Its radiance sweeps the beholder up into an *eros* and rapture, under the attraction of what is revealed in Christ.[59] Von Balthasar writes,

> The Gospel presents Christ's form in such a way that 'flesh' and 'spirit', incarnation to the point of suffering and death, and resurrected life, are all interrelated down to the smallest details. If the Resurrection is excised, then not only certain things but simply everything about Jesus' earthly life becomes incomprehensible . . . [his] death and resurrection . . . are comprehensible only if they are understood as the transformation of this earthly form by God's power, and not as the form's spiritualisation or apotheosis.[60]

David Bentley Hart's theological aesthetics[61] is closely related to von Balthasar's approach.[62] The self-revealing phenomenon of beauty comes on its own terms and transfigures the world of our experience. It makes its own space, and keeps its own distance, for it eludes any fixed structure of apprehension or control.[63] The beautiful form gives itself, not as a pleasurable satisfaction, but as summoning to a self-transcendence in the light of the truth and value it represents. The beautiful crosses over all boundaries, and all types of being. It permeates creation in such a way as to subvert the totalising goal of ideology, be it of a mythic, conceptual or pragmatic kind.

Hart's theological aesthetics are especially focused in the resurrection. The rhetoric celebrating the form of the risen One possesses 'an infinite power of expression' eluding all efforts to silence it.[64] In reference to Luke 24:13–35, Hart remarks:

> as the disciples who encountered the risen Christ on the road to Emmaus discover, Christ can now no longer be recognised as an available and objective datum, a simple given, but must

---

59. Medard Kehl, 'Hans Urs von Balthasar: A Portrai', in Medard Kehl and Werner Löser (eds), *The von Balthasar Reader*, translated by Robert J Daly, SJ, and Fred Lawrence (Edinburgh: T&T Clark, 1985), 47–48.
60. Von Balthasar, *The Glory of the Lord*, 467.
61. David Bentley Hart, *The Beauty of the Infinite: The Aesthetics of Christian Truth* (Grand Rapids, Michigan: Eerdmans, 2003).
62. Hart, *The Beauty of the Infinite*, 15–28.
63. Hart, *The Beauty of the Infinite*, 15–16.
64. Hart, *The Beauty of the Infinite*, 334.

be received entirely as a *donum*, as gift in the breaking of the bread, in the offer of fellowship given anew even when all hope of fellowship seems to have been extinguished.[65]

For Hart, as for von Balthasar, the resurrection does not figure simply as an aesthetic principle. It radically subverts all totalitarian pretensions, be they political, cultural or intellectual. The dehumanising forces of culture appear triumphant in the crucifixion. The cross is their final word in their effort to determine the form of the world.[66] Yet at that very point, the Word of God is definitively and inexhaustibly pronounced: Christ is risen.

The Resurrection as 'Flesh'

The phenomenon of 'my body' or 'flesh' is saturated with a special sense of immediacy and intimacy. While it is 'mine', it is the field of communication with the other. The body or 'flesh', so intimately constituting the subject, gives the possibilities of intimate self-giving and self-disclosure, as in the case of erotic or maternal love. In this sense, the flesh is a field of mutual indwelling, a being with and for the other. In the eros and generativity of love, my bodily being is re-experienced in the flesh of the other.[67] This is to suggest that embodied existence transcends the status of being simply a physical body in a material world, for the human body is the zone of incarnated relationships.[68] The body of my conscious being is affects, and is affected by, the larger phenomenon of the world. My body, therefore, is at once my 'natal bond' with the world, an immediate exposure to it, an immediate participation in it, and a primal communication within it.[69]

In this respect, the phenomenon of the resurrection is a communication of the 'body' of Christ in the Pauline sense, or of the 'flesh' of the Risen One, to use a more Johannine expression. In the Pauline vocabulary, of course, the 'flesh' has negative connotations. Nonetheless, Paul envisages a transformed physicality in a bodily sense: 'For just as the body is one and has many members, and all the members

---

65. Hart, *The Beauty of the Infinite*, 334.
66. Hart, *The Beauty of the Infinite*, 334.
67. Marion, *Le phénomène érotique: Six meditations* (Paris: Grasset, 2003), 185.
68. Marion, *Le phénomène érotique*, 170.
69. Marion, *In Excess*, 100; *Le phénomène érotique*, 170, 180–1.

of the body, though many are one body, so it is with Christ' (1 Cor 12:12). With the diversity of the many spiritual gifts, '. . . you are the body of Christ and individually members of it' (1 Cor 12:27). The shared breath or living atmosphere of the body is the Holy Spirit: this one Spirit is manifested in the diversity of gifts. In this one Spirit, 'we are all baptised into one body . . . and made to drink of the one Spirit' (1 Cor 12:13). To change the metaphor, with some reliance on Merleau-Ponty, the Spirit of Christ is the 'inspiration' and 'expiration' of the risen One invigorating the whole body of Christ.

The transformed body or flesh of the risen Lord is also transformative in its effect. The Word became flesh; and in that flesh, he is crucified, and raised from the dead and taken up into heaven.[70] The flesh, with all the organic and social limitations that are implied, is still, after the resurrection, God's chosen field of communication. For the Christian phenomenon is not accessible to the order of thought alone. It is disclosed only in the phenomenality of body, flesh and 'incarnation'. Ps Dionysius speaks of *pati divina*, 'to experience the things of God' as transcending all thought and imagination. This venerable phrase has a strongly mystical overtone, and figures as such in the elaboration of negative theology. Nonetheless, the tradition it represents must never be separated from the bodily event of the resurrection of crucified One. Experiencing 'the things of God' such as are revealed in the death and resurrection of the incarnate Word, presupposes the mediation of crucified and risen of Jesus *in the flesh*. The Christian connotation of the mystical phrase, *pati divina*, includes the possibility of interpreting it as *pati humana et carnalia*—the experience of God in the flesh and body of Jesus Christ. In Tertullian's cryptic wordplay, *caro est salutis cardo*, the flesh (*caro*) of Christ is the turning point (*cardo*) of our salvation of our embodied existence—as the philosopher Michel Henry so vividly appreciated in his understanding of the Gospel of John. To emphasise the incarnation is not to suggest that the risen Lord is giving expression to a new theology, or that Christians are involved in an ongoing theological seminar. Rather, Christ is the form and source of incarnate, bodily communication. God made him 'the head of all things for the church which is his body, the fullness of him who fills all in all' (Eph 1:22–23).

---

70. Marion, *Being Given*, 239.

The phenomenology of the body inevitably strains against excessively spiritual interpretations. Yet the Church is the body of Christ. He is the head, and we the members. In the Johannine idiom, he is the vine and we the branches, with his flesh given for the life of the world. In this regard, Christ's flesh/ body is the field of his relationship to the world. In that communication, he is both affecting and affected by the manifold reality of our incarnate co-existence. Though now transformed, his risen body continues to be his 'natal bond' with the world. It expresses the immediacy of his exposure to the world in the process of its transformation in him. Through the body, he, the Word incarnate, is constituted in a primal communication with all incarnate beings, and continues to affect the material universe. In that transformed bodily being, he breathes his Spirit into all his members, so that there is one Spirit-vitalised body—even if he is risen and his members on the way to be transformed as he is.

Through incorporation into that subjective-body of Christ, the world is disclosed to his members in its original and eschatological significance. Consciousness is illumined with the 'light of life' (Jn 8:12). Though he has come and remains in the flesh, his vitality emanates from the very life of God: 'What came into being in him was life and the life was the light of all people' (Jn 1:3-4). The primordial generative mystery of the Father is thus revealed in the flesh of the Son: 'Just as the Father has life in himself, so he has granted the Son to have life in himself' (Jn 5:26). In answer to Philip's request, 'Lord, show us the Father, and we shall be satisfied' (Jn 14:8), Jesus replies, 'Whoever has seen me has seen the Father ... Do you not believe that I am in the Father and Father is in me?' (Jn 14:10). Life flows from a source beyond time and space into the living flesh of Christ, and into those united to him. It constitutes the phenomenological condition of Christian corporate existence. This gives rise to an extraordinary sense of inter-subjectivity and mutual indwelling within the incarnational field of divine communication. Jesus prays, '... that they may all be one. As you, Father, are in me, and I in you, may they also be in us' (Jn 17:21). The incarnate 'Word of Life' (1 Jn 1:1) takes the form of a communal existence:

> This life was revealed, and we have seen it and testify to it, and declare to you the eternal life that was with the Father and was revealed to us ... so that you may have fellowship with us; and

truly our fellowship is with the Father and with his Son Jesus Christ (1 Jn 1:2–3).

The life of the vine flows into the branches (Jn 15:5), just as the Head of the Body governs the activity of each of its members. The incarnation, already reaching its fulfilment in him, is extended into a living corporate form of the Church. For those who are 'members, one of another' (Eph 4:25) are united in a life of charity: 'for no man hates his own flesh, but nourishes and cherishes it, as Christ does the church because we are members of his body' (Eph 5:30). The Letter to the Ephesians does not hesitate to appeal to the most intimate, ecstatic and generative human experience of the body in sponsal love to express Christ's relationship to the ecclesial body of believers. Just as man and woman become 'one flesh' (Gen 2:24), the risen One is one flesh with communion of believers. As Wittgenstein appositely remarked, 'It is *love* that believes the resurrection'.[71]

Though Jesus is glorified, his body it is still marked by the wounds of the cross. This represents his compassionate involvement with humanity in its sufferings and with the whole groaning reality of creation (*cf* Rom 8). The power of his resurrection extends into the alienated and mortal sphere of our corporate existence, for 'even when we were dead through our trespasses, [God] has made us alive together with Christ . . . and raised us up with him' (Eph 2:5–6). A new field of incarnate relationships opens up is disclosed in the resurrection of the Crucified. His rising from the dead does not mean disincarnation, but a new form of incarnation. The former sphere of fleshly divisions is now relocated, as it were, in a new form of incarnate existence (Eph 2:14–22). Its vitality derives from Christ's self-giving love, in order that, 'we are to grow up in every way into him who is the head, into Christ, from whom the whole body, joined and knot together by every joint with which it is supplied, when each part is working prop-

---

71. L Wittgenstein, *Culture and Value*, translated by Peter Winch (Chicago: Chicago University Press, 1980), 83. The paragraph reads:
    What inclines even me to believe in Christ's Resurrection? . . . If he did not rise from the dead, then he decomposed in the grave like another man . . . but if I am to be REALLY saved—what I need is certainty—not wisdom, dreams or speculation—and this certainty is faith. And faith is faith in what is needed by my *heart*, my *soul*, not my speculative intelligence. For it is my soul with its passions, as it were with its flesh and blood, that has to be saved, not my abstract mind. Perhaps we can say: only *love* can believe in the Resurrection (83).

erly, makes bodily growth and upbuilds itself in love' (Eph 4:15–16). Physical existence is transformed. A bodily 'mutation' has occurred, as the love that possessed the Head conforms his members to him. His self-giving love is embodied: 'the bread that I will give for the life of the world is my flesh' (Jn 6:51). By sacramentally assimilating his flesh and blood, given and outpoured for the life of the world, believers are conformed to his risen life: 'Those who eat my flesh and drink my blood have eternal life, and I will raise them up on the last day; for my flesh is true food and my blood is true drink' (Jn 6:55).

In the risen Christ, therefore, communication in the flesh does not cease, but opens out to an unimaginable fulfilment. The mutual indwelling and openness to the other, which characterised the earthly experience of the flesh, is now actualised in a new mode of mutual co-inherence: 'Those who eat my flesh and drink my blood, abide in me and I in them' (Jn 6:56; *cf* 15:4, 6). In this paschal realm, believers 'abide in the Son and in the Father' (1 Jn 2:24; *cf* 3:24), and so inhabit a field of love in which earthly *eros* is subsumed into the *agape* of the divine self-giving: 'God is love, and those who abide in love, abide in God, and God abides in them' (1 Jn 4:16). To the degree faith assimilates his flesh and blood and breathes his Spirit, there is new sight, hearing, touching, tasting, eating and drinking, feeling and indwelling—enlivening all the 'senses' of faith, as Origen recognised so clearly.[72] Because of its unobjectifiable immediacy, the flesh earths and embodies faith in the risen One with fresh directness. It counteracts the tendency to abstraction, either in thought or symbol, that ill serves what has been uniquely given.

The Resurrection and the Face of Christ

The phenomenon of the face overbrims with significance, even if in a more distanced manner compared to the intimacy of the flesh. George Orwell expressed something of this in his verse tribute to the 'crystal spirit' on the face of the young Italian militiaman with whom he served in Spain (and in contrast to the terrifying emptiness written on the face of 'Big Brother'). Whenever he read a moving piece of writing, Orwell found himself conscious of 'the face somewhere

---

72. Hans Urs von Balthasar, *The Glory of the Lord,* volume VII: *Theology: The New Covenant,* translated by Brian McNeil, CRV (Edinburgh: T&T Clark, 1989), 308–9.

behind the page, which is not necessarily the actual face of the writer', but as he put it, 'the face that the writer *ought* to have'. Here, he had Charles Dickens especially in mind.[73] This reference conveniently leads into the elusive but ever arresting phenomenon we here consider.

When 'faced' with the other, I am not looking at something amongst other objects in the world, or at a 'somebody' in the crowd. When someone looks at me, I meet with a striking otherness. It lays claim to my attention and concern. Here Marion is influenced by Levinas's widely influential account of 'the other', especially in his/ her suffering. To faced with this other is to feel the force of the question, Where were you, given what you now see?[74] The face paradoxically makes visible the invisible totality of the other. It resists objectification. At the same time, this 'you' calls for a respect and regard, in such a way as to render inhuman any gaze that is just a mere 'looking at', as in the inspection of objects. The centre of gravity is shifted; not *here*, in the perception of the self-contained ego, but *there*, in the other, whose look stops us in our tracks. In this sense, the face of the other is a commanding presence.[75] The face of the other does not reflect back to me what I desire to possess or dominate. It takes me out of myself, into the disturbing world of responsibility, respect and love. The face is not a mirror in which I see myself, but more a window through which the light of arresting otherness breaks through. It calls forth a self-transcendence that goes beyond any symmetries of an 'I and Thou' relationship. For this other who confronts me, face to face, breaks into my awareness as an inviolable uniqueness: 'thou shalt not kill'—despite the disruption it causes in the self-secure world of the ego.

In terms of Christ, we have to admit that the New Testament, when speaking of the risen Jesus, shows no interest in describing a face in any conventional terms. Icons, of course, and the long tradition of Christian art already referred to, have sought to serve revelation and faith by expressing, in Orwell's terms, the face somewhere behind the biblical accounts of Jesus deeds and words. But at its best, faith seek-

---

73. See Michael Sheldon, *Orwell: The Authorised Biography* (London: Minerva, 1992), 343.
74. Emmanuel Levinas, *Ethics and Infinity: Conversations with Philippe Nemo*, translated by Richard A Cohen (Pittsburg: Duquesne University Press, 1985), 85.
75. Marion, *Being Given*, 216; *God Without Being*, 19.

ing to find its best artistic expression is intent on the face of Christ, as the icon of the self-revealing God. Paul speaks expansively of Christ, 'the image of the invisible God (Col 1:15). But the otherness of the transcendent must allowed to appear on its own terms—looking us in the face, rather than being a projection of our look.[76] The only appropriate attitude when faced by the icon is prayer, adoration and self-surrender. The unenvisageable and invisible is rendered visible only to faith, hope and love. Surrender to this kind of evidence exceeds any measure of cognitive or conceptual comprehension. It enjoins a waiting and longing for its final appearance, typified in the earliest recorded Christian prayer, Maranatha, 'Come, Lord'! (1 Cor 16:22; Rev 22:20).[77] The face of Christ as the one who is to come allows for a deferral and delay, filled with an endless diversity of significations through the course of history.

The face of Christ is the face of each other that would call forth the biblical prohibition against killing, and so demand reverence and care, for all bear the image of God. In fact, Christian faith looks upon the Jesus who has in fact been killed by human agencies. He has been raised up, as the embodiment of God's self-giving love: 'They shall look upon the one whom they have pierced' (Jn 19:37). In this kind of gaze, faith anticipates in the world of dim reflections the future 'face to face' vision (1 Cor 13:12). Yet, in the bold Pauline idiom, there is already a kind of experience of the face of Christ who is turned toward us in a light from beyond this world: 'For it is the God who said, 'Let light shine forth out of darkness', who has shone in our hearts to give the light of the knowledge of the glory of God in the face of Christ' (2 Cor 4:6). The most striking aspect of the face of Christ is not so much our seeing, but that of 'being seen through'. In its apocalyptic rhetoric, the Book of Revelation gives a visionary description of the face of Jesus with 'eyes like a flame of fire' (Rev 1:14; 2:18), who declares, 'I know your works', 'your affliction and your poverty', and 'where you live' (Rev 2:2, 9, 12, 19; 3:1, 8, 15). He identifies himself as 'the living one, I was dead, and see, I am alive for evermore' (Rev 1:18). The transparency of all to him pervades the Gospels accounts (for example, Lk 9:47; 11:17; Jn 1:48). Before there are any 'resurrection appearances', before the chosen witnesses see him, he sees them (for

---

76. Marion, *Being Given*, 232.
77. Marion, *In Excess*, 124.

example, Jn 20:27–29). They experience themselves as being 'seen through', and so faced with him as the truth of who they are and what they now called to be.

From Phenomenon to Meaning

After these initial correlations of the resurrection to Marion's list of saturated phenomena, his question lingers: 'Could not theology's demands allow phenomenology to transgress its own limits, so as finally to attain the free possibility at which, from its origin, it claims to aim?'[78] In the present context, we do not presume to teach anything to phenomenology, but rather to receive a fresh orientation from phenomenological attentiveness. Theology must go on, patiently making correlations and picking its way beyond univocity and equivocity in order to say what it can be said with its own criteria and evidence. Resurrection-faith displays its own rationality. It must take account of a singular datum. It is not as though God is giving us a saturated phenomenon, nor even new range of concepts and suggestive analogies. With the revelation of Christ, the whole of creation in him is newly sensed in its original and final coherence (Col 1:15–18). When the crucified Jesus rises from the tomb, there is a sense in which our reason and our powers of perception also rise the place of death and decay. Reason begins to occupy its place in a world made new, and our experience expands into the domain of what is new-in-the-making. In short, Christian phenomenology must learn to account for the God-given phenomenality of perceptions of faith, hope and love.

The phenomenon is of the resurrection is productive of various dimensions of meaning. In this respect, meaning in the rhetoric of the New Testament unfolds in three great arcs.[79] First, Christ is presented as the fulfilment of all the promises of God—for he is the 'yes' to all God's promises, and the 'amen' to all our prayers (2 Cor 1:20). Secondly, to live, now and forever, is to participate in what he is, be it in a Johannine mutual indwelling and communion (Jn 17:20–21; 1 Jn 1:1–3), or in the Pauline idiom of being baptized into his death and resurrection (Rom 6:3–11). Thirdly, in the resurrection the cosmic

---

78. Marion, 'Le possible et la revelation', 228.
79. See *Evocations of Grace*, edited by Joseph Sittler, in Steven Bouma-Prediger and Peter Bakken (Grand Rapids: Eerdmans, 2000), 92–116.

expansiveness of God's design in Christ comes to light, with everything created in him, through him, for him, so that in him 'all things hold together' (Col 1:15–18). Christ is, at were, the divine 'univocity', even if the human mind, impatient to capture it, would veer toward a Gnostic ideology. Theology must be content with a nexus of analogies and fragmented perceptions, ever ready to defer to what can be revealed only in the end. The phenomena we have correlated to the resurrection are 'saturated' only because that is the way creation-in-Christ actually is. At the risk of putting it all too crudely and forcing terms beyond any reasonable extension, phenomena are saturated because the risen Christ saturates all phenomena. There is a giving and a given-ness in, before, and beyond, anything the phenomenal world can give.

The supersaturated Christic world is productive of meaning.[80] This meaning is *effective*; it shapes the world in different ways: if Christ is risen, then there is work to be done. The violence of oppressors must not go unchallenged, neither must the suffering neighbour be left without hope, nor the sinful and the guilty be left without mercy and forgiveness. The meaning of Christ, crucified and risen, is also *communicative*. It forms an historical community, living from and mediating 'the resurrection and the life' (Jn 11:25). Such meaning is also *constitutive*: it informs human consciousness to affect one's sense of self and its experience of subjectivity: 'If Christ has not been raised, your faith is futile and you are still in your sins' (1 Cor 15:17). More ontologically, the meaning of the resurrection is *cognitive*. Theology affirms *this*, not *that*, *something* and not *anything* or *nothing*. It knows the differences between plenitude and emptiness, life and death, truth and illusion, divine action and human response, seeing and believing, and all the rest. Note that NT Wright and JD Crossan in their exchanges would seem to agree in every domain of meaning except the cognitive.[81] Yet without that objectivity, the salvific realism of faith is lacking.

Paradoxically, the salvific realism inherent in the cognitive dimension of faith's meaning is most served by a disciplined return to the phenomenality of the resurrection. The adjective 'salvific' is used to

---

80. Here I am using Lonergan's four dimensions of meaning as found in his *Method in Theology*, 76–81.
81. See *The Resurrection of Jesus. John Dominic Crossan and NT Wright in Dialogue* edited by Robert B Stewart (Minneapolis MN: Fortress Press, 2006).

highlight the precise kind of realism involved. It is not contrary to the respective realisms of phenomenological, historical, metaphysical, scientific and anthropological methods. Each has its own limitations, particular concerns, traditions of interpretation, criteria of evidence. Salvific realism is focused on a unique event. It is, first of all, intent on being receptive to the phenomenality of that event which is the focal point of faith, and a shock at the foundations of every theology.[82] If the methods of other forms of phenomenological disclosure and patterns of knowing end by declaring the resurrection to be a non-reality, a non-event, the problem could largely be an unexamined prejudice against the singularity and effectiveness of historical phenomena. If this is the case, it is not helped by a theological method, either unaware of what is at stake, or simply taking for granted what should be taken *as* granted, and, therefore, to be respected in the singular conditions of its 'given-ness'. It is of greatest theological importance not to be distracted into apologetics before discerning the unique form of what has been given. Apologetics is at its most persuasive when Christian faith risks being rejected for the right reasons. Only in this way, can the resurrection be perceived as reasonable, and reason be receptive to the 'resurrectional'. The phenomenology of resurrection faith has reasons that Enlightenment reason has forgotten or is yet to discover.

---

82. For extensions of the 'resurrection effect' into trinitarian theology, ethics and interfaith dialogue, see Kelly, *The Resurrection Effect*, 153–172.

Beginning Again

To write again, if not perfect poems,
at least to feel that excess of meaning
awkward in corridors and too loud in libraries,
cluttering desks, a distraction at prayer--
and unsettling the agenda generally.
Its the old thrill, to write freely
not knowing what you have to say,
but being written in a way . . .
Lower case inspiration, you might call it . . .
Whatever the case, despite the theories,
things get given: there's store enough
in nostril and tongue, in skin and eye and ear,
and in the push and pull of being here,
to say nothing of a larger undertow
of presence and absence somehow --
so enjoying the limits of vocabulary,
and resonance and dance,
and the times being as they are,
to wait, pencil poised, or fingering a keyboard,
listening . . .

Exploration Into God

In any exploration into God the preposition, 'into', is important. If the mystery of God is infinite, then the exploration is necessarily open-ended; and, in the deepest sense, inconclusive. Indeed, theologians have long stressed that even in the beatific vision of God face to face, one aspect of that vision is to see that God is absolutely uncontainable and never fully graspable by any finite mind. Indeed, only God can really 'get' God. Even in the bliss of the blessed, the infinite mystery can never be exhausted, for it calls forth an endless kind of joyous exploration. It gives a knowledge that leads into an ever-continuing knowing, a love that keeps on being love for the infinite goodness and beauty that are revealed, a delight that draws ever more fully from the divine joy and bliss.

We can lament over the strange kind of amnesia that can come into cultures and even creep into religious studies and theological systems, church communications and interreligious dialogue—a forgetfulness of God, even though the light that God is underpins all searchings for meaning, value and beauty. Each step along the way of exploration into God opens to new perspectives. There can be no definitive statement. After all, theology deals with the darkness and light of God, the analogical character of our knowing, the singularity of revelation, and the absolute and limitless Be-ing of God. The words of the Fourth Lateran Council continue to be a wholesome reminder: 'between creator and creature no similarity can be noted without a greater dissimilarity being noted' (*DS* 806). Nonetheless, there are some conclusions that may be drawn, each pointing the way forward into a greater sense of the mystery into which believers have been drawn.

The Absent Frontier

There is what has been called 'an absent frontier' in so much of our religious and even theological conversation, with the result that references to God become stale and banal. Cultural conditioning plays a part in making the frontier seem so distant and, indeed, absent. Further, our very familiarity with religion, theology, liturgy, and religious expression, theoretical and practical, can desensitise us to the most radical and crucial of all questions, 'where is your God?' (Ps 42). One question begets many: How is God to be found? What are we looking for? And why bother? The first chapter of John's Gospel, after hymning the incarnation of the Word of God amongst us, prepares believers to receive the whole message of the Gospel. It is worth noting, therefore, that the first words of the Word addressed to the disciples who have begun to follow Jesus, are a question, 'what are you looking for?' (Jn 1:38). Questions keep recurring in every time and culture as to where God is to be found, and how is God the fulfilment of all we long for. Such questions lose none of their edge in our present situation when they are ignored. The pressures of culture from without, and our oppressive familiarity with religious practices and expressions from within, make it necessary to refresh, as best we can, the boundless horizon in which we think and act and pray—all aspects of an orientation to the mystery that attracts us as nothing else can. The idea of God, In Nietzsche's vivid language, is not meant to be a spider sucking the vitality out of human existence, but the mystery that is the 'transfiguration and eternal Yes' to what life is about. He wrote:

> The Christian conception of God—as god of the sick, God as a spider, God as spirit—is one of the most corrupt conceptions of the divine ever attained on earth. It may even represent the low-water mark in the descending development of divine types. God degenerated into a *contradiction* of life, instead of being its transfiguration and eternal Yes! God as the declaration of war against life, against nature, against the will to live! God—the formula for every slander against 'this world', for every lie about the 'beyond'! God the deification of nothingness, the will to nothingness pronounced holy.[1]

---

1. Friedrich Nietzsche, *The Antichrist*, in *The Portable Nietzsche*, edited and translated by Walter Kaufmann (New York: The Viking Press, 1972), 585–586.

The culture of the present is in a state of flux. It has entered into a postmodern situation in which 'God is dead' sounds all too certain, while affirming the opposite in this pluralist age has value only as a personal conviction leaving the wider world untouched. Part of the problem is language. A literal-minded age may not recognise the flexibility and range of reference in language attempting to name all dimensions of reality. Hence, theology stresses the special character of analogical language: words and ideas born of experience in the routine world can be stretched, as it were, toward what is other. When that evocative and creative character of language wanes, words drown in the flood of advertising and media chatter.

There are problems also as to the character of knowledge itself. If theology is traditionally described as 'faith seeking understanding', it might be considered as an odd type of knowledge, at best as an emotive or mythological rhetoric. Things look different with the realisation that a form of faith—and love, too—pervades all efforts to understand. In a paradoxical sense, the more self-involved we are in mind, heart and imagination, the more we come to know realities beyond the routine scope—as when the love of nature informs ecological and environmental sciences. It is not extreme to claim that a commitment to love God with all one's heart and mind and soul and strength results in a special kind of knowledge of God as it is expressed in the Bible and in the mystics, great and small.[2]

It is widely recognised that 'God' can easily as appear as serving both idolatrous and mythological fundamentalism. Indeed, there are classic resources to be retrieved in Aquinas' notion of God as sheer, all-actual, Be-ing, that is, not as a 'supreme being' among many 'beings'. Such a notion need not distract from the personal and concrete sense of personal faith and replace it with a vague colourless abstraction. The sheer, all-actual Be-ing of God forms the horizon in which all biblical, doctrinal and experiential data on the character of God can be appreciated in their depth and singularity. Not to attempt this can lead to a flat fundamentalism. Expressions of faith lack a sense of wonder and incapable of speaking with conviction in the dialogical situation of faith today, especially concerning God as life's 'transfiguration and eternal Yes', as Nietzsche suggests.

---

2. For example, Anne Hunt, *The Trinity: Insights from the Mystics* (Collegeville, MN: Liturgical Press, 2010).

We now briefly pause on the sense of God inherent in our experience

God-Ward Orientation

Exploration into God does not begin with a big idea of God, or even with an idea of a big God. There is no question of demeaning of the divine mystery, or subjecting it to something outside itself. Rather, we begin, not with a big idea, but with what precedes all ideas—the fundamental orientation of our conscious being. Here, as elsewhere, we gratefully acknowledge, the influence of Bernard Lonergan when he writes:

> Now an orientation to transcendent mystery is basic to systematic theology. It provides the primary and fundamental meaning of the name, God. It can be the bond uniting all men despite cultural difference. It provides the origin for inquiry about God, for seeking assurance of his existence, for endeavouring to reach some understanding of the mysteries of faith, at the same time it is quite in harmony with the conviction that no system we can construct will encompass or plumb or master the mystery by which we are held.[3]

The following seven points are worth noting:

i) An orientation to transcendent mystery to basic to theology. Such an orientation is based in that self-transcending movement of mind and heart as it looks beyond any present attainments to search for the ultimate meaning of all that is found meaningful, to find the ultimate worth of everything that is worthwhile, good, and valuable, finally to enjoy fully the beauty and the love that persistently filled the heart with longing;

ii) This orientation based in the self-transcending dynamism of our conscious being provides 'the primary and basic meaning of the name, God'. In other words, and in a traditional idiom, God is named first of all as the One who alone can 'save our souls', where

---

3. Bernard Lonergan, *Method in Theology* ((London: Darton, Longman and Todd, 1972), 342.

'soul' means the self-transcending movement of existence toward fulfilment and ultimate rest only in absolute truth and absolute goodness;

iii) This orientation is such that it can bring together those who are culturally divided and inspire interreligious dialogue in the light of the ever greater God;

iv) This orientation leads to limitless questions but also anticipates ultimate answers: we would not be seeking God unless, in some way, we had already found him, or even more deeply, unless the grace of God had already founds us;

v) From this orientation comes the search for a proof, or intimation or assurance of the existence and presence of God in a world of meaning which cultures can be hostile to religion, to what transcends the world and is opposed to what disturbs their self-containment;

vi) This orientation finds explicit expression in faith, and faith as a self-transcending openness to the Other, seeks understanding of the mysteries of God as articulated in the Scriptures, in the teachings of the Church, and as explored in the long labour of theology to enrich understanding with a deeper knowledge of what has been revealed;

vii) The orientation toward God is dynamic and can never congeal into a closed system, lacking a sense of the limitless mystery of God and of the singularity of what has been revealed.

In his *Method in Theology*, Lonergan describes religious believers as drawn to a higher form of self-transcendence. They undergo a conversion in an event that 'dismantles and abolishes the horizon in which their knowing and choosing went on and sets up a new horizon in which the love of God will transvalue our values and the eyes of that love will transform our knowing.[4] Consequently, we cannot but agree with Karl Rahner's more specifically theological statement that the 'experience of God really constitutes the very heart and center of Christianity itself and also the ever-living source of that conscious manifestation which we call "revelation".[5] For his part, Hams Urs von

---

4. Lonergan, *Method in Theology*, 106.
5. Karl Rahner, 'The Experience of God Today', in *Theological Investigations XI*, translated by David Bourke (London: Darton, Longman and Todd, 1974), 164.

Balthasar specifies the relation to God as 'the movement away from myself, the preference of what is other and greater'.[6] Such approaches find solid support in biblical accounts of the experience of the prophets and in the Gospel's narrative of the challenges faced by Jesus' disciples in proclaiming the Kingdom of God.

The question of God and of any exploration into God has suffered enormously by being cut off from religious experience, especially the mystical or 'sub-mystical' as the living field of reference. A muscle-bound rationality favoring (or attacking) objective doctrinal expressions tended to push to the margins any consideration of the experience out of which doctrines arose. As a result, knowing God became more and more to be regarded as an assent to a cerebral proposition regarding divine existence and the Trinity of persons. The self-communication of God going on in the humble dress of ordinary experience was hardly registered. However, in the push and pull of daily experience, people feel the tug of truth in their dealing with one another and the insistent impulse to love and to keep on loving even to the point of continuing prayer and acts of forgiveness.

All exploration into God, however, must encounter the problem of evil. The encounter with evil however stark, oppressive and piercing, must take a larger picture into account, made up of the accumulated experience of many other aspects of reality and dimensions of human experience. The problem of evil collides always with the 'problem' of goodness and beauty, of hope and moral goodness, the problem of why anything exists—including ourselves—and the character of that consciousness in which these 'problems' occur. Moreover, a religious attitude intensifies the problem. The more there is a sense of God, the more evil in all its forms and influences is felt to be grotesque and obscene. To that degree, there is a point in oft-repeated adage: 'religion is the wound, not the bandage'!

In the experience of the good and beauty—and of the parasitical presence of evil in whatever is good and beautiful—the great Mystery beckons, at once from within, and yet from beyond the time-and-space-bound limits of human existence. It is the conviction of faith that God acts in order that human beings may find their ultimate ful-

---

6. Hans Urs von Balthasar, *The Glory of the Lord I, The Glory of the Lord. A Theological Aesthetics I: Seeing the Form*, translated by Erasmo Leiva-Merikakis, edited by Joseph Fessio, SJ and John Riches (Edinburgh: T&T Clark, 1982), 237.

filment in the divine life. It is not as though our searching discovers God or somehow attracts divine favour. The initiative is all on God's part. Paul, in his discourse to the Athenians, emphasises that precise point:

> ... [God] allotted the times of their existence and the boundaries of their places ... so that they would search for God and perhaps grope for him and find him—even though he is not far from each one of us. For 'in him we live and move and have our being...' (Acts 17:26–28)

In the face of the atheism of our day and the idolatries embedded in our culture, faith in the One God is a counter-cultural stance, as already mentioned.[7] Biblically speaking, faith in God is always a choice against obvious cultural deities—the 'false gods', whatever they might be: 'You shall not have strange gods before me' (Deut 5:7). In biblical terms, God is not *Baal*, the deification of nature (cf 1 Kgs 16–18), nor *Moloch*, the idol of political power (Lev 18–20; 1 Kgs 11:7), nor *Mammon*, the idol of greed and possessions (*cf* Mt 6:24, etc). True faith cannot serve both the One God and false gods. In the end, idols inspire, not the liberating self-surrender of faith, but the sacrifice of what is most properly human within us. And so, by contesting all forms of cultural self-enclosure, commitment to God is a source of creativity within history and society. In the face of the emptiness and universal doubt that hugely affect the modern era, faith in the One God lays the foundation for the continual renewal of hope. When there is a loss of the sense of the transcendent, a prevailing mood is that of cosmic despair while public agnosticism is presumed in the social, intellectual and moral conversation of the time.

Despite the cultural incubus, commitment to God has a transformative effect. Lonergan speaks of a fundamental Godward orientation taking for the form of a radical self-transcendence. A deep and far-reaching conversion is set in motion and leads one into 'a new horizon in which the love of God will transvalue our values and the

---

7. Note the following remark of Bernard Lonergan on authentic religion:

   > ... a religion that promotes self-transcendence to the point, not merely of justice, but of self-sacrificing love, will have a redemptive role in human society inasmuch as such love can undo the mischief of decline and restore the cumulative process of progress (*Method in Theology*, 55).

eyes of that love will transform our knowing'.⁸ In the language of tradition, charity informs all virtues, and works in human consciousness to produce wisdom, a depth and intimacy of knowing, that can savor the mystery of God. The path of exploration into God is necessarily accompanied by a love, wisdom and selflessness as notable gifts of the Spirit.

The metaphysical objectivity of the scholastic tradition privileged theoretical precision and intellectual rigor in our knowledge of God. However, the rich account of affectivity of the heart that accompanied this highly intellectual approach of mind has often been overlooked, specially the role of the Spirit permeating Christian consciousness: '... no one comprehends what is truly God's except the Spirit of God. Now we have received not the spirit of the world, but the Spirit that is from God, so that we may understand the gifts that are bestowed on us by God' (1 Cor 2:9–10). A new field of communication is the result: 'And we speak of these things in words not taught be human wisdom but taught by the Spirit, interpreting spiritual things to those who are spiritual' (1 Cor 2:9–13).

Faced with these and similar New Testament texts (for example 1 Jn 2:27), theological systems were somewhat at a loss. There is a gifted excess, in the gift of the Spirit and in the knowledge it leads to. It gave rise to the tradition of 'spiritual senses', as found with different emphases in the writings of Origen, Augustine, Bonaventure, Ignatius of Loyola.⁹ Such authors presumed that a lively expanded and embodied experience accompanied all knowledge of God.¹⁰

The love that informs faith, not only unites believers to God, but also locates them in the community of faith. Faith is a social bond which gives rise to shared scriptural, doctrinal, institutional and moral beliefs, expressive of shared sense of what has been revealed and must now be passed on to future generations. In this shared awareness or sense of faith makes its own the body of attestations,

---

8. Lonergan, *Method in Theology*, 106.
9. Von Balthasar, *The Glory of the Lord*, 365–380. For a variety of historical perspectives, see *The Spiritual Senses: Perceiving God in Western Christianity*, edited by Paul Gavrilyuk and Sarah Coakley (Cambridge: Cambridge University Press, 2012).
10. See, for instance, Pierre Rousselot, SJ, *The Eyes of Faith and Answers to Two Objections*, translated by J Donceel and Avery Dulles (New York: Fordham University Press, 1990).

narratives and judgments as found in the Gospels and other writings of the New Testament. That appropriation of the earliest written tradition can hardly be separated from the Church's liturgical action (as we will soon mention). The common celebration in adoration and thanksgiving of what has been revealed in Christ is the site in which Word of God, in Scripture or proclamation, lives and works its transformative effect. Within the developments of its history, faith is further focused, and the beliefs that express it are more sharply articulated in the words of the creeds, in symbolic communications, in the witness of saints, doctors and martyrs, in the rise of theologies, and in the development of the arts—musical, figurative, architectural and so forth.

'Letting Go'

Perspectives on how the reality of God is known and experienced lose nothing by being earthed in the deep cultural movements of our time. Martin Heidegger can instruct us on this level, even if he drew back from any theological or religious commitment. In his *Discourse on Thinking*,[11] we find the philosopher's notion of *Gelassenheit*—translatable as 'releasement', with connotations of 'abandonment', 'detachment' and 'letting go' in regard to everyday patterns of knowing and choosing. The goal is a receptive and courageous attachment to the real ground of existence.[12] For Heidegger, the modern malaise is a flight from 'meditative thinking', that is, contemplative attunement to the wholeness and originality of being. The modern fragmentation of thinking and distraction from the wholeness of being is the product of a technological culture. What is needed is a refreshed openness and receptivity to counter the technological style of calculative thinking and the manner of existence it promotes. This entails a 'letting go' of the compulsions, control and preoccupations that have cramped existence into an alien pattern.[13] To be released from all this opens the possibility of welling in the world in a new and wholesome way. Consequently true thinking is not locked in itself, but looks beyond

---

11. Martin Heidegger, *Discourse on Thinking: A Translation of Gelassenheit*, by John M Anderson and E Hans Freund (New York: Harper Torchbooks, 1969).
12. Heidegger, *Discourse on Thinking*, 53–56.
13. Heidegger, *Discourse on Thinking*, 58–61.

itself to the mystery that already possesses us. It means entering the 'region' of the whole truth of being which is really our home and native place, even if it cannot be represented or reduced to the categories of the routine world of ordinary perceptions and activities.[14] Compulsive manipulative habits of action must yield to a more centered and serene style. It manifests itself as a kind of non-acting compared to the preoccupations of routine busy-ness and control, just as it points to the need of receptivity and waiting for the whole truth to reveal itself. This whole truth is impervious to analysis or control, and yet constitutes the proportion in which the human being exists in a wholesome and thankful manner.[15]

The existential attitude that Heidegger evokes has remarkable similarities with the concerns of the eminent Christian thinkers referred to above. Lonergan presupposes a pre-conceptual orientation to God preceding and grounding all eventual expression, and working as an undertow in the consciousness of faith. Rahner placed consistent emphasis on the ever-present, incomprehensible mystery affecting all our knowledge and love and action. Von Balthasar interprets knowing God as demanding a continuous looking away from oneself and one's activities or abilities, for the sake of the inexhaustible mystery. How much these eminent thinkers drew inspiration from Heidegger is not for the present writer to say, except to observe a notable convergence of concerns, despite the differences in language and idiom. They all sought to allow for a transcendent horizon of self-transcendence in order that the human spirit might breathe.

Gifts of the Spirit

In this context, the traditional theology of the gifts of the Holy Spirit is important. One way or another, it influenced the theologians just cited, and may even have indirectly influenced Heidegger through the German mystical writers familiar with the writings of Aquinas, especially Meister Eckhart. He wrote, 'All that God asks you most

---

14. Heidegger, *Discourse on Thinking*, 64, 73, 80.
15. Heidegger, *Discourse on Thinking*, see especially 81–90. The text is so highly evocative as a whole that attempts to give precise references seem like relapsing into calculative thinking!

pressingly is to go out of yourself . . . and let God be God in you'.[16] As regards Aquinas' *Summa*, despite its emphasis on objective intelligibility, logical precision and systematic exposition, it intriguingly included, and repeatedly made room for, what could never be systematized, namely, the gift of the Spirit. For St Thomas, the gifts of the Spirit lead to both an intimate knowledge of God, and union with the divine will in every domain of action. These gifts work in a supra-rational manner and enable heart and mind to have a sense of God in ways that can never be reduced to the routine frameworks in which we construct and understand our world.

The seven gifts of the Holy Spirit are traditionally enumerated as wisdom, understanding, counsel, fortitude, knowledge, piety and fear of the Lord. Aquinas presents these gifts as saturating every aspect of our knowing and choosing, so enabling the faithful to respond to the movement of the Spirit and to act in a manner that is 'beyond the human measure'.[17] While the life of faith engages the hardy world of objective and rational theological discourse, the gifts of the Spirit represent a vertically-given excess, extending, or even disrupting, the horizons of reason alone. Intelligence must be receptive, and waiting, as it were, on the gift from above, in order to know and to act in a way that respects the transcendent character of the Spirit's action. Each gift is, therefore, an aspect of transforming grace of the Spirit and specifies a particular buoyant receptivity within Christian consciousness to the Spirit's 'supra-rational' action. The gifts of the Spirit contrast, therefore, to the muscle-bound rational systems that can so easily take control of theological exploration. An appreciation of these gifts, therefore, leads to a healthy deconstruction of a one-dimensional rational or calculative mode of thinking, while suggesting other domains of spiritual perception.

The Thomist account of the gifts recognises a certain strain or dislocation inherent in the life of faith and its present way of knowing God. There is an essential cloudiness and limitation in our human mode of knowing. While there is a native aptitude for the pursuit of the good and the truth proportionate to this present mode of human

---

16. *Meister Eckhart: The Essential Sermons, Commentaries, Treatises and Defense*, translated by Edmund Colledge and Bernard McGinn (New York: Paulist Press, 1981), 184. For an excellent chapter of Eckhart, see Hunt, *The Trinity: Insights from the Mystics*, 73–98.
17. *III Sent* d. 34, q. 1 a. 1; *STh* 1-2, 70, 4.

existence in the world, such a proportionate attunement is lacking when it comes to knowing the revealed God and participating in the divine life. Hence, the gifts of the Spirit are necessary complement to the life of faith in that they attune the mind and heart of the believer to the divine milieu in which faith must now live, guided by 'an instinct and movement of the Holy Spirit'.[18] A mono-dimensional rationality would tend to go against the kind of receptivity and surrender that the gift of the Spirit entails. The gifts of the Spirit have, therefore, a healing effect for they equip the faithful with a special instinct. Faith can thereby reach beyond mundane patterns of calculation, to know God in a more intimate and experiential manner.[19]

Knowing God comes to mean more than having bright ideas or making correct deductions. There is the gift of Spirit-infused 'wisdom' providing a special 'taste' (*sapientia*, translated as wisdom, from *sapere*, 'to taste') for the things of God.[20] 'This kind savoring experience gives faith a 'feel' for the totality of God's self-revelation in Christ. Then, there is the gift of "understanding" (*intellectus*) implying a clear-eyed perception of the uniqueness of divine revelation, and protecting it from the general impressions and projections that would dim its unique originality and reduce it to some general class of religious phenomena.'[21] The gift of 'knowledge' (*Scientia*) likewise bears on the singular uniqueness of divine revelation, saving its universal significance from being lost in an empty and meaningless contingency.[22] Then there gifts of another type, more related to our choosing and loving. Through the further gift of *pietas* (often

---

18. *STh* 1-2, q 68, a 2.
19. In the activity of the theological virtues is found the radical condition for the operation of the gifts. The movement of the Spirit is recognized in charity: 'faith is about what is not seen, hope is concerned with what is not possessed, but the love of charity concerns the one who is already possessed, for the beloved is somehow within the lover, and also the lover is affectively attracted to be united with the beloved' (*STh* 1-2, 66, 5). The work of Francis X Clooney, *His Hiding Place is Darkness: A Hindu-Catholic Theopoetics of Divine Absence* (Stanford, CA: Stanford University Press, 2014) invites further applications of the gifts to interfaith dialogue, as it accents the primacy of love, the darkness and absence that affect knowledge of the Beloved, and the need for a theopoetics to evoke the full reality of the particularity of Christian revelation. See his concluding remarks, 140–141.
20. *STh* 2-2, q. 45, a. 1–6.
21. *STh* 2-2, q 8, a 1–8.
22. *STh* 2-2, q 9, a 1–4.

poorly translated as 'piety'), Christian consciousness is disposed to live with an intimate sense of filial relationship with the God of love and mercy. The gift of 'fear of the Lord' (*timor Domini*) brings with it a radical poverty of spirit, along with a reverent sensitivity to the ways God and a readiness to surrender to divine providence.[23] In the domain of moral action, the gift of 'counsel' (*consilum*) is the special Spirit-guided instinct for responding to the divine will in the details of individual and social life.[24] The spirit of 'fortitude' is manifested in a vigorous choosing of the ways of God and in a rejection of the contrary.[25]

These brief remarks on the gifts of the Spirit suggest a certain buoyancy and assurance in any exploration into God. The gifts act in a supra-rational way and surpass the scope of reason alone—what Heidegger would call 'calculative thinking'. The gifts are identified within the history of religious and Christian experience as enabling an attitude of 'letting go' and self-surrender. They allow the mystery of the ever-greater God to have its way in the mind and heart of the believer. Thus, the consciousness of faith is lifted to new levels. To that degree, knowing God entails being always open to the surprises that only the Spirit of God can give.

Liturgical Action

It might seem to some that this exploration is an eccentric mixture of metaphysics and mysticism, theology, and exalted abstractions. Any exploration worthy of the name, however, must come down to earth, and keeps its feet on the ground. A deliberate act of grounding occurs above all in the liturgy. The *opus Dei* of the liturgy is not a matter of more thinking, nor a keener and more mystical manner of experiencing, nor living with an expanded consciousness. Nor, for that matter, does liturgy so concentrate on the nameless Other that our exploration into God must exclude a wide and deep experience of life in this world. The liturgy is not about doing or producing something. Rather, its essential form is to enact, in the time and space, and in the midst of all the contingencies of life, the real sense of God

---

23. *STh* 2-2, q 19, a 1-12.
24. Cf. *STh ll*, 2-2, q 52, a 1-4.
25. Cf *STh* 2-2, q 139, a 1.

in all creation, and, indeed, of all creation in God. Liturgy is at once an earthed and englobing activity, not in the sense of reducing the manifold of the world to a narrow band of religiosity, but of opening the pluriform reality of the world to both its real depth and its ultimate future. And yet, positioned in the here and now, it is at once an affirmation and a hope. From that perspective, liturgical activity is resistance to the sheer oppressive weight of what is often called the 'secular' as opposed to the 'religious'. Yet this resistance is not based on a calculation of greater strength or power, as though the religious dimension subverts or swallows the secular. The service of God, if it is of *God*, and not of an idol of human construction. Nor, indeed, is it some kind of group-dynamic of demonic possession or narrowly focused obsession. Liturgical action, in contrast, is possible only in poverty of spirit. It moves in a humility resulting from the openness and abandonment that arise from being left with nothing but God and what God can do. It is the conduct of patience, poverty and surrender to God in the world, and of finding all we call 'the world' in God. Indeed, from that point of view, the Church is that part of the world that brings to expression the universal mystery at work in every aspect of the world.

In this sense, liturgy is a refusal to allow the spirit of our common humanity to be suffocated by the spurious opposition of the religious and the secular: the secular is too important for that, situated as it must always be within the horizon of God's creative action; and the religious, in its explicit relationship to the Source of creation and salvation, is more real than a decorative addition to the rituals of a particular culture. To act liturgically, is to 'do God'—in word, symbol, in art and community, in the time and space of the here and now, even while being exposed to ideology and mono-dimensional secularism. Yet the liturgy humbly presses on in its daily, weekly and yearly round. However poor and naked, it gives expression to the presence of God in the world, and of everything we call 'the world', in God.[26] The liturgy 'does' faith (and hope and love) in God—'doing God'—in the limitation and poverty of a moment in space and time. It means not holding to exalted moods, beautiful words, or noble sentiments,

---

26. I am indebted to an as yet unpublished lecture of Kevin Hart, "'Poverty's Speech": On Liturgical Reduction'—especially in reference to Jean-Yves Lacoste, *Experience and the Absolute: Disputed Questions on the Humanity of Man*, translated by Mark Raferty-Skeban (New York: Fordham University Press, 2010).

but being left with nothing but God, and with what God is doing as all creation anticipates its fulfilment in God. To that degree, liturgical action is the expression of a radical poverty and cultural nakedness, even a non-experience compared to the vividness of ordinary secular experience.

Nonetheless, the liturgy, as the service of God, is world-forming, in its wholeness, and in its openness to the depths and heights of the present, and to the eschatological future. Liturgical acts are characterised by patience, poverty and hope, taking place in time, but toward that future when God will be all in all.

From this point of view, Christian liturgy bears clear resemblances to all kinds of sacred rituals and their ways of offering participation in sacred space and sacred time. From a specifically Christian perspective, a number of particular features could be mentioned if the liturgy is to be presented in terms of an exploration into God—the inspired scriptures, the sacraments, the real presence of Christ in the Eucharist, the transformations of grace, the communion of saints and so forth. Here two remarks can be made.

The first treats of the confession of sins, a typical introductory rite in all Christian liturgical activities. In this respect, the Christian liturgy concretely actualizes exploration into God, but not so as to present the faithful as conquering heroes or daring explorers. We are sinners who are confronted with the truth of evil we have caused or contributed to, and, therefore, unable to proceed further into God without invoking the divine mercy for healing and forgiveness. Such a confession is allied to the way of negation. The confession of sins and prayer for mercy mark an exploration into the God who is 'out of this world' in terms of its structures of identity and moral judgments. For in the present world, justice moderates society by declaring the accused guilty or not guilty. Courts of law have the power to draw conclusions from any finding of guilt or innocence. In a society armed with the laws and procedures of justice, it is dangerous to admit to moral guilt and to ask forgiveness, for that would be a form of public nakedness and vulnerability. Any such confession can be manipulated, perhaps to be portrayed as a symptom of weakness and lack of integrity. But in the liturgical confession of sins, the community of believers stands before God to acknowledge how it has resisted the will of God in thought word, deed and omission, 'through my fault, though my most grievous fault'. To admit sinfulness in this way, publicly, even if with due discretion, is an intensely counter-cultural act. It establishes the liturgy as a movement into the God who cannot be contained in even the most respectable structures of the world.

Second, there is the liturgy focuses on Christ. The readings from scripture place liturgical activity within the corporate history of Old and New Testaments. The Bible is not a compilation of information, but an invitation to enter through faith into the history of God's self-revelation. Divine revelation continues as an ongoing and inexhaustible event, centered in the promise and fulfillment that have occurred in Christ. In that frame of mind, the Eucharist is celebrated within the horizon of the universe of God's creation in Christ. Consequently, the liturgy occurs in a God-charged field in which the universe is being transformed into God's new creation, centred in Christ, 'the firstborn of all creation' (Col 1:15).

In all its acts, the Eucharistic liturgy envisions, and even enacts, the world 'otherwise', as it is before God. Christ has occupied the depths and the heights of that world through his death, resurrection, and his ascension to the fullness of his humanity with God. The liturgical doxology, 'through him, with him and in him' evokes the reality of the new creation in Christ as a field of communion and mutual indwelling. His disciples inhabit the world in a new way, as a community based in the unity the Father and the Son: 'that they may be one as we are one' (Jn 17:11). Jesus' ascent to the Father relocates believers into a space of holy communion and mutual indwelling: 'As you, Father, are in me, and I am in you, may they also be in us, so that the world may believe that you have sent me' (Jn 17: 20–21).

Each Eucharistic liturgy realises an answer to the prayer of Jesus, 'that they may all be one. As you, Father, are in me and I in you, may they also be in us . . . I in them and you in me, that they may be completely one' (Jn 17:21–22). By implication, the liturgical horizon unfolds in the inter-relationships and mutual indwelling deriving from the union existing between the Father and the Son. Each is *in* the other for the life of the other. By being from the other, for the other, and so, *in* the other, the liturgical praise of the Father, Son and Spirit arises from participation in God's own Trinitarian life. This is to say that the Eucharist is not 'virtual reality' in any sense. It is a Spirit-inspired form of actual reality, communicating Christ as the 'real food' and 'real drink' of eternal life. In this regard, the liturgy of the Eucharist brings together what is often kept apart—the reality of

God, consciousness of the self in relation to others, and the emerging universe itself. As the sacrament centred on the 'real' presence of Christ, liturgical consciousness is not a distraction from the reality, but an immersion into it. The liturgy, therefore, 're-members' and brings together in a new integrity the fractured experience of humanity on many levels. As holy communion, it joins believers to Christ's Body, and summons them to participate in its growth. The risen and ascended Christ, he is not *here* in any sense of worldly location, but present beyond any worldly measure or containment. Christ is not located in the world because that world now exists in him (Col 1:16).

In liturgical consciousness, elemental notions such as 'world', 'heaven', 'time' and 'place', 'change' and 'body' need to be recast. If Christ is risen and scended into heaven, then, in and through him, humanity, together with the world in which it is inextricably immersed, has entered into a new mode of existence. Liturgical experience is not shaped by Christ absent from the world, but as related to that world in a new way—just as humanity has not been discarded in the Christ risen from the tomb or ascended into heaven. Heaven, in Christian terms, therefore is not a vague celestial and unreal location, but communion with God in Christ in a creation transformed. By moving into God as revealed in Christ, humanity and the created universe find a new integrity. The liturgy, then, is an enactment of how, in Christ, the world has irreversibly ascended into the life of God, and God descended into the life of the world. The liturgy is, therefore, not an imaginative attempt to fit Christ into an unredeemed world; nor is it a memorial to his past presence after his disappearance into a vaguely determined heaven. Rather, the liturgical synthesis or 'reduction' consists in seeing both the world and heaven embodied in him: something new has irreversibly begun; time and space are newly configured in Christ. With him as the centre and focus of God's action, the corporate faith of the Church grows, from generation to the next, as an exploration into God.

At the end of exploration we find ourselves, not so much the end of the road, but looking back to a series of signposts, each pointing further into God. We begin to recognize more accurately the self-made frontier that we have allowed to bound our lives. It is also moving beyond it, to find a land and a region unbounded, our homeland. Yet always, the exploration into God goes on...

Letter to the Hebrews (Hb 12:18–24)

To this place you have come --
stumbling, hesitant or apalled --
not to something that can be touched
and held in a fist of skin or mind;
but neither, do remember, is it ethereal,
as though less than flesh and bone and feeling,
not less given than anything in all this earth is given;
not less there, so to speak,
even if intangible . . .
Nor is it fire, blazing and leaping,
untouchable in that other sense,
as being too fierce for touch,
a flame untamed and all-consuming.
Nor, as darkness and gloom,
is it visible or invisible:
eyes fix in vain
on some dread or shining shape
measured against an horizon of light or darkness
in clear perspective.
Nor does it result of some sudden change in season,
not a winter storm, not a summer squall,
not, in short, a tempest heaven-sent,
or calmed by the sleeping Christ;
for nature shows no theatrics here --
the drama now is otherwise:
if you hear, and I suppose it is hard not to listen,
it vibrate in a silence deeper than any sound,
more arresting than the trumpet blast,
more summoning than that voice
that was all too terrifying
in our previous acoustic range.
But you have come
now, to this place, this holy ground,
led on without knowing,
taken by surprise on the crest of a winding road
by the mountain of meeting
on which every Jerusalem is built:
here are walls of light

here houses of welcoming,
and heaven a-building;
here angels, resting from cosmic labours,
make festival and move radiantly;
and you can hail all the assembled
whose names are written in heaven
by the unwieldy graphite of this world,
to await a more precious birth.
And so to God, about whom this is all about,
the resonance of truth,
the light in which we see light --
and, as I said, all holy ones are there,
in luminous vitality,
pure and perfect now in that glory,
still neither flame nor storm
nor trumpet blast nor heavenly symphony:
just this tortured man shedding blood
in evidence of new innocence.

Christ, Risen and Ascended, and Interfaith Dialogue

The ascension marks the ending of the visible mission of Jesus in the world. And this connotes a departure and an absence, where before he was present. And yet the ascension makes the disciples see the world differently. Neither the Church nor the world can contain Christ. He has ascended into the boundless glory and grace of the Father—whence comes the gift of the Spirit and the promise of Christ's return. As the Spirit witnesses to him, and as faith awaits his return, Jesus is not occupying some ever receding vanishing point, but is present to the Church in a way that outstrips the possibilities of any earthly familiarity with him—as Magdalen found out (Jn 20:17). It breaks open any notion of presence experienced in the ordinary converse of social life.

Faith sees the world differently in the light of Christ's ascension. The coming of the Spirit, and the promise of the return of the ascended, both Jesus form a particular horizon in which Christian life is lived. The inexhaustible witness of the Spirit is calling to mind all that Jesus was, is, and will be, in word, deed and in the paschal event of his death, resurrection, ascension and eventual return. The Spirit inspires the faith that which, while 'not seeing' in the way Thomas saw, still is not sightless, for faith has its own eyes. Further, there is the promise of his return so vividly impressed on the experience of the early Church and the early communities out of which the writings of the New Testament emerged. It suggests a presence in absence: at one extreme, Jesus is no longer present as he once was. At the other extreme, he has ascended into the boundless, invisible mystery of the Father. The Johannine rhetoric in this regard is varied: Jesus 'goes', 'returns', 'ascends' to the Father. His communion with the Father, at the prayer of Jesus, extends to include all who believe in the ages to come. In short, he is present in a new way, once ascended to the Father. We note that the entire New Testament has been written in this light. The crucified, risen and ascended One draws all to himself. In that drawing, a deeper reading occurs of the recollections of incidents in his life on earth and the teaching by which he formed his early disciples. He is 'lifted up', not only on the cross to manifest the divine glory of self-giving love but 'taken up" into the invisible and boundless dimensions of the Father.

Jesus and the Samaritan Woman

With such presuppositions, we return to John 4, dwelling briefly on Jesus' dialogue with the unnamed Samaritan woman—a representative of the quasi-indigenous population of that region of the Palestine of those days.

In the ever-widening circle of John's Gospel, the Father's love for the world moves Jesus on: 'He had to go through Samaria' (Jn 4:4). At this stage of his journey, Jesus is found at Jacob's well, outside the city of Sychar. He is described as exhausted by his travels, and his mission is proving costly. His tiredness and thirst foreshadow his passion (*cf* Jn 19:28), and 'the lifting up' by which he would draw all to himself (12:32). Left behind by his disciples who had gone off to buy food, he is alone, until a Samaritan woman comes to draw water from the well. He initiates a conversation with an abrupt demand: 'Give me a drink' (Jn 4:7). A disconcerting other is entering her life. She registers the anomaly, for cultural and religious boundaries are being broached: 'How is it that you, a Jew, ask a drink of me, a woman of Samaria?' (Jn 4:9). Though, by the end of this episode, this stranger would be acknowledged by her people as 'the Saviour of the world' (Jn 4:42), he is at first dismissively reduced by the woman to his obvious ethnic and religious status. For his part, Jesus does not accept the segregated world that allowed no communication between a Jew and a Samaritan—let alone between a man and a woman in these circumstances. Despite the prohibition of contact between these two antagonistic groups (Jn 4:9), Jesus is obedient to another will. He will not be part of such a polarized world. Accordingly, he responds to the woman in terms the Father's all-inclusive self-giving love (Jn 3:16).

The woman is being invited into another realm of divine grace and life. The well was historically connected with former blessings

('. . . our father Jacob who gave us this well' (Jn 4:12. Cf Gen 33:19; 48:22; Josh 24:32). Now it emerges as a symbol of the life-giving depths of another kind—the gift of 'living water' as 'a spring . . . welling up to eternal life' (Jn 4:14). It is the divine gift which alone can slake all human thirst in ways that surpass all past forms of divine giving. The Word who speaks is now breaking open the world moulded by the antagonisms, and even by particular gifts, of the past. Sensing something indefinably new happening, the woman responds in a tone of measured respect: 'Sir, you have no bucket and the well is deep. Where do you get that living water?' (Jn 4:11).

Still, she is confused, unable to respond on the level at which Jesus promises this life-giving gift. She insists that any promised future is determined for her by what is already in possession. There is no room for anything other or greater: 'Are you greater than our father Jacob?'(Jn 4:12). She reduces the proffered 'gift of God', the promised 'living water', to her own mundane needs, demanding in her turn: 'Sir, give me this water . . .' (Jn 4:15). But her sense of initial impossibility is about to be confronted by impossible possibilities of the gift of God now opening up.

In the exchange that follows, the woman is shocked into new realization. She is being intimately addressed by one who truly knows her. He knows her, and sees more in her that she has previously dared admit. His presence is unsettling, as if to stimulate her real questions and her real search—in a way reminiscent of the first words of the Word to the disciples in the question, 'What are you looking for?' (Jn 1:38).

She arrives at a new appreciation of Jesus. He is no longer 'you, a Jew' (Jn 4:9) or even 'Sir' (Jn 4:11, 15, 19a). She is brought to a religious level of engagement with him: 'Sir, I see you are a prophet' (Jn 4:19). She identified him as one who speaks in the name of God, even if he is a Jew. And so she invites him to clarify the radical point of antagonism between Jew and Samaritan: 'Our fathers worshipped on this mountain but you say that the place where people must worship is in Jerusalem' (Jn 4:20). Under the shadow of holy Mount of Gerizim, she is limited to the categories of her ancestral religion. Samaritan tradition associated this mountain with Abraham's sacrifice of Isaac and Jacob's dream, and so revered it as a special dwelling place of God. Jesus addresses her out of a light 'from above', unshadowed by the purely human perspective with its succession of sacred times and its geography of sacred places. Jacob's dream of the ladder between heaven and earth, and his waking declaration that 'this is no other than the house of God and this is the gate of heaven' (Gen 28:12, 16–17) is about to be reshaped in the light of the vision of 'opened heaven' (Jn 1:51), centred on Jesus himself. Here is the text itself:

> Jesus said to her, 'Woman, believe me, the hour is coming when you will worship the Father neither on this mountain nor in Jerusalem. You worship what you do not know; we worship what we know, for salvation is from the Jews. But the hour is coming, and now is, when the true worshipers will worship the Father in spirit and in truth, for such the Father seeks to worship him. God is spirit, and those who worship him must worship in spirit and in truth.' The woman said to him, 'I know that the Messiah is coming, he who is called Christ. When he comes, he will show us all things.' Jesus said to her, '"I am" is the one speaking to you' (Jn 4:21–26).

The hour has arrived when God would be definitively revealed as the God of everyone, irrespective of the limitations of the cherished traditions of the past. In this sense, Jesus is not concerned to act in the traditional prophetic role of confessing the one true God against what is false and idolatrous. For all previous modes of worship, both the genuine and the defective, are relativised. He is at once more than a prophet and greater than the patriarch Jacob. He presents God as no longer contained within the limitations of the past ('our fathers'), but as '*the* Father' whose worship is not restricted to particular places, however holy, nor confined to those who have been part of the privileged economy of divine revelation in the past: '. . . neither on this mountain nor in Jerusalem' (Jn 4:21).

While transcending previous traditions in this new hour of grace, Jesus nonetheless locates himself within the history of God's giving. As a Jew (*cf* Jn 4:9), he acknowledges the 'anonymous Judaism' of the Samaritans: 'You worship what you do not know' (Jn 4:22a). Such worship has been without the benefit of the universal dimension of God's design. In contrast, 'we worship what we know, for salvation is from the Jews' (Jn 4:22b). In the history of Israel, the saving will of God has been manifest in the many gifts preparing for this hour when an ultimate universal salvation would appear: 'Turn to me and be saved, all the ends of the earth! For I am God, and there is no other' (Isa 45:22). Jesus' use of the inclusive 'we' in regard to the faith of Israel intensifies the sense of all that was positive in its long history of familiarity with the one, true God. That history has included the Word 'coming to his own' (Jn 1:11). Despite rejection and incomprehension that mark his relations with 'the Jews', the darkness has not overcome the light (Jn 1:5), with the result that 'We worship what we know...'

A new time of grace has arrived when true worshippers will come into their own. They will adore God, not as one contained in the hallowed sanctuaries of either Gerizim or Jerusalem, but as the Father to whom they will turn in unreserved intimacy and assurance. They will worship the Father 'in spirit and truth' (Jn 4:23a). This promise of universal access to God is already being realised: 'and now is here' (Jn 4:23b). As the Gospel unfolds, the meaning of both 'truth' and 'spirit' will be progressively filled out. For example, Jesus will promise to send 'the Spirit of truth' from the Father, to testify on his behalf (Jn 15:26). In the Johannine range of reference, the significance of these two key words unfolds like fractal patterns, endlessly replicating themselves in wider dimensions. In the immediate context of Jesus' encounter with the Samaritan woman, worshipping the Father 'in spirit and truth' is first of all contrasted with her narrow and distant sense of God. She is being drawn out of herself into a new realm of relationship to God. For the worship of the Father 'in spirit' implies going beyond all previous localisations and objectifications of the divine. The true God can never be an instrument of self-glorification, nor an individual or national possession. The Father is not kept anywhere nor owned by anyone. He is worshipped in his self-giving love for the world (Jn 3:16)—in the truth incarnate in his Word, and in the Spirit of his measureless generosity (Jn 3:34). Faith must now live in the expanse of the 'opened heaven' (Jn 1:51), and not within the world enclosed in its history of antagonisms and rivalries.

In apposition to worship in 'Spirit', is worship in 'truth'. The gifts, restrictions and ambiguities of former situations are now brought to their moment of truth. Through Jesus, God is proving true to himself in an all-surpassing communication. His Son will declare himself to be the way, *the truth* and the life (Jn 14:6). Holding to his word will mean 'to know the truth, and the truth will make you free' (Jn 8:32). Previous economies structured on rigid exclusion mean nothing in the presence of the Word. He has come into the human situation, and speaks; for he is the hinge on which a new final phase of the revelation of God will turn. As the communication of the truth, his words to this woman reach out to all actual and potential believers.

Still, while Jesus is the revelatory focus of what is happening, his words and action always look to the Father, the origin of all his communication. What he offers is the gift *of God*. As if to emphasise the divine origin of his mission, he explains, 'for the Father seeks such as these to worship him' (Jn 4:23). This statement suggests the very purpose of John's Gospel, which is to witness to the Father actively seeking out those who will relate to him as he relates to the world. The Father's seeking enables his genuine worshippers to respond in accord with his unreserved love—the measureless generosity of the Spirit in which he has given his Son. God is revealed as the love that knows no bounds and acknowledges no boundaries. Hence, 'God is spirit, and those who worship him must worship in spirit and in truth' (Jn 4:24). The indefinable reality of God must be met with the unconditional self-giving of true adoration. The Father himself has defied the measure of all earthly criteria, breaking open the little worlds of 'religion' to another sense of proportion. His seeking out true worshippers is an aspect of his unreserved love for the world, as it invites believers to participate in such love and to witness to it (cf 1 Jn 4:11–12). This 'gift of God', given in the spirit of all-embracing love, given in the truth of all that it claims to be, inspires a response proportionate to it.

Faith in Christ Now

As often pointed out, our historical present is marked in a special way by the travail of being born into a new stage of history. The change that is taking place provokes trans-cultural consciousness, thereby making imperative a new global integration of human relations—international, inter-religious and inter-cultural. There is inevitably a world-wide turbulence: previous rigid patterns of division break down, and crises of identity, community and moral responsibility ensue.

Something of profound historical importance is taking place. A development of global consciousness is occurring, deeper and broader than any reductively economic description of the phenomenon. Far from occasioning a breakdown in Christian faith, there is no reason why this troubling of former cultural, national and ethnic boundaries should not result in a breakthrough into a new stage of benign co-existence with hitherto alienated or threatening others. Indeed, an expansion of global consciousness accords with a fresh appreciation of the transcendent character of the risen and ascended Christ. He has risen beyond the containment of any culture or any one stage of history, to be 'the light of the world' in its entirety. This is to say that the risen Jesus has ascended, as it were, to be the space of both fulfilment and reconciliation in a way which anticipates and provokes fresh forms of global solidarity and dialogue. There is no denying the discomfort occasioned by the collapse of the old boundaries behind which human, or even the Christian cultural identities, functioned in their respective forms of self-containment. The crisis of particular historical forms of culture is the pain of a rebirth into another realm of communication, more religiously radical and open compared to anything experienced in the past, promising larger dimensions of life and new horizons for human selfhood and community.

Christ is risen and ascended into the heaven of God. The event of God's incarnation and self-emptying is not for the sake of producing an idol formed by the projections and supposed excellence of any particular culture or religious history. Rather, Christ is the icon of the invisible God (Col 1:15), through whom the light of God's universal saving purposes shines. Compared to the historical limits in ancient Palestine, the ascended Jesus now belongs to 'all nations' and to all times (Mt 28:19), calling for a worship of the one true God 'neither on this mountain nor in Jerusalem' (Jn 4:23). Peter found two millennia ago, as he journeyed from Joppa and then—to the scandal of his Jewish sensibilities and connections—he entered the house of the pagan Cornelius: there are no human limits to the saving will of God (Acts 10: 34; *cf* 10:1–48). The risen glory of Christ does not mean the glorification of the heritage of Israel, nor that of the Christian West, nor that of any other culture or location.[1] By entering into our hitherto locked cultural and historical rooms, the risen One in ascending to the Father is the luminous space in which the limitless world beyond is disclosed as the theatre of God's saving purpose. In him, Christian

---

1. David Burrell, *Faith and Freedom: An Interfaith Perspective* (Oxford: Blackwell, 2004) points to the medieval experience of interfaith communication as a model, and in some measure an antidote for the 'monocultural attitude *certainty* in which we know we are right' (255).

faith experiences not only the opening of heaven (Jn 1:51), but the opening out the world to new proportions.[2]

This trans-cultural openness of faith in the risen Jesus is not simply an extrinsic property of Christian existence; nor is the resurrection an apologetic proof for the truth of Christianity, nor is his ascension a rather commonplace mythic extravagance. Nor is it an incitement to that kind of energetic proselytizing that leaves one's own culture and faith beyond criticism; and the value of other cultures and religious beliefs unrecognised.[3] The ascension of crucified and risen One inspires an expanding sense of universality: 'And I, when I am lifted up from the earth, will draw all people to myself' (Jn 12:32). To this degree, Christ's ascension relativises all cultures and locates each of them in a universe of grace. Jesus' departure from the conditions of earthly existence into the realm of the Father creates a field of new communion with him. His departure was the condition for the Spirit's coming. In that ever-new space is found 'the advantage' (Jn 16:7) of the Spirit witnessing to 'the many things that Jesus' disciples could not previously bear (Jn 16:12)—'the things that are to come' (v 13). Faith ascending with Jesus to the Father reaches out to a limitless otherness. In accord with the words of the risen Jesus, 'As the Father has sent me, so I send you' (Jn 20:21).

The Logos Incarnate has become the site of dialogue with all peoples, in the Spirit formed space of *dia-Logos*, in witness to the God who 'desires everyone to be saved and to come to the knowledge of the truth' (1 Tim 2:4). The accomplishment of God's universal eschatological purpose embodied in the resurrection and ascension of the Crucified as Jesus reveals himself in the act of sending forth his disciples to all nations and throughout all time.

As regards the future, Christian hope has a vital mediating role. If Christians must never give up hope even for their enemies and persecutors, there is surely a lot that can be said—or left unsaid in the necessary darkness of our present perceptions—regarding the ulti-

---

2. See William M Thompson, *Jesus, Lord and Savior: A Theopathic Christology and Soteriology* (New York: Paulist, 1980), especially chapter 9, 'Exploring the Christ-Experience IV: Thomas Merton's Transcultural Christ', 250–276.
3. On the inadequacies of the standard 'inclusivist-exclusivist-pluralist' distinctions, see Lieven Boeve, 'Resurrection: Saving Particularity: Theological-Epistemological Considerations of Incarnation and Truth', in *Theological Studies* 67 (2006): 795–808.

mate reconciliation of their friends and partners in dialogue. There in a breadth and length and height and depth of the mystery (Eph 3:18) that is yet to be discovered. The love of Christ 'surpasses knowledge' (Eph 3:19). It includes all in whom the Spirit of love and hope is moving. Whatever the impasse in the practice of dialogue, Christians must wait on the unfathomable freedom of the One 'who by the power at work within us is able to accomplish abundantly far more than all we can ask or imagine' (Eph 3:20). The mission of dialogue must, in short, wait on its prayers to be answered, and for the revelation of Christ to fully unfold.

The Experience of Dialogue

The conduct of dialogue indicates a certain change of consciousness. It involves something more than research, and the drafting of agreed documents. There is a movement from objectively articulated expressions of religious belief to the inter-subjective field of communication. In that setting, truth exercises its attraction primarily by being lived and incarnate in a communication with the 'other'. While past traditions need interpretation, dialogue is an encounter occurring in the interpersonal present. It takes place as a new event in the Now, in *this* critical moment of history. The dialogical event happens as a gift, the unpredictable grace of those previously estranged coming together in a shared openness to a latent, indefinable excess of what might yet be. It is a moment of openness to heaven!

Second, dialogue does not consist in episodically overhearing what the other has to say. A common conduct of listening is presupposed, attentive to the historical particularity of each one, and allowing each and all to emerge from the anonymity inevitably associated with typical generalizations that have previously held sway. To that degree, the dialogical attitude undermines our tendencies to expect 'more of the same'. It envisages unity in difference in the light of the One who is never to be possessed or clung to, who has departed into the realm from which he will return as the fulfilment of history. It is a moment in going with him into the realm of the Father, a moment of openness to indefinably divine horizons. Any homogenized sameness and lack of hope is called into question. The ideology of uniformity undermines the experience of the new, as if the other is to be converted to *us*, rather than *we* being converted to the radically new of the Ascended One, in a more inclusive communal history.

A dialogical overture to the new derives from a refreshed sense of God as the transcendent and all-inclusive Other. In the wide world of divine creation, the creator is to be, not possessed, but adored and praised in all that is given.[4] God must be left free to act and to give in ways always hidden to human comprehension. He is ascended . . .

Third, on a more explicitly religious level, dialogue in an 'inter-faith' or 'inter-religious' context can give the impression that the faith/religion concerned is a fixed entity, a body of religious positions, with clearly defined boundaries, doctrines and classic texts, and so forth, which we speak 'about'. It creates the impression that discussions occur from behind fixed positions in the shape of a body of clearly articulated beliefs. While it would be destructive to suggest that dialogue means that those involved should hold their beliefs in suspension, it may prove more realistic to refer to 'inter-hope' dialogue—in regard to the other and to the universe itself. Admittedly, hope is sustained by faith and articulated in beliefs. However, inter-hope suggests an eschatological overture that brings a larger proportion to the exchange, and makes for more self-involved and properly open communication. For example, I might say with all the weight of Christian and Catholic tradition, that I hope to share eternal life, in a transformed creation already anticipated in the risen Christ, with *you*, and all peoples as the beneficiaries of a limitless love, destined to see God face to face. At least, this would suggest something wonderfully indefinable, a horizon of excess that reduces the force of present religious, spiritual or philosophical differences. Exchanges on the level of hope cannot but engender a more engaged and lively dialogical attitude.[5]

Doubtless, this is an exalted ideal. But affecting any reciprocal exchange of hope is a relationship that can only be described as love. Love means affirming the existence of the other in all the sincerity of their convictions, personal goodness and dedication to the absolute truth and good. It means, too, a readiness to share what each has found to be most precious and liberating, and destined for all, despite

---

4. For a specifically Thomist account, see Anthony J Kelly, 'A Multidimensionsal Disclosure: Aspects of Aquinas' Theological Intentionality', in *The Thomist*, 67/3 (July 2003): 335–374.
5. See Anthony J Kelly, *Eschatology and Hope* (Maryknoll, NY: Orbis, 2006), 15–17; 25–28.

the failures, lost opportunities and mutual intolerance that have minimized the possibilities of God's most abundant giving.

Concluding Remarks

This brief reflection began by recalling the perspective in which the New Testament was written, namely, in the light of the risen and ascended Christ. We then proceeded to meditate on John 4, and the Father's seeking true worshipers 'in spirit and in truth'—in a way that cannot be limited to Mt Gerizim or Jerusalem, or Rome or Alice Springs—a realm defined only by God's life-giving love. We noted, too, that resurrection and ascension of the Lord is always associated with a mission to all peoples, beyond any limits of space and time. Then followed a reflection on the phenomenon of contemporary dialogue itself—an act of hope in a future definable only the ultimate and sheer gift of God.

The New Testament does not seem to envisage a world as of urbanely conducted dialogue. The figure of the enemy and the persecutor is never far away. The Gospels presume that the world that God loves, and that Christ comes to save, will be in neuralgic reaction against the Risen One who disturbs the human condition with his summons to love, to forgive, and to renounce oneself (Lk 6:27-31; Jn 16:1-4). The world, and even in its religions, is the milieu in which the crucified Jesus is a multi-dimensional scandal (1 Cor 1:22-25). Admittedly, Christian hope can never foreclose on the limitless range of God's mercy, nor turn from the possibilities of reconciliation even in adverse situations; nor, for that matter, dare we place any limits on our hope for the salvation of all (1 Tim 2:3-4). How such an eschatological hope will be realized is not given to the mortal mind or imagination to conceive (Rom 11:33-34). What must remain clear is that any Christian conception of the fulfilment of life must not give way to defeat, or limit itself to the present dimensions of the fear-locked room in which the community of disciples gathered: the crucified and risen Jesus appears among them, and sends them forth in the power of his Spirit (Jn 20:19-23).

Our historical present is marked in a special way by the travail of being born into a new stage of history. The change that is taking place provokes trans-cultural consciousness, thereby making imperative a new global integration of human relations—international, inter-religious and inter-cultural. There is inevitably a world-wide turbulence: previous rigid patterns of division break down, and crises of identity, community and moral responsibility ensue. For example, what been termed 'the over-fed ego'[6] of Western cultural and political domination is being provoked into becoming a more dialogical self. The Northern Hemisphere has become aware that the wide world contains a hemisphere of the South, more populous, more religious in its way, not predominantly white, politically unstable in a post-colonial phase, and certainly poorer.[7] The hitherto unknown or unregarded 'other' cannot be ignored. Hence, there arises the critique of the kind of mono-cultural globalism that is unaware of the vast, differentiated cultural inheritance of the whole of humanity—while the purely economic globalism that serves multinational corporations and leaves the billions to live in poverty is being subject to a new audit.

Such distortions are not the whole story. Something of profound historical importance is indeed taking place. A development of global consciousness is occurring, deeper and broader than any reductively economic description of the phenomenon. Far from occasioning a breakdown in Christian faith, there is no reason why this troubling of former cultural, national and ethnic boundaries should not result in a breakthrough into a new stage of benign co-existence with hitherto alienated or threatening others. Indeed, an expansion of global consciousness accords with a fresh appreciation of the transcendent character of the risen and ascended Christ. He has risen beyond the containment of any culture or any one stage of history, to be the light of the world in its entirety. This is to say that the risen Jesus has ascended, as it were, to be the space of both fulfilment and reconciliation in a way which anticipates and provokes fresh forms of global solidarity and dialogue. There is no denying the discomfort occasioned by the collapse of the old boundaries behind which human, or even the Christian cultural identities, functioned in their respective forms of self-containment. The crisis of particular historical forms of culture is the pain of a rebirth into another realm of communication, more religiously radical and open compared to anything experienced in the past. The hand that hurts is the hand that heals. In a new phase

---

6. William M Thompson, 'The Risen Christ, Transcultural Consciousness, and the Encounter of the World Religions', om *Theological Studies*, 37/3 (1976): 381–409.
7. For an informative and challenging reflection, Philip Jenkins, 'Believing in the Global South', in *First Things*, 168 (December 2006): 12–18.

of history, larger dimensions of life and new horizons of human selfhood and community are coming to light, as, in the words of the poet, 'For each age is a dream that is dying, / Or one that is coming to birth'.[8]

Christ is risen, but not as an idol formed by the projections and supposed triumph of any particular culture or religious history. He is given as the icon of the invisible God, through whom the light of God's universal saving purposes shines. Compared to the historical limits in ancient Palestine, he now belongs to 'all nations' and to all times (Mt 28:19), calling for a worship of the one true God 'neither on this mountain nor in Jerusalem' (Jn 4:23). Peter found two millennia ago, as he journeyed from Joppa and then—to the scandal of his Jewish connections—as he entered the house of the pagan Cornelius, that there are no human limits to the saving will of God (Acts 10:34; cf 10:1–48). The resurrection does not mean the glorification of the heritage of Israel, nor that of the Christian West, nor that of any other culture or location.[9] By entering into our hitherto locked cultural and historical rooms, the risen One is the luminous space in which the limitless world beyond is disclosed as the theatre of God's saving purpose. In him, Christian faith experiences not only the 'opened heaven' (Jn 1:51), but the opening out the world to new proportions.[10]

This trans-cultural openness of faith in the ascended Jesus is not simply a contingent property or of Christian existence, just as his resurrection is more than an apologetic proof for the truth of Christianity. Nor is it an incitement to that kind of energetic evangelization that leaves one's own culture uncriticised—and the value of other cultures unrecognised. The resurrection floods Christian consciousness with an expanding sense of universality: 'And I, when I am lifted up from the earth, will draw all people to myself' (Jn 12:32). To this degree, Christ's rising from the tomb and consequent ascension relativises all cultures. It draws each of them out of itself in order to find

---

8. Arthur O'Shaughnessy, *'Ode' Albatross Book of Verse*, edited by Louis Untermeyer (London: Collins, 1966), 480.
9. David Burrell, *Faith and Freedom: An Interfaith Perspective* (Oxford: Blackwell, 2004) points to the medieval experience of interfaith communication as a model, and in some measure an antidote for the "monocultural attitude *certainty* in which we know we are right" (255).
10. See William M Thompson, *Jesus, Lord and Savior: A Theopathic Christology and Soteriology* (New York: Paulist, 1980), especially chapter 9, 'Exploring the Christ-Experience IV: Thomas Merton's Transcultural Christ', 250–276.

itself anew in a universe of grace. If Jesus is the life and light of 'the world', faith in him is necessarily an outreach to all peoples. In this regard, his departure from the conditions of earthly existence into the realm of the Father creates a field of new communion with him. It reaches beyond the exclusions and limitations of the past. In that ever-new space is found 'the advantage' (Jn 16:7) of the Spirit witnessing to 'the many things that Jesus' disciples could not previously bear (Jn 16:12)—'the things that are to come' (v 13). Faith thus reaches out to the limitless otherness beyond it. In hearing the words of the risen Jesus, such faith must respond to the original Other from whom he comes: 'As the Father has sent me, so I send you' (Jn 20:21).

One of the great signs of hope today is the many levels of interfaith dialogue taking place. Those who speak for the deeper places of the heart and the higher reaches of the spirit are playing a part in the emergence of a global human culture. Such a meeting of religions and spiritualities cannot but make the world more hospitable to the values of peace and justice, compassion and human dignity. Eminent missiologists recognise the eschatological or hope-oriented aspect of this dialogue.[11] Engagement in such dialogue is a manifestation of the outreach of the Kingdom of the God who 'desires everyone to be saved and to come to the knowledge of the truth' (1 Tim 2:4). But what we wish to emphasise is that this eschatological universality is an effect of the resurrection and ascension of the Crucified. That singular event is the effective disclosure of the actuality of God's reign in history and creation. As such, it is the ever-productive impetus to the Church's mission. The risen Jesus reveals himself in the act of sending forth his disciples to all nations and throughout all time.

Despite the differences and conflicts that have shaped the past of the various religious traditions, the future is what all have in common. At the point where all look forward to a hoped for future, Christian hope, centred on the glorification of the crucified Jesus, has a vital mediating role. If Christians must never give up hope even for their enemies and persecutors, there is surely a lot that can be said—

---

11. Standard references here are: Stephen B Bevans and Roger P Schroeder, *Constants in Context. A Theology of Mission for Today* (Maryknoll, NY: Orbis, 2004); and the much-discussed Jacques Dupuis, *Toward a Christian Theology of Religious Pluralism* (Maryknoll, New York: Orbis Books, 2001) and his more succinct, *Christianity and the Religions: From Confrontation to Dialgue*, translated by Phillip Berryman (Maryknoll, NY: Orbis, 2002).

or left unsaid in the necessary darkness of our present perceptions—regarding the ultimate reconciliation of their friends and partners in dialogue. There in a breadth and length and height and depth of the mystery (Eph 3:18) that is yet to be discovered. The love of Christ 'surpasses knowledge' (Eph 3:19). It includes all in whom the Spirit of love and hope is moving. Dialogue may reach an impasse, and will certainly pose its problems, but the Christians involved must wait on the unfathomable freedom of the One 'who by the power at work within us is able to accomplish abundantly far more than all we can ask or imagine' (Eph 3:20). The mission of dialogue must, in short, wait on its prayers to be answered and for the revelation that has occurred in the resurrection of Christ to keep on being revelation in ways still to be disclosed. If such an attitude is criticized as too specifically Christian, at least it will criticised for the right reasons—for having too much hope—in the Other, and for all others in their longing for the fullness of life—rather than too little. In the light of Christ, these 'others' are not identified as individuals on the level of past conflicts and mutual incomprehension. It is not a question of a religious subterfuge, but rather of receptivity to the gift embodied in 'the resurrection and the life' that includes all. The other side of such receptivity is the readiness to take the last place in the service of all who together are called to eternal life.

John The Baptist

Would that I could make clear,
and cleanly real now,
the way it is these days,
the whole damn wonderful way
it all is now:
I have no skill in proclaiming
non-dreadful things --
just this need to goad
all the demeaning witless
unfeeling of life into something else . . .
Maybe flame and darkness
are not more understood;
but at least now we will sweat blood
in a million luxuriant Gethsemanes,
and to us it will be given to see the lilies,
waving splendid in the threatened field;
and that wretch at the gate
will have a place, if not at our tables,
well, at least in the awakening heart.
Let sins have the proper scale,
to test the stuff of mercy . . .
if not, then be utterly lost . . .
in a huge and negative praise
of straighter, narrower ways:
Now no need now to tip-toe,
as when most, neither saints not sinners,
feared to alarm lazing demons,
shuddered to make idols tremble,
or summon too quickly the holy ones.
It's different now:
reality is so climactically appalling.

Creator and Father Almighty

Three topics that often prove to be an obstacle to s deeper exploration of God are conveniently summarized in the article of the creed, 'I believe in God the Father Almighty. Maker of heaven and earth'. Hence our concentration in what follows on the meaning of 'Father' and the 'Almighty' and the universal extent of God's creative act.

A Theological Horizon

But first a general comment. In our exploration into the reality of God, we are concerned with the divine mystery and its relationship to the world. We may well give the impression that God is mysterious, and that the world, by contrast, is a clearly understood entity. That is to assume that we know already what the world is. It makes a difference, however, if the world is understood in relation to God, its creator. The question returns: what, then, is the world? In a theological sense, the world is not known until the world as God's creation as the object of God's love and mercy is made manifest.

Jeff Bloechl observes that 'the life of faith moves perpetually between distance and nearness, and thinking that attends to such a life must reckon with both of them'.[1] In this respect, the notion of secular is as old as the distinction between the Creator and creatures. Furthermore, relating to God in mind and heart is itself a distinct way of being in the world. Indeed, liturgically and sacramentally, the consciousness is formed of being in the world understood as charged with the grace and redemptive love of God in Christ. This leads a

---
1. Jean-Yves Lacoste, *From Theology to Theological Thinking*, viii.

view of the world in a certain affective tone and mood—quite different from that of scientific objectivity, and at variance with a blinkered reductive scientism.

As a classic expression of Christian faith, the Creed's 'I believe in one God, the Father almighty, maker of heaven and earth, of all things visible and invisible' provokes continuing reflection. This first article of the creed introduces the one, all-creating mystery of God in, through and for whom all exist (Acts 17:28). The boundless mystery of God is connoted as the atmosphere and milieu of all existence, so that God can be invoked as the beginning and end of all that is.

The distinctive way in which 'the Father, the Almighty' is the primordial 'maker' of everything is usually expressed in the term of God's role as 'creator'. The divine mode of making, doing and acting in creating is expressed in a great variety of images in the scriptures which Christians share with Israel (cf Gen 1–3; Sirach 16:26–17:19; Wis 7:22–25). In that biblical understanding, God's making extends to all that is—in all the tenses of the verb 'to be', and all the modes of actual and possible being—in all that is, was and will be; in all its being and becoming. That must include everything connoted in phrases such as 'I am', 'you are', 'we are', 'they are' and 'it is', in all the differences and relationships and actions implied in *all* this. God's way of 'making' is, therefore, not like any other kind of action or creativity contained within the bounds of 'heaven and earth'. That is to underline, therefore, the uniqueness of God's creative activity. The 'Almighty Father' does not act as one agent among a myriad others in determining the shape of the world. God is not busy in the great unfolding process of the universe as a particular agent collaborating with the rest of known, or as yet unknown, agents and energies that make things the way they are. God's making is different. The divine agent is present at the roots of all existence and in every creature's capacity to act. The creative activity of God is, therefore, not set simply alongside the rest, as one factor, however important, in the varied influences that determine the shape of the real. For God acts out of a sheer and unconditioned originality. As the source of all being, the creator God is the ground of why there is something rather than nothing, and of why every being continues to exist in the way it is, from one moment to the next. God, in this biblical and creedal understanding, is the all-embracing cause of all being and becoming.

From such a sense of creation flow the wonderful insights which are the common possession of the biblical tradition.

In the first place, as creator, the One God is more intimately present to creation than the creature is to itself. The more the creature comes to be, the higher the degree of its life and love and creativity, the more God is involved and present, and the more does that created reality participate in the creativity of the divine. Our capacity as persons to be and to act is the outcome of what God has done, and is doing. God is ever engaged in creating what and who we are, as participants in the wonder of existence. Divine Be-ing is the limitless matrix 'in whom we live and move and have our being' (Acts 17:28), present and active in all creation as 'one God and Father of all, who is above all and through all and in all' (Eph 4:6).

Second, in creating the universe, God acts freely. What is created is not a necessary or automatic overflow from some great reservoir of being. This is to say, that God's creative freedom is unconditioned, and depends on nothing external to itself. The acknowledgment of God's freedom in creating leads to the realisation of creation as loved into being in the deepest possible sense. The creative freedom of God means that at the source of all creation, there is the exuberance of infinite love. That is to say that the universe, and everyone and everything in it, is primarily a gift. Since creation need not have happened, the universe of all that is, in its very fabric and every fibre, is given into existence. It is therefore loved into being, and occurs as a gift.[2]

Third, the divine creative act presupposes nothing. As sheer gift, the universe is made 'out of nothing'—a more negative way of saying that it is loved into being. For God has acted so that something other than God should exist to share in the divine joy in being, and to receive the gift and the giving that God is. And all this is for the sake of that perfect fulfilment to occur when 'God will be all in all' (1 Cor 15:28). Inevitably, imagination envisages some kind of some kind of raw material on which God acts or which is presupposed to the divine act of creation. Beyond the limits of imagination, however, is the moment of wonder. Any 'raw material', any presupposed cos-

---

2. Werner Jeanrond, *A Theology of Love* (London: T&T Clark, 2010) is a valuable resource in the discussion of love in is divine and human forms, especially 239–259, for a concluding summary.

mic energies or life-forces are themselves created. In short, the divine freedom presupposes nothing except divine creativity and generosity.

More deeply still, there is no goodness prior to God's action, or apart from the goodness of God. There is nothing outside God that somehow entices the Creator into the act of creating. God's own overflowing goodness is the only reason why there is anything at all: 'the love of God infuses and creates the goodness in reality' (*amor Dei infundens et creans bonitatem in rebus*) as St Thomas Aquinas notes.[3] The universe as a whole and in each of its particulars, in all its structures and processes, is loved into being; and so manifests the unconditioned goodness of God. Infinite Good spreads itself, shares itself, and gives itself so that all that is good might exist and be enjoyed.

The Divine Artist

If creation is not like any other kind of making or doing, how can we speak of it within our world of limited making and doing? Language must here be analogical. We can dimly describe the divine creative act only in terms of the human experience of making and producing. For example, in a moment of inspiration, the artist is possessed of profound, original creativity. That moment of inspiration animates all the distinct actions and elements involved in the production of any work of art. All the varied elements and phases, be they notes or words, paint strokes or shapes and movements, are born out of an imaginative conception of the whole. The creative moment, as distinct from the demanding effort to 'realise' it in some concrete form in a certain medium, is experienced as in some way wonderfully 'given'. It springs forth within the fertility of the artistic imagination, already anticipating the whole of what is to be produced or performed. Of course, the transforming moment of real art is prepared for by the long formation of the artist in a chosen medium. Even Mozart had to practise his scales, learn from others, and become familiar with the capacities and limitations of the various instruments at his disposal. But within those limits, his originality was seemingly limitless; and the world continues to enjoy his amazing art. Along with all artists in their respective media, he gave expression to what was original within him, and in what was other than him in the notes,

---

3. *STh* I, q.20, a.2.

the scales, the harmonies and the instruments employed. The ecstatic self-expression of artists affect this human world by lifting it out of its routines of shape, sound, colour, image and movement to a point of surprise and wonder. The after-effect of art is that the world can never be the same again.

Artistic creativity, therefore, can be taken as a dim metaphor for divine creation. God's creative action springs forth, as were, from the divine imagination, in utter originality. No medium is presupposed, nor is there any other to appreciate it—except in so far as it too is created. In this respect, God is pure originality, pure self-expression. The creative act brings forth what is other than God so that this other—and others, ourselves included!—is not only the expression of the divine goodness and beauty, but also that it might share, in its own scope for self-expression, in the creative love of God.

Though the word, 'incarnation', is usually reserved to the Word made flesh in Jesus Christ, we can understand it in a more extended sense in the context of creation, and so regard the world, and the universe itself, as the incarnation of the love and imagination of God. This cosmic incarnation finds its culminating moment in the personal self-expression that occurs when the Word personally becomes flesh. In Jesus Christ, the original meaning and promise of creation takes explicit shape.

There is another analogical way of understanding what creation means. The original human community was made in God's self-image: 'Let us make humankind in our image, according to our likeness . . . male and female he created them' (Gen 1:26–27). Living images of their creator, human beings, in the generative capacities of body and spirit, go on to 'make' one another in love and communication.[4] Through the creativity of nature and culture, in the family, and society, the human person is formed in a way that far transcends any ordinary instrumental meaning of making. This communal, mutual creativity, through all the exchanges of human relationships, actively shares in the divine creativity imaged in our co-existence. In this experience of 'making', and of procreating the other, we grow to a deeper sense of how God creates us and the universe in which we exist.

---

4. Brendan Purcell, *From Big Band to Big Mystery: Human Origins in the light of Creation and Evolution* (Hyde Park, NY: New York City Press, 2011).

In this perspective, we are finally led to the distinctively Christian and most intimate understanding of creation as it is envisaged in the creed. All divine making flows from the trinitarian life of God. In that primordial mystery, divine life is eternally unfolding through an ever-original self-expression, namely, in the Father 'speaking' the Word and begetting of the Son. This self-expression can never be separated from God's ecstatic self-giving, for the Spirit is breathed forth as the love motivating and informing all the gifts of God. In this regard, creation is an extension into time of the eternal circulation of divine life. What God creates bears traces (*vestigia*) of its trinitarian origin: in the sheer wonder of existing, as coming forth from nothing, creation radiates a sense of the limitless Be-ing of the One-who-is, the eternal source and origin, confessed as 'the Father'.[5] In its particularity and varied forms, as *this* rather than *that*, in *this* actual universe, the universe participates in the divine self-expression characteristic of the Word. Each reality can be named in its own individuality, illumined as a ray of divine light and appreciated as the manifestation of infinite wisdom. Then, when creation is received as an interconnected and inter-related whole, moving into greater communion and deeper life, the universe images forth the presence of the Spirit, the love the inspires all loves and all gifts. Creation in its deepest reality is, therefore, an icon of the Trinity. The trinitarian source of creation finally crystallises when, through the power of the Spirit, the Word becomes flesh. Faith can glimpse how the perfect form and deepest meaning of creation is climactically embodied in Jesus Christ, 'the image of the invisible God, the firstborn of all creation' (Col 1:16).

All in Heaven and Earth

To confess God as 'maker of heaven and earth' amounts to a declaration that there is, in effect, nothing outside the scope of the divine creating. The creativity of God embraces the whole of creation despite the temptation to divide it into two separate domains—the heavenly and the earthly. The scope of God's creative activity, therefore, is not limited to purely spiritual creation, as though it were involved exclusively with the production of souls and spiritual realities. God also

---

5. Larry W Hurtado, *God in the New Testament* (Nashville: Abingdon Press, 2010), 38–47.

creates the material world and all the physical energies presupposed in the structure and processes of the world as it is—the inanimate, the biological, and all the pre-personal structures, forms and dynamics that, one way or another, support human existence—including the sexual—which tends to be unevenly accommodated in our spiritual traditions.

It is important to underscore the involvement of God in material creation for two reasons. First, modern scientific exploration of the physical origins of the universe leads us to awe at the quite uncanny emergence and astonishingly inter-connected totality of the physical world. That overall sense of things cannot be dismissed as of no religious value. Admittedly, religion has been traditionally more at home with spiritual realities, with 'heaven', and 'the invisible'. For its part, modern scientific culture has become marvellously familiar with 'earth', 'the visible', and the material. Despite the tension resulting from such different emphases and perspectives, faith in creation insists that the two realms are related in the one reality of God's creative self-expression.

Furthermore, stalking religious consciousness down the ages has been a noxious alternative—of belief in a material, or even evil principle somehow co-existent with, and even resistant to, God's creative power. Such a belief holds to a dark side of creation. Under the influence of such a dualistic view, the religious mind becomes intolerant of the bodily and the material. Dualistic spirituality favoured an escape from the physical, in the conviction that the visible and the material belonged to an inferior and spurious mode of existence. In Christian history, there has been on different occasions an unhealthy emphasis on a 'spirituality' nourished exclusively on the 'invisible', as if we human beings were pure spirits haunting the earth instead of inhabiting it. The early Manichean heresy gave doctrinal expression to the tendency to dematerialise the integral goodness of creation. Preceding such a position, however benignly, there was an anti-matter, anti-body influence stemming from classical Platonism. As a result, mutilated versions of Christianity down the ages have been both deeply suspicious of the body and sexuality, and hostile toward scientific activity because of its involvement with physical reality.

In contrast, the movement of God's creation is toward Incarnation. The invisible is embodied in the visible, while the divine mystery is present in the physical and material. God's creative love encompasses both heaven and earth, to bring the two together in the one blessed creation. The polarities present in our one human existence do not result in competing dualisms. There need be no rivalry between these two dimensions of created existence. Genuine spirituality does not demean the material and the physical, the bodily and the sexual, or the scientific exploration of matter. Likewise, true worldliness does not mean a lessening of contact with the transcendent, the divine, the spiritual, or the heavenly. The larger ecology of creation allows for different, interrelated realms and principles. Neither the spiritual nor the material can be ignored, unless to the detriment of both. For instance, an holistic sense of creation demands that faith make room for the proper independence of the secular, and the true value of the world in itself. Our hope for the life of the world to come cannot demean the worth of our present life in this world. On the other hand, life in the secular world will lack its full meaning if it represses the domain of the spiritual. Cut off from ultimate hope, it will be going nowhere: God is, therefore, confessed as 'the maker of heaven *and* earth'.

Out of a sense of the wholeness of God's creation, believers must accept the whole gift and bear the whole weight of that creation. As complex beings, we praise the creator, in and through that complexity. Whatever the diversity in our callings, life-styles and philosophies, faith in God the Creator excludes any mono-dimensional vision of existence. It likewise counters the dualism that compartmentalises our experience of the world so that the underlying unity of creation is missed. Indeed, belief in God as maker of heaven and earth keeps us in a healthy awareness of the complexity of the creation in which we live, and the continuing need to make room for the whole. However complex the world is, faith in the Creator enables us to understand it as a 'universe'. That means both respecting and going beyond the purely physical cosmos of modern science. While faith need have no problems with the brilliance of modern 'grand unified theories', or a 'Theory of Everything', it must insist that however brilliant such mental constructs might be for correlating the four forces affecting all material things, there is still the larger consideration of the transcendent origin, form and goal of the totality of material and spiritual existence. Only as created by God is reality in all its aspects, phases, levels, structures and dimensions finally appreciated as a *uni-verse*, the one reality of creation. The doctrine of creation supports the most comprehensively holistic appreciation of reality, and keeps the '- holic' in the *catholic*—the universal dimension of Christian faith.

Belief in creation attunes faith to recognise the universe as a great symphonic event. Nothing in all its manifold dimensions of order and spontaneity, of nature and history, is outside the scope of God's creative activity. God's making includes the past, present, future; and all the dynamics of cosmic emergence, biological evolution, spiritual freedom, intellectual achievement, artistic expression, ethical action. God creates not merely 'things', but all the variety and levels of conscious existence, in which the great symphony of creation springs into awareness. Since God is the source of all that is, everything and everyone is inter-related in the one universal event of creation. Each element and energy participates in its own particular way in the one universal event of what God has made, and is making.

The universe is the totality of what is, of all that is already known, or is yet to be discovered. Faith in the Creator occurs within the universe that has brought us forth, in the many billion years of cosmic history. The creed is sung on the air of one of the planets of one of the hundred billion stars of one of the hundred billion galaxies of the known cosmos. No doubt there are forces and energies, dimensions and life-forms that remain to be discovered—or rediscovered. Here I note the excess of reality that the liturgy celebrates in its exuberant listing of ranks and hosts of angels. If we adore the creator and if we wonder at the dimensions of the universe, we are must be slow to believe that human intelligence has exhausted God's creative power, and that the human is the only spiritual presence in the whole of God's creation. But wherever we turn, from quarks to quasars, from protons to super-novas, from the Big Bang to black holes, from the human brain to dark matter, from the beginnings of life to the defiant death of the martyr, from the brilliance of scientific exploration to the grandeur of simple moral goodness, from the human soul to the seraphim and archangels, there is one source from which everything derives

Ongoing Creation

God keeps acting. Creation continues. Divine creativity is not limited to the past. Unless the creator continues to create, the universe would fall back into nothingness. Today, however, the continuing creative activity of God can be understood in greater depth. God's continuing creation not only prevents the universe from falling back into nothing, but enables it to increase its being in progressive levels of becoming. God creates the world, not as a fundamentally finished reality, but as an expanding event. An all-engendering love is still at work, creating the universe in its capacity to become more, and to unfold to its ultimate dimensions. We can picture God creating the world less from 'on high' or 'from above', and more as the infinite energy acting 'from within', enabling it to emerge into new intensities of consciousness and communion. As the Spirit of God acts within all being and becoming, in all matter and life, it has brought forth human consciousness. In the human mind and heart, the world has become conscious of itself as an event of divine creation. In the contemplation and prayer, creation becomes intimate with its source, to wait on the final self-revelation of the reality from which everything has come forth.

In its coming forth from God, however, created reality remains genuinely other than God. It is given to exist in its own real, finite right. It has its own freedom, spontaneity and principles of action and interaction. The creator God, therefore, lets creation be itself. Being-created does not mean that God crowds reality with a kind of overwhelming presence which never allows the creature to be genuinely other before God. Rather, created existence is a kind of dependent independence—*dependent* since God is always the ultimate ground of its being; *independent* since it truly does exist, with its own nature and scope of operation. When thinking of God's creation as an act of God, we think of the total dependence of everything on God. When we consider creation as a noun, as what God in fact has made and is making, we are struck more by the total independence it enjoys, right to the point, in the case of freedom, of standing for or against God. The creator has thereby risked, as it were, the true freedom of the creature. While this is an insoluble enigma, both sides of the reality of creation must be affirmed if we are to appreciate its mystery. For, by creating, God is committed to having time for creation, for letting it be itself, and for making space for what has come from the divine hand. God is not a big reality mixed in with multiplicity of creation. For in its own domain, the world of creation is intelligible in its own right and on its own terms. Herein lies the foundation for the integrity of all scientific exploration. Indeed, no idea of God can be allowed to distract the mind from exploring what God has made.

More practically, cosmology, physics, chemistry, biology, psychology and so on, have their own subject matters. They are not be confused with a theology of creation even if such 'subject matters' are aspects of the one creation and are the activities of human consciousness. Ideally, all human modes of exploration properly exist in a conversational interaction, each and all with a sense of the one overwhelming, manifold mystery. Given this growing multiplicity of specialisations, how to prevent confusion, how to promote interaction and collaboration within the one great, all-involving event of the universe, are exciting questions. The task of the theology of creation is to remind science that, in exploring any kind of reality, it is not edging out the reality of God. God is not part of creation. The Creator acts both within and from beyond the scientifically accessible structures and dynamisms of the material world. On the other hand, in exploring ultimate reality, there is no need to demean or ignore any aspect of reality that is scientifically accessible to human investigation. To be created is to be given to exist, in its own right and with its own self-organising powers.

If all beings are given into existence out of the generosity of Infinite Be-ing, God is never foreign to creation. Everything is essentially related to God as its abiding source, sustenance and goal. In the limited and varied being of the created universe, the sheer, unlimited Be-ing of God is, so to speak, materialised, embodied, expressed. The Incarnation of the Word is, in the sense we suggested above, a culminating incarnation of God—the Word coming into his own, as the full, personal self-communication of God (Jn 1:11).

We can therefore suggest that believing in creation frees the mind to be completely untrammelled in its explorations of reality. While intelligence delights in what is achieved though the scientific explanation of the universe on intra-worldly terms, it must also appreciate the genuine creative reality of mind in the midst of creation. The mind can keep expanding as the reality it explores brims with questions: What is the explanation of all the explanations? What is the sufficient reason for all our sufficient reasons? What is the ultimate value of everything we have find worthwhile? Before what or whom we do we finally stand? What does the consciousness of being a self suggest, a self that enjoys so much, that thinks, explores, acts, creates, cares and wonders? Belief in creation, then, inspires the ultimate adventure in thinking, as the mind and heart refuse to rest in anything but the ultimately intelligible, the finally good, and the unified whole.

And yet creation includes the astonishing variety of real things, in all their inter-relationships, processes and levels of existence. Why is this *all*, this *whole*, so intricately varied and differentiated? Evolutionary biology gives its answer in terms of the history of life's emergence. Physics and chemistry point to all the elements and forces and patterns necessary for the universe to be what it is. Modern ecological awareness appreciates the wondrous diversity and interconnectedness of life, so as to warn the human generations against carelessly tearing or upsetting the web of life on this planet. In pondering the question of why there is such variety in creation, St Thomas Aquinas gives a deceptively simple answer. God chooses a varied creation to express more fully the richness of divine Be-ing:

> God is . . . the most perfect agent. Therefore, it belongs to him to induce his image in created things in the most perfect way in a manner that befits created nature. But created things cannot attain to the perfect image of God in a single form: the cause exceeds the effect; for what exists in the cause in utter simplicity, is realised in the effect in a composite and pluriform manner . . . It is fitting, then, that there be a multiplicity and variety in created things so that God's image be found in them perfectly in accord with their mode of being.[6]

However, interwoven with the varied wonder of creation is the force of evil as was mentioned earlier. Disease, catastrophe, the perversions of human freedom, death itself, permeate what God has created. If belief in creation excludes any evil principle in rivalry with God, why then is evil such a force, and such a presence? Why is creation burdened with such a problem of evil?

The Excess of Creation

The history of Christian thinking largely leads to silence, hope and waiting. We human beings would have more chance of hearing silence

---

6. Aquinas, *Summa c Gent*, book 2, ch 45.

and seeing darkness than of understanding evil. It is the oppressive absence of the good we need and seek. In the face of the excess of evil, faith does not attempt a philosophical answer. It offers no solution except that of opening the way to a more complete surrender to the mystery of love, in order to participate in the transforming and healing power of love and mercy. For the 'almighty' source of love is also an excess beyond human comprehension. The excess of God's love is displayed as it exposes itself to our problem of evil in the incarnation, suffering and death of the Son. Such love is not turned to vengeance, but keeps on being love in its ultimately transforming power. It has already triumphed over evil in the resurrection of the crucified, thereby anticipating an ultimate victory. God's love shows its patience in having time for the whole of human history against the day of a final, universal judgment when evil will be revealed for what it is. In the meantime, the omnipotence of love assures us of the forgiveness of sins, and promises an ultimate transformation in 'the life in the age to come'.

There is, then, no instant solution for the conflicts and clashes, the destruction and limitations, the disease and ambiguity we experience. Nonetheless, God, the Father Almighty promises an ultimate universal judgment to justify his way of creating and redeeming, and so, to allow time and history to follow their course. As faith waits for this final evidence, it is summoned to stand with the Son, who 'for us and our salvation', has immersed himself in the cosmic process, thereby making himself vulnerable to the risk and tragedy of human history. A suffering creation finds its hope in the knowledge that God suffers our sufferings even more than we do ourselves.

The Canticle of Daniel calls us back from cosmic sadness to the defiant affirmation of universal praise. The inspired writer summons all 'the works of the Lord to bless the Lord'. In our present knowledge of the wonder of the universe and emergence of life within in, such praise can be extended into a thousand other forms. The biblical prayer of praise runs through the realities of the natural world—sun, moon and stars, night and day, heat and cold, sea and dry land, wind and rain, animals, birds and fish, angels and human beings. But today the contemplative appreciation of the universe leaps to new possibilities. God can be glorified in the uncanny providence that guided the universe through its astoundingly improbable journey to this present moment. It now brings forth to awareness of the vast, intricate scope of the universal event.

'All you works of the Lord, O, bless the Lord!'—cosmic forces, galaxies in their billions, matter in all its varied forms, consciousness in all its glimmerings, both the sturdy predictabilities and the strange randomness of nature, its order and its chaos, in all the ten million species of living things with whom we share this planet, in every instant of the billions of years that have gone into our making, in all the elements of the stardust from which we are made: 'to him be highest glory and praise forever'.

Faith in creation is not limited to the 'invisible', that is, to what is outside the immediate range of human experience. It includes 'the visible'. To know the Creator means not to reject any aspect of creation. Prayer, contemplation, and intelligence itself cannot exist save as earthed in what we see and hear, touch and taste, smell, hear and feel. Sense, feeling, imagination, and all delight in this world, serve to bring home to the human mind and heart the mystery pervading all creation. Every level of our human awareness has its place in faith's experience of the one creation in which everything is related.

This sense of universal interconnection is the foundation of all analogical knowledge of God. The *invisible* is known through the *visible*. What is immediately accessible as, say, food and drink, as light and fire, as water and earth, as sexual love and family intimacy, is, in its largest frame of reference, a symbol of the beyond, of what is present but inexpressible. Above all, the humanity of Jesus is the incarnation of the divine, for the Word made flesh is the ultimate analogy: 'In him we see our God made visible, and so are caught up in love of the God we cannot see' (The First Preface of Christmas). Flowing from the climactic event of the incarnation is the special sacramental awareness of faith. Familiar human symbols become 'visible signs of invisible grace'. More provocatively, our neighbour 'whom we can see', must be loved as condition of loving God 'whom we cannot see' (1 Jn 4:20).

The creed's confession of God, the Creator, far from permitting a disjunction in our experience, unites the visible and invisible domains of reality as the one self-expression of God in creation. The visible is a path to the invisible, not a distraction from it. The Word is incarnate in the visible, and not concealed behind it. As St Augustine preached,

'Through the invisible made visible, we pass from visible things to the invisible.'[7]

The result is a distinctive kind of Christian realism. When ultimate reality is disclosed in the earthly, familiar realities of immediate experience, the world cannot be treated as a mirage. It is not a veil behind which an unknowable and unknown reality is concealed. In the native patterns of human experience, reality is accessible, to be known and revealed in its ultimate dimensions. In this respect, the created totality in which the visible and invisible are related is the condition for the development of Christian civilisation. The world of the senses, the expanding horizon of the human meaning and value, and the reality of the spiritual, are all united in the one universe of God's creation. The instinct of Christian faith to embody itself in a given culture is, at root, a refusal to let the visible, the native element of our experience expressed in work, art and imagination, be consigned to non-creation, or to the non-divine. Faith is a public matter, a cultural fact, and not an individual private refuge, nor a private revelation. It is a social communication. The revelation of God occurs in the rough and tumble of actual history, not merely in the inner domain of the spiritual. That is to say that faith can never desert the visible for some disembodied realm.

In treasuring the visible, faith claims the world of the senses. It has eyes, just as it hears, tastes, inhales the presence of God. It senses the mystery in realities of the world, in the symbols of its sacraments, in the form of its words, in the face of its neighbour. The invisible comes to us through the visible as the *icon* of the one 'who is'. It follows, then, that both the experience of the senses and the creativity of imagination are integrated into the ecstasy of faith. Signs, symbols, sacraments, the incarnation itself—all point beyond themselves to what transcends our world. Since faith is never a mere matter of having a good look at the visible, believers never simply see God— either in themselves or in others; nor, for that matter, in the entire event of the universe. Nonetheless, the invisible domain is not unfelt; it too is experienced. The realm of the invisible stirs in the depths of our consciousness, in all the dynamics of knowing and loving, judging, deciding and relating to the other and to the whole. It turns consciousness into conscience, and lifts that conscience to its ultimate

---

7. Christmas Day Sermon (c 410 AD), *Sermo* 190.2.

height in the experience of being loved, and of being called to share in the life of love: 'No one has ever seen God; if we love one another, God lives in us, and his love is perfected in us' (1 Jn 4:12).

There is, therefore, an interior dimension of creation. In that invisible *within*, God's Spirit stirs in the manifold activities of our conscious selves, as well as in creation as a whole. Creation is going on; it happens both in the scientist's understanding the universe, and in the physical universe itself. Creation includes both the artist's self-expressive activity and the objective work of art. It contains both the mind at work and the reality it understands or produces. It is there in the silence of the mystic and in inspired words of faith and devotion; in the integrity of good conscience and in the good deeds that are done.

In other words, creation is not simply 'already out there', as though we are spectators. It is also 'in here', making us participants through the creativity of human consciousness, in all the modes of its loving, praying, exploring, acting, dreaming and communicating. In that way, creation occurs, as the *visible* becomes conscious of itself in the *invisible* reality of mind and heart and spirit. And this *invisible* expresses itself in the visible domain of the material, public, social world. Adoration of the creator leads to a truly bodily indwelling in the wonder of creation: matter and spirit, senses and mind, the exterior and the interior, are interrelated as in the one created universe.

To inhabit the world with a vivid sense of its being God's creation is to live with an awareness of everything as sheer gift, as we have previously stressed. Thanking becomes the condition of true thinking. All creative thinking and acting, all the loving and doing—all likewise participate in God's creation. The creativities of mind and heart, of eye and hand, of word and art communicate in the unfolding of what is coming to be. The divine Spirit is at work in the scientist and the scholar, in the inspired productions of the artist, in the contemplative and the mystic; most of all, in the moral activity of good men and women working together in love and justice to make the world both a human place and a biosphere hospitable to life in all its forms. And so, to be part of creation and to adore the Creator brings both a gift and a responsibility. We live the wonder of existing, belonging and acting in the universe of God's creating.

To believe in one God is to turn to the infinite Light which cannot be fully known within the bat-like vision of human knowledge: 'No one has ever seen God' (Jn 1:18). Yet faith in Christ makes us familiar with what, to human vision, is the blinding glare of too much light, and which, for human intelligence, is an impenetrable darkness. Hence, the need to appreciate what has been given from beyond: 'It is God the only Son, who is close to the Father's heart, who has made him known' (Jn 1:18). The Word incarnate reveals the human face of God, and the Spirit enables faith to hear that inexpressibly fullness of that Word (Jn 16:12–14).

In the confession of the One God, the faith of Israel and the faith of the Church are united 'you shall love the Lord your God with all you heart, and with all your soul, and with all your mind, and with all your strength' (Deut 6:4, Mk 12:29, Mt 22:34–40, Lk 10:25–28). God is to be loved with the best energies of our being, with all our powers of knowing, loving and doing. In God, our minds adore the all-surpassing truth which summons them, and our actions find their scope and fulfilment. In adoring, loving and entrusting ourselves to this One, we belong together most fully as 'we', and enter a community of love and forgiveness. The commandment connected to the summons to love God unreservedly is this: 'You shall love your neighbour as yourself' (Mk 12:31). There is not going up to God unless it includes going out to our neighbour. Consequently, we cannot come to God, isolated, alienated from others, and loveless in their regard. It remains, however, that all our capacities to explore this present world, and to be drawn beyond it into the fullness of life, find their point of rest in the One God: 'For with you is the fountain of life; in your light we see light' (Ps 36:9).

Certainly, the Christian experience of God is shaped by the disconcerting vision that Jesus brings into the situation. He comes, looking upward to his origin with the Father; and outward—to the scope of what the Father is bringing about through the mission of the Son. His entry into the historical scene opens it to dimensions of 'spirit and truth' (Jn 4:23). The Samaritan woman's God of our 'fathers' is now revealed as 'the Father', loving the whole world and seeking true worshippers 'in spirit and truth' (Jn 4:24), in a way that cannot be limited to Mt Gerizim or Jerusalem, or to Rome or Rio, Melbourne or Tokyo—a realm defined only by God's life-giving love.

If true worshipers of God are not limited to any particular time and place, that is because, within the mystery of creation, God can no longer be 'kept in his place'. The world itself is newly defined as that into which the Father has sent his Son. The world has lost its self-made boundaries through the coming of the Son and the sending of the Spirit. Union with God does not mean, therefore, losing oneself in an infinite solitude, since this One God does not live in self-contained isolation. God lives in the vitality of interpersonal love and relationship. The life of God, Father, Son and Holy Spirit, is communication and endless giving to the other, so that God is one as a unity-in-communion. The divine communion enfolds believers into itself—that they may dwell in God and find their unity within the divine life:

> The glory that you have given me I have given them so that they may be one, as we are one, I in them and you in me, that they may be completely one (Jn 17:22).

The Intelligence of Faith

Belief in creation and faith in the Creator do not mean that believers are always trying to 'prove the existence of God'. The opposite seems to be the case when believers are more intent on proving, not God's existence, but the genuineness of their own existence in the light of the mystery into which they are drawn, as their origin and end. Still, to live the gift of faith does not entail intellectual paralysis. Faith cannot be isolated from the intellectual or moral concerns of life, nor cut off from the sheer wonder of existing at all, and the wonder of the universe itself. In this respect, faith is to be lived, not as stupidity or ignorance or indifference to the real world, but as the wisdom that can integrate every dimension of life—in surrender to God and in the service of our neighbour.

On the other hand, out of its long experience of the ways of God, Christian tradition does recognise some proofs or arguments for God's existence, as previously mentioned. Perhaps the word *proof* is far too cut and dried. It may suggest that the existence of God could be established as one more fact, pinned down by rational control—one factor among many, within a philosophic or scientific system. But God is outside any system, and beyond the reach of any mind. Proof, in a naive, superficial and logical sense, cannot conclude to the reality Christians adore as *God*. Even 'arguing' to God's existence, whilst more modest in its connotation, is still all too heady a description of the 'searching and groping' that St Paul speaks of (Acts 17:27).

The word, 'intimation' suggests something of heart and mind moving together to what must remain beyond our grasp, even if 'not far from each of one of us'. It connotes both God's action—intimation in an active sense—and our experience of it—intimation in a passive sense. Human beings cannot evade questions arising out of the depths of what and who they are in this world. Such questions arise within human consciousness as it unfolds through all the relationships that make up an individual, personal life. When life is fired at us point blank, the uncanny fact of the sheer existence—of the universe and of ourselves within it—demands explanation.

Believers, therefore, take part of the time-honoured exercise of attempting to give reasons why 'God' can mean in fact what faith already lives. As faith expands its capacities to reflect and understand, it expands with a growing appreciation of the universe as God's creation. The more believers gather to themselves the diversified wonder of the universe, the more inclusive is their cosmic praise:

> O all you works of the Lord, O bless the Lord!
> To him be highest glory and praise forever (Canticle of Daniel, v 1).

Arguments for God's existence were traditionally based on the objective inexplicability of the world. For instance, there had to be a first cause since no one element of reality, nor all of it together, is a sufficient explanation of why anything exists, nor why the universe has emerged in the astonishing way it has. True, this is not so much 'proving the existence' of God as arguing that the world is ultimately not self-explanatory. Intelligence owes itself an intelligent explanation, and so asks why any such explanation is truly ultimate in not presupposing anything else.

In recent times this line of argument has been taken further as the billions of years of cosmic time and space have been gradually explored through a series of astonishing discoveries. The Big Bang, the formation of the galaxies and the appearance of our tiny planet Earth, the emergence of life, and the way the universe is aware of itself in the consciousness of the human mind and heart—all suggest a richer context. In fact, the wondrous event at the origin of our universe has made science itself remarkably open-minded on the possibility of an original, provident and limitless Mind behind it all. After the pondering such possibilities, an outstanding modern philosopher suggests some fascinating questions facing the modern thinker about the character of God as 'charged not only with unfathomable wisdom, power and exuberant generosity, but also with dazzling "imaginative" creativity',[8] working through a creative synthesis of both law and order, on and the one hand, and chance, risk, spontaneity, on the other.

Faith in God does not exclude believers from the conversation that makes up human culture. They share in the adventure of intelligence, wonder and creativity, to insist, however, that the ultimate question must not be suppressed. Moreover, they point to a special kind of data drawn from the millennial experience of religious people in their adoration of the One God and with which their own experience resonates. Believing in God, therefore, does not mean surrender to absurdity. In fact, for believers, at least, faith is the supremely meaningful act. The question that aches in all our efforts to understand concerns the final meaning of everything we understand. We hunger for meaning and cannot live without it. It is the essential sustenance of the mind. In this search for meaning, human knowledge has expanded in a myriad ways, above all in the 'knowledge explosion' of our times. Our minds unfold in this world of meaning. We are plunged into a limitlessly intelligible world which emerges ever more brightly as the human mind explores it. We are participating in a universe of meaning and existing in an intelligible world which cannot be explained by repressing intelligent questions. Science and scholarship collaborate in celebrating the fact that questions *do* have answers, and that reality overbrims with meaning to an astonishing degree. To believe in, and to adore, the One God is to have a sense that there is a meaning, an ultimate all-comprehending meaning implicit in all that we have found meaningful.

Faith in God, then, is not an option for absurdity. It is, rather, a celebration of meaning and a confirmation of our restless search for truth. Intelligence ponders on the 'sufficient reason' for something being *this* rather than *that*, for intelligence feeds on meaning and sufficient reason. A sense of being beholden to truth pervades all intellectual activities as the mind seeks to find a point of rest in a sufficient reason that is truly sufficient. In this respect, the absolute is the intel-

---

8. W Norris Clarke, SJ, 'Is Natural Theology Still Viable Today?', in *Prospects for Natural Theology*, edited by E Long (Washington, Catholic University of America Press, 1992), 181.

ligence and love of God, the truth that grounds all truth, the sufficient reason for all sufficient reasons, the solid ground and foundation of truthful existence.

Moreover, believing in God is not immoral, but an assent to absolute good and value, the source and foundation of everything we most prize and of all that we find worthwhile. The fact that conscience can find peace only in honesty, justice and generosity suggests that we live in a universe based on value and the truly good—a universe grounded in an original goodness—indeed, occurring as the gift of primordial love. Hence, believing in the one God implies that moral decisions really count in a value-friendly universe.

Believing in God, then, is not a self-destructive option, nor a form of self-enclosure. It is not moving away from who or what we are, individually, socially and culturally. Believing means living in the presence of the mystery for which our personal being, individual and social, most hungers for its confirmation and fulfilment. Our hearts home to the supremely personal reality, to the One in whom we are most alive, in whose embrace each of us is named and recognised and destined for the fullness of life. Human existence means being involved in an elemental 'love-affair' (Sebastian Moore) with the infinite Good. This has been described as a 'natural desire to see God' so that to be human means to be waiting on the Mystery to manifest itself. Faith occurs when the Word is spoken in the hearing of creation, and when the Spirit gives a listening creation the power to listen further and respond. In that sense, to exist is to stand on holy ground in the presence of the Infinite mystery which summons and attracts. St Anselm, in the first chapter of his *Prosologion*, prays in words applicable to us all,

> Teach me to seek you, and reveal yourself to me as I seek, because I can neither seek you if you do not teach me how, nor find you unless you reveal yourself. Let me seek you in desiring you; let me desire you in seeking you; let me find you in loving you; let me love you in finding you.

Two Obstacles: 'Father' and 'Almighty'

There are two designations of the one God which today have proved problematic. First, to name God as 'Father' seems, in the context of the current critique of patriarchy, especially when intensified by feminists concerns, opens the way to patriarchal idolatry. Secondly, the creedal invocation of God as Almighty and omnipotent raises modern suspicions of totalitarianism and psychological oppression. A word, then, of each of these.

'Father'

To name God as 'Father' without the awareness of context is to risk reducing its meaning to some cultural sense of fatherhood, either ancient or modern. That would project onto God a cultural idol in some form. In contrast, the Christian meaning of 'our Father' is revealed only through the incarnation of his Son and through the gift of his Spirit dwelling within us. Adoring and invoking God as 'Father' manifests faith's conviction that God, the Father, is the absolute 'beginning'. Divine initiative precedes all creation, all time and all human action—even the action of Jesus himself.[9] For Paul, 'the Father of our Lord Jesus Christ' is the original actor 'who has blessed us in Christ with every spiritual blessing', who has chosen us in Christ 'before the foundation of the world' to be present to him in love (Eph 1:1–3). In the vision of faith, everything comes into being out of God's generative and creative love. God creates the universe 'out of nothing'. When God creates, nothing is first 'there', as it were, as some kind of raw material. More positively, God creates purely 'out of love', so that all creation is loved into being, the manifestation of sheer loving on the part of God.

God is Father first as the inexhaustible fount of all life—both within God, in the life of the Trinity, and in the universe of divine creation. God is, therefore, invocable as 'Father', not merely as the source of creation, not only in his gracious relationship to us in time, but also in the eternity of his loving self-expression in the Son and in the grace of his Spirit, named and adored, therefore, as 'the Father of our Lord, Jesus Christ'.

Everything derives from this divine personal source as a gift. The Father's love precedes all creation, all time and all human action; it enfolds all becoming, and is the end of all fulfillments. Faith's rela-

---

9. For example, Jn 1:18; 3:16, 35; 4:23, 34; 5:18–21, 26–28, 30, 36–37; 6:32–33, 37–40, 44–45, 57, 65; 7:16.

tionship to God as Father cannot be determined by sacred sites or ethnic loyalties: '... you will worship the Father neither on this mountain nor in Jerusalem' (4:21). God the Father is beyond all the limits and boundaries the historical world imposes.

Naming God as 'Father' in a Christian sense is the culmination of the experience of all the gifts of God, especially in the sending of the Son and in the further gift of the Spirit. Consequently, thanksgiving (Greek, *eucharistia*) offered to the Father precedes and accompanies all religious thinking. Paul accordingly encourages the early Christian community, to move forward,

> joyfully giving thanks to the Father who has enabled you to share the inheritance of the saints in the light. He has rescued us from the power of darkness and transferred us into the kingdom of his beloved Son, in whom we have redemption and the forgiveness of sins (Col 1:11–14).

When notions of God's fatherhood congeal into oppressively patriarchal patterns, part of the remedy is being aware of the genesis of faith's confession of God as Father. Although the Father is 'the first divine person' in the trinitarian formulation of faith, it is the Holy Spirit, usually referred to as 'the third divine person', who comes 'first' in our experience of God. For the Spirit reveals Christ to faith so that, in the words of the liturgical doxology, 'through him and with him and in him, in the unity of the Holy Spirit, all glory and honour' is offered to the Father Almighty. The circle is complete, since the Father is the One from whom Jesus, the Son, comes, in whose presence he lives, and to whom he has returned. And so, as sons and daughters in the Son, we are freed to be free with God:

> For you did not receive the spirit of slavery to fall back into fear, but you have received a spirit of adoption. When we cry, 'Abba! Father!' it is that very Spirit bearing witness with our spirit that we are children of God (Rom 8:15f).

Almighty

Equally ultimately revealing and presently problematic is the confession of the Father as 'almighty'. Just as the faith undermines any idolisation of God as a patriarchal figure, it likewise subverts any notion of divine power as brute power or caprice. In contrast, God's 'glorious power (Col 1:11) is can be understood only in terms of the reality of Christ and the Holy Spirit, and in relation to the free creation that the Father calls into being.

Nonetheless, the 'almighty' character of God (*omnipotens; pantokrator*) does mean that there is nothing outside God's creative and providential scope. The whole of history unfolds before the Father's gaze, and is brought to its climax in the life, death and resurrection of Jesus, the only Son. Confessing 'the Almighty' in these terms, therefore, is an act of limitless hope:

> Now to him who by the power at work within us is able to accomplish abundantly far more than all we can ask or imagine, to him be glory in the church and in Christ Jesus to all generations, forever and ever. Amen (Eph 3:20–21).

In short, the Father's omnipotence is not an unbridled force aiming to stun and shock all lesser powers with some kind of super-energy. In contrast, the power of God acts, as Elijah experienced it, 'as the sound of sheer silence' (Kgs), and, as history unfolds, in the Word made flesh. In the incarnation, divine power surprises creation with the revelation of God's own involvement in our humanity, beyond the scope of what eye can see, what ear can hear or the human heart conceive. That kind of power is compatible with a divine vulnerability. God refuses to appear in our world save in the form of the crucified humanity of the Son. In this sense, the crucified Christ is both 'the power of God and the wisdom of God' (1 Cor 1:24).

In short, the almighty character of God is primarily instanced in the supremely personal gift of the divine Word becoming flesh. Only God can communicate in this way. The world of finite persons, despite the generosity evident in our various forms of gift-giving, there are limitations. We have to acknowledge a limit beyond which human giving is either destructive for oneself or oppressive and manipulative of the other—or even both. In contrast, such is the power of the Father's love that it does not diminish his divinity or overwhelm our humanity. His Word becomes flesh with us, (*Emmanuel* = God-with-us), to offer believers the fullness of God's gifts. The Spirit comes to be, as it were, God-within-us, to enable our free and ever growing acceptance of the Word. In these gifts of the divine Word and Spirit, the 'almighty' character of God is displayed in the unreserved character of the Father's giving. Divine omnipotence, therefore, does not enter into competition with human freedom, as though the more of the one means less of the other. Rather, God acts to create, enlarge and fulfil our liberty, as the creator and fulfilment of freedom. Where the human autocrat exercises power over 'subjects', the Almighty Father works within the freedom of the children of God, in order to bring about true liberty of spirit and true autonomy. The greater our freedom, the more creative our response, the more the omnipotent freedom of God is displayed.

Another aspect of the omnipotence of God is patience. God has time, and, indeed, *makes* time for the whole of human history to grow into its true grandeur and scope. The patience of the Almighty is not defeated by human evil. The power of God is incalculably at work, despite the reality of evil, healing, forgiving and leading to an evergreater good. Though the patience of God is manifested in time, it is not endlessly frustrated or resisted. The will of God *will* be done. God acts, however, not as a brute force or grandiose display, but out of the inexhaustible imagination of love. Beyond all human limits, conditions and calculations, such love achieves its own success. The crucified Jesus is raised from the dead. The evidence of this all-transforming event is such that it discloses to faith the triumph of God over evil, and yet allows for the freedom of each one to surrender in hope to the life-giving power of God, the Father Almighty.

The omnipotence of God is a life-giving and person-forming power. It works beyond the tiny limits of our own self-making. To confess the Father Almighty, therefore, is to enter the realm of true life, only to receive it as a gift and a grace: 'All things can be done for the one who believes' (Mk 9:23). Though we might long for the eternities of life, love and universal communion, reaching such fulfilment is impossible in terms of any human abilities. But such limitations are not imposed on the almighty love at work through the universe: 'For men it is impossible, but not for God; for God all things are possible' (Mk 10:27). Consequently, faith in God, the Father Almighty, is the foundation of hope. The last word on the human predicament is not swallowed up in the dark silence of suffering, guilt, death and failure. Working within, with, and through that groaning totality of the way things are, is God's limitless and loving power.

The almighty, all-comprehending compass of God's power is not contradicted by an evolutionary understanding of the world, which can be entirely appropriate from a scientific point of view. It remains, however, that the 'almighty' power of God is not compromised by any cosmic forces or evolutionary processes. The dynamics of emergence and evolution are indifferent to individual fate, and even to the continuance of the species—perhaps even to the continuance of planetary life itself. In contrast, the almighty power that is the object of faith and the ground of hope, is intensely personal. In God's creative intention, no one is left out or left behind, and, in terms of human history, no one generation is closer to God than another, and no self-sacrifice for others is lost. Those who have died out of the world, those who have given their lives for the sake of others, are not mere raw material for progress. They have died into the depths of the mystery at work, and are embraced by the healing and creative action of the almighty Father.

Admittedly, the totality of what is in the making cannot be known to the human mind. It must be left to the omnipotent wisdom which operates in God's way and in God's time. The central icon of the emerging wholeness of creation is the Risen Christ. The Spirit's transforming power is manifested in the crucified and risen Jesus, overflowing into the whole of creation and the whole of history. Nothing and no one is outside its universal care: 'We know that all things work together for good for those who love God, who are called according to his purpose' (Rom 8:28).

In the face of evil, omnipotent goodness is displayed in a new intensity. The divine capacity to turn evil into good is manifested as mercy and forgiveness. The inexhaustible resources of God's love thus break the vicious circle of revenge and domination by inspiring the spiritual and moral risk of being 'merciful as your heavenly Father is merciful' (Lk 6:36). Christian hope grows in a world where the limitless power of divine goodness, though seemingly defenceless, is the ultimately decisive factor:

> If God is for us, who is against us? He who did not withhold is own Son, but gave him up for all of us, will he not with him give us everything else? . . . No, in all these things we are more than conquerors through him who loved us. For I am convinced that neither death, nor life, nor angels, nor

rulers, nor things present, nor things to come, nor powers, nor height, nor depth, nor anything else in all creation, will be able to separate us from the love of God in Christ Jesus our Lord (Rom 8:31–39).

God's omnipotence confronts the omnipotent pretensions of human culture—'the principalities and powers' of this world. The almighty character of God's love subverts the totalitarian pretensions that lie at the root of the world's self-destructive pride. In this regard, the loving power of God works to exorcise our most familiar demon, the lust for power which infests human history. God alone can topple the idols that distract us from the one thing necessary, to obscure our true finitude and to mask our dependence on the Other. The Father, the Almighty, acting in the subversive force of love, leaves us with nothing but the disarmed reality of our own humanity—yet as always loved by God, and offered true life as a gift. The humbling outcome is a new awareness: 'God's foolishness is wiser than human wisdom, and God's weakness is stronger than human strength' (1 Cor 1:25).

The active experience of prayer makes us familiar with the manner in which God's almighty power works in our world. God does not act as one more vector of force among countless others. Rather, God works in all causes, and acts in all activities. However, the almighty power of divine love does not act from the outside, but from within the reality and dynamics of the world of divine creation. The seeming powerlessness of prayer works within, as the most life-giving and ultimate of all energies. In this respect, God is not changed by our prayers, as though our Father is made aware of some aspect of our needs or some detail of possible good which previously escaped his notice. The opposite is the case: the sheer bounty of God's love inspires human freedom to express itself in prayer in order that the heart be made more open to the gift-giving God. In this manner, God's power changes believers into intercessors, as they open their lives and the lives of others, and the life of the world itself, to the ultimate gift.

In all this, God acts as creator and redeemer by being intimately self-involved. As already mentioned, the climactic instance of God's self-involvement is the incarnation of the Word and the outpouring of the Spirit. This is to say that God is with us, within, behind and before us, in all the pushes and the pulls that determine our lives. God acts in all influences from above and from below, in the formation of the structures that determine our being, in the intelligence that guides us, and in the transformation that awaits us in the life of the world to come. Everything issues from the Almighty, but with the gentleness of light, and in both the patience, and the impatience, of love.

When all is said and done, God is almighty, not in the sense of being capriciously at work from beyond our world, but as integrating all that makes up our world so as to make it serve an ultimate and all-inclusive purpose—to communicate the divine self-gift to creation.

> In summing up, the words of the ancient sage of Israel cannot be bettered:
>
> We could say more but could never say enough; let the final word be: 'He is the all'. For he is greater than all his works . . . Glorify the Lord and exalt him as much as you can, for he surpasses even that . . . do not grow weary, for you cannot praise him enough (Sirach 43:27–30).

To conclude: the power of God's love is revealed in patience and respect for the structures and dynamisms of the created world. The power of God has had time, indeed, made time and made space for us, in the billions of years needed for the universe to unfold, for life to emerge, and for human consciousness to awake in wonder. Dante wrote of 'the love that moves the sun and the other stars' (*L'amor che muove il sole e le altre stelle*). Today, we can think of that love creating and moving the universe from the first moment of the Big Bang, to the formation of the galaxies and the stars, planets, and finally of our earth. There followed the emergence of primitive life three and half billion years ago, until it eventually broke through in human life. And in the human mind and heart, the universe became aware of itself as a gift of limitless wonder. Omnipotent love has time for the whole of human history to grow to its own grandeur and to reach its fulfilment.

Bede

He is well content now:
All along, an empty shell
on this lost shore
lapped by the luminous plentitude
of teeming seas
as they wash
the uncanny island
of the world.

Trinitarian Connections: Inside Knowledge

David Bentley. Hart has structured his profound treatment of our experience of God around the classic Hindu notion of God in terms of as being, consciousness and bliss—*sat, chit, ananda*.[1] Not only does such a tripartite attribution have profound metaphysical consequences, but invites a phenomenological approach to the experience of a triadic, even if not triniarian, mystery of God,[2] in a way that offers a good beginning for a specifically trinitarian theology of God.[3]

An Intra-Trinitarian Standpoint

The classical doctrinal mode confesses God as Trinity in a communion of the three divine persons, Father, Son and Spirit. Any effort to relate the Christian experience of God to a contemporary worldview cannot bypass the centrality of the Trinity. In the vision of faith, to be created is to be invited into the divine love-life: God communicates in the incarnation of the Word and through the outpouring of the Spirit—and, indeed, in the final face-to-face revelation of the Father.

There is no suggestion, therefore, that being united to the One God means intimacy with infinite solitude. The One God does not live in self-contained isolation, but in the vitality of communion of interpersonal love and self-giving. The life of God, Father, Son and

---

1. David Bentley Hart,*The Experience of God: Being, Consciousness, Bliss* (New Haven: Yale University Press, 2013, 42–43.
2. Hart, *The Experience of God*, 44.
3. See Hurtado, *God in New Testament Theology*, for the section, 'The Triadic Shape of God-Discourse in the New Testament', 99–109. Also Richard Bauckham, *Jesus and the God of Israel* (Grand Rapids, Michigan: Eerdmans, 2008), 127–151.

Holy Spirit, is that of communication and endless self-giving to the other. God is one, but n a unity-in-communion. Furthermore, the divine communion enfolds believers into itself—that they may dwell in God and find their unity within the divine life. The words of Jesus in the Gospel of John are a focal reference:

> The glory that you have given me I have given them so that they may be one, as we are one, I in them and you in me, that they may be completely one (Jn 17:22)

The surprising thing, textually and rhetorically, is the pervasive presence of triadic formulations in the New Testament writings. Even the earliest letter, 1 Thessalonians (AD 58?) speaks in a straightforward uncomplicated manner about the threefold character of God (1 Thes 1:1–5). It is assumed that everyone will understand what is meant in such expressions. While there is no need to be uncritically maximalist in this regard, the seemingly spontaneous use of a triadic rhetoric celebrating the New Testament experience of God's presence and action is striking. It certainly requires an explanation, especially given the long struggle for adequate doctrinal formulation which would occupy the Church in the four centuries to come. A triadic manner of speaking imposes itself, for example, in Paul's discussion of the law (Gal 3:11–14) and Christian freedom (Gal 4:4–6), just as it pervades his expressions of thanksgiving (2 Thess 2:13; Col 1:3–8). It is noticeable also in the way he expresses his prayers (Rom 15:30; Phil 3:3–6; Eph 3:14–16). Moreover, the unity and giftedness of the Christian community are presented with explicit reference to the divine three (1 Cor 12:4–8). A number of creedal and liturgical formulations are even more explicit. At the conclusion of Matthew's gospel, the Risen Lord commissions the disciples to go forth and baptize the nations 'in the name of the Father and of the Son and of the Holy Spirit' (Matt 28:19). The most likely explanation of a deliberately ordered triadic pattern is a settled liturgical usage, the most well-known being 2 Corinthians 13:14.

Inchoately Trinitarian elements in the early rhetoric of Christian faith can be further specified. They are evident in the two forms we name here as iconic and schematic, even if they are often interwoven (*cf* Acts 1:4–8; 2:23, 28; 9:17; 10:38; 11:15–17 in reference to the following).

Iconic forms occur where New Testament language works to construct an image of the divine mystery involved in the work of salvation.

- These are detectable principally in the Synoptics such as the various depictions of the baptism of Jesus: the Spirit descends in the form of a dove, the heavens are opened, the divine voice proclaims Jesus as the beloved Son (*cf* Matt 3:16–18; Mk 1:9–11; Lk 3:21–23; and also Jn 1:32–34).
- Then, the Infancy Narrative (especially Luke) gives something like a holographic impression of God's saving presence: the Holy Spirit is the divine power at work, Jesus is uniquely the Son of the Most High (Lk 1:32–35).
- Transfiguration passages speak of the cloud of glory (the *Shekkinah* of the Spirit?), the voice from heaven, the proclamation of Jesus as the Beloved Son (Matt 17:1–8; Mk 9:2–8; Lk 9:28–36).
- Jesus rejoices in the Spirit, to express the intimacy of his communion with the Father, and his role in inviting others into it (Lk 10:21–22).
- In his Ascension (Lk 24:50–53; Acts 1:6–12), Jesus as the Risen Lord ascends to the divine realm, from which he will send the Spirit, as 'the promise of my Father' (Lk 24:49).

Schematic instances accent less a symbolic content, but more the conceptual presentation of the fullness of salvation in Christ. Some Pauline passages approach a systematic presentation of the divine mystery—though without any awareness of the problematical nature of what is presented. Note the manner in which major sections of Romans (for example, Rom 8), Galatians (for example, Gal 3), 1 Corinthians (for example, 1 Cor 12) and Ephesians (for example, Eph 1) are constructed: there is a strong emphasis on three aspects the mystery of salvation:

- the initiative of the Father;
- union with Christ;
- living in the unity and power of the Spirit.

One example of this kind of schematic structure is the following:

> There is one body and one Spirit, just as you were called to one hope that belongs to your call, one Lord, one faith, one

baptism, one God and Father of us all, who is above all, and through all and in all (Eph 4:4–6).

As we consider John's Gospel, it would seem that the evangelist is not only giving a coordinated account of the fullness of grace and truth now present to the world in Jesus Christ (Jn 1:14), but evidently attempting something more systematic. He is presenting the divine three in the one mystery of God. No doubt, he is influenced by the problems that inevitably arose from the preceding triadic proclamation of the grace of salvation. It is not anachronistic, therefore, to suppose that John is already beginning to face a doctrinal challenge. If salvation begins with the Father who so loved the world (Jn 3:16), if the Son he gives for the world's salvation is to be confessed as 'My Lord and my God' (Jn 20:28), if Jesus departed to send the other Paraclete from the Father (Jn 15:26), then the question could not be long in coming: How are these divine 'three' related to one another?[4]

A significant inflection of Johannine rhetoric is its expression of the communion existing between the Father and the Son. To this degree, it points to a dialogue or conversation going on between them. The Word made flesh has a dialogical existence: his origin in from the Father, his identity is to be this Father's Son, just as his mission is to the Father's will. Existing from and for the Father, he is sent from the Father, receives everything from him, yet is one with him. Still, 'the Father is greater than I' (Jn 14:28), for he is the origin and goal of all that Jesus is. No one goes to the Father but by him, but no one can come to Jesus unless drawn by the Father (Jn 6:44). The speech of the Son and the silence of the Father who speaks only in this Word, express the character of the transcendent mystery into which all believers are drawn. The prayer of Jesus in John 17 is the climax of this kind of rhetoric: 'that they may be all be one even as you, Father, are in me and I in you, that they also may be in us' (Jn 17:21).

Compared to the interaction of Father and Son, the presence is the Spirit is not as directly expressed in John's Gospel. On the other hand, full attentiveness to the Word depends on the presence of the Spirit. For this 'other Paraclete', 'the Spirit of Truth', whom the Risen Jesus sends, 'will teach you all things, and bring to mind all that I have

---

4. See Francis J Moloney, SDB, *Love in the Gospel of John: An Exegetical, Theological and Literary Study* (Grand Rapids, Michigan: Baker Academic, 2013, especially 37–69, 201–210.

said to you' (Jn 14:26). The Gospel can speak of the Father and the Son because the Spirit gives, and continues to give, his testimony (Jn 15:26). The Paraclete guides successive generations of believers into all truth (Jn 16:13). The Spirit is, therefore, a pervasive and implicit presence in John's Gospel, inspiring the understanding of Christ and guiding its development. A problem seems to have clearly occurred to the evangelist: how was the presence of the Spirit related to the dialogical relationship existing between the Father and the Son? How did the Spirit figure in the communication taking place between the Father and the Son?

> I have many things to say to you but you cannot bear them now. When the Spirit truth comes, he will guide you into all truth, for he will not speak on his own authority, but whatever he hears he will speak, for he will declare the things that are to come. He will take what is mine and declare it to you. All that the Father has is mine; therefore I said, he will take what is mine and declare it to you (Jn 16:12–16).

In this presentation, the Spirit of Truth is the one who hears, and receives what is going on between the Father and the Son, that totality of communication that comes from the Father to the Son, and from the Son to the Father. The Spirit is 'of truth' in that he makes this communication open to believers, and draws them into it. The least that can be said is that John is aware of the problem in the rhetoric of faith. He begins to face it by presenting the mystery of the whole in the form of a logic serving to structure a way of thinking about the divine Three. Such logic draws its force from a sense of the divine as a field of loving communication characterised by an attitude of self-surrender to, and for the sake of, the other. The Son lives for the Father. The Father gives everything to the Son. Father and Son give everything over to the activity of the Spirit. The Spirit speaks not on his own authority, but from what he has heard from the Son, and, by implication, from the Father—to order to glorify them both.

The God of Communion

The above remarks are a brief indication of the beginning of trinitarian theology and of the logic shaping its development. In the Johannine perspective, the divine Three are being presented in a unity which is at once a communion of life, and a community of inter-related persons. Subsequent doctrinal formulation and systematic theology will necessarily address such issues.

At every stage, the New Testament offers an enriched cognitive sense of the meaning of God. In all that happens, the one God of Israel is at work, but with a singularity concentrated in a unique form of communication lived out between the Son and the Father. This is in contrast to any kind of mono-dimensional orthodoxy that would presuppose that God is not only one, but also that this God is ultimately alone, the absolute solitary. In contrast, the self-revelation of God, Christian faith insists, leads to understanding of Jesus, as Word and Son, as utterly and originally 'Father-ward', in eternity and in time (*cf* Jn 1:1, 14, 18; 5:19, 30, 43). Likewise, the Father's 'Son-ward' communication is stated in various ways: 'The Father loves the Son and shows him all he himself is doing' (Jn 5:20). This 'showing' includes the 'work' of raising the dead and giving life 'to whom he will' (Jn 5:21, 26). Still, it is not only a matter of the Father's *showing*, but *giving* to the Son—the gifts of 'all judgment' (Jn 5:22), of having 'life in himself' (Jn 5:26), of the 'authority to execute judgment' (Jn 5:27), and of 'the works' that are his to accomplish (Jn 5:36). Further, the Father both sends and bears witness to the Son (Jn 5:37). What emerges is a differentiated unity enlivened by mutual relationships and inter-subjective communication. Though the axis of the inter-relationship is here presented along the lines of the Father above and the Son below, the prologue (cf Jn 1:1–2) has already expressed the supra-temporal dimension of divine communion which will presented more fully in John 17.

By attending to the data of this distinctive experience, later theology and Church teaching will be led to affirm a singular mystery of divine self-communication. Thereby is implied a transparent reciprocity of relationships between the Father and the Son. The Son is constituted, as it were, in his identity and mission through his relationship to the Father. For his part, the Father is constituted in his paternal self-giving in relationship to the Son. In every aspect of the being and action of the Word, there is the 'verb' of the Father's timeless self-utterance and engendering. The 'subsistent relationship' of the Father is revealed in his ceaseless generation of the Son, even while the identity and mission of the Son in intelligible only in his continuing coming forth from the Father, in order to reveal him as the source of life and light.[5]

Two problematic expressions deeply affect any interpretation of the Johannine experience of God. The first is a straight declaration on the part of Jesus: 'I and the Father are one' (Jn 10:30). The second gives expression to the hope that, through his performance of his Father's works (Jn 10:37), 'you may know and understand that the Father is in me and I am in the Father' (Jn 10:38). Neither of these statements collapses the Son's relationship with the Father into undifferentiated metaphysical identity. Nor do they reduce the action of the Father to one of simple collaboration with what Jesus is doing. The Father is 'in' the Son not as contained by him nor as confined to his scope of action. Rather, what is at stake is the Father's generative initiative in all that affects the life and mission of Jesus: 'My Father . . . is greater than all' (Jn 10:29). Immense and complex theologies have struggled to appreciate each element of these statements. Themes such as the unity of the Son with the Father, their reciprocal co-inherence (*perichoresis*), and the sense in which the Father can be understood as 'greater' than the Son in a manner which excludes both the Arian and Sabellian extremes, will allow theology no rest.[6] The exploration of such high doctrinal issues begins from, and forever returns, to the compact experience that is constitutive of Johannine sense of the gift of eternal life emanating from the Father.

If Socrates had counseled that 'the unexamined life is not worth living,'[7] life, in the terms of the Gospel, is both examined and summoned to its highest reach, namely, communion with the Father and the Son: '. . . that they may be one even as we are one, I in them and you in me, that they may be perfectly one' (Jn 17:22).

---

5. On the necessity of understanding this divine reciprocity of relationships in an active and 'verbal' sense, see G Lafont, *Peut on connaître Dieu en Jésus-Christ* (Paris: Cerf, 1969), 272–277.
6. As Aquinas notes, in reference to Jn 10:30: 'a twofold error is here excluded: that of Arius who divided the divine essence, and that of Sabellius who confused the persons. We escape both Charybdis and Scilla, because when he [Jesus] says *"one"*, he frees you from Arius, because if "we" are "one" there is no diversity. But in that he says *"we are"*, he frees you from Sabellius, for as "we", the Father and the Son are different subjects [*alius et alius*].' *In Evang B Joannis Expositio*, c. 10, 4. For an Athanasian treatment of these issues, TF Torrance, *The Trinitarian Faith*, 110–145.
7. *Apology*, 38A.

The coming of the Spirit is a further gift of an overwhelming positive significance in relation to the disciples, to Jesus himself, and to the Father. First of all, the Spirit of truth will guide the disciples into 'all truth' (Jn 16:13). Second, as the Spirit of *truth*, he will glorify Jesus, taking what is his to declare it to the disciples (Jn 16:13). Third, in declaring the truth of Jesus, the Spirit will be declaring 'all that the Father has' is to be found in Jesus (Jn 16:15). In the light of these relationships, the Spirit is, so to speak, a luminous field of presence in the history of faith, through which believers can penetrate ever more deeply into what has been going on between the Father and the Son. Post-biblical doctrinal developments will speak of the Spirit as a 'subsisting relationship' between the Father and the Son.[8] Already at this stage of faith's expression, the Spirit is identified as 'in-between-ness' which makes possible the believers' entry into communion with God and into the fully bounty of the divine gifts. He is the God-given presence of the 'revealed-ness' of what the Father has communicated to the Son and, through him, to the disciples.

And yet the full significance of the hour of Jesus will take its own time: 'I have yet many things to say to you but you cannot bear them now' (Jn 16:12). Though the whole truth of Jesus' words will be the truth that heals, frees and gives life, the disciples at this time find themselves on the dark side of the cross. In sorrow and fear they have a foreboding anticipation of their Master's violent exit from the scene. The full truth of the revelation to be accomplished in his death and resurrection is beyond what they can either imagine or expect. God's self-revelation takes time; and all the events of the hour must run their course. Even if the disciples were to receive verbal instructions from the lips of the Master, the 'many things' yet to come cannot be fully communicated (Jn 16:13c). The Word made flesh will be fully incarnate among them only when, in the flesh of his existence, he will be glorified in the event of the cross. The realisation of this event looks to the coming of the Spirit if it is to be grasped in its abiding significance.

As given into the limited horizon of the disciples, the Spirit will abide in them and be among them (Jn 14:18). As the field in which the

---

8. For a thorough survey and comment, see Gary D Badcock, *Light of Truth and Fire of Love*, 35–82; 145–170. Rowan Williams, in his *On Christian Theology* (Oxford: Blackwell, 2000), makes insightfully compares Johannine pneumatology with the Pauline and the Lukan types. See especially 115–121.

full meaning of what is taking place will be progressively unfolded, the Spirit will guide the disciples into 'all truth' (Jn 16:13a). The Paraclete not only acts against the darkness, but also for the light, bringing home to the community of faith 'the fullness of the gift of truth' that Jesus embodies (Jn 1:14–18; 14:6). He will guide the followers of Jesus into the way of living truth opened up through his passing over to the Father (Jn 14:6). Hence, the Spirit will not speak independently, but will communicate only what he himself hears (Jn 16:13). The Spirit has come, not to replace the message and mission of Jesus, but to make it a living reality in the history that is to unfold. In this sense, the Spirit is the light in which the opened heaven will be seen in all its truth (Jn 1:51).

Nonetheless, neither Jesus,[9] nor the Paraclete, is the originator of revelation. Both are sent by the Father (Jn 14:16, 26; 15:26), each serving the one revelatory communication of the Father—the Son, in the course of his coming from God and going to God (Jn 13:3); the Spirit, by coming after the departure of Jesus to bring out the saving fact that 'the Father had given all things into his hands' (Jn 13:3). The Spirit will remain with the disciples as the Father's permanent gift, in the 'forever' (Jn 14:16) which is in contrast to the 'little time' (Jn 16:16–19) of Jesus' physical presence to them. Because of the coming of the Spirit, time is no longer a pointless succession of instants; nor a continuing cycle endlessly repeating itself; nor is it a memory of a privileged past. Time is experienced as moving to a divine fulfilment, for the Spirit comes to declare what is to come (Jn 16:13). There is a dynamism inscribed in time that looks to the fullness of divine revelation. Jesus and the Father will come to make their home with those who, despite the conflicts that history will produce, have made the persistent, yet peaceful, journey of faith (Jn 14:23). With the gift of the Spirit released through the death and glorification of Jesus (Jn 7:39), the worshipping community will move to meet the Father 'in spirit and truth' (Jn 4:23–24).

Guiding the disciples in all truth, the Spirit of truth 'unpacks' the full meaning of the Word incarnate in the historical conversation of faith. The Spirit will glorify Jesus, to communicate all that he has and is to present and future believers (Jn 16:14). As sent by the Father, the Spirit is impetus to a continuing mission of witness to the world (Jn

---

9. *Cf* 3:32–35; 7:16–18; 8:26–29, 42–43; 12:47–50; 14:10.

15:8). The Spirit of truth witnesses to the most original truth—that of Jesus' oneness with the Father; the Son is sent into the world from the heart of this unity.[10] The Spirit, however, proceeds from the Father and is sent by Jesus (Jn 16:7; *cf* 15:26). As their joint gift of the Father and the Son, he is the first witness to the unity that reigns between them, the divine and personal communicator of that all-enfolding unity to the world. The Father is not hidden, as one unknown, behind the mask of the Son. Rather, under the guidance of the Spirit, the community of faith finds in Jesus the true face of the Father turned lovingly toward it.

The Enfolding Trinity

Unfortunately, doctrinal controversies have often reduced this most illuminating and life-giving of Christian mysteries practically to the point of absurdity—at least in the minds of most Christians. What should have been a celebration of God as the absolute Being-in-Love in all things, the divine community enfolding all conscious creation into its own love-life, has been reduced to an exercise in supercelestial mathematics in which one could neither be multiplied, nor divided, by three. On the other hand, in recent years, trinitarian theology has been undergoing a considerable renewal,[11] so that a distinctively Christian vision and moral practice is informed by a Trinitarian faith, and the theological perspective is sharpened.

First of all, God, as the one ultimate reality, is revealed as relational. In John's Gospel, for instance, the transparent reciprocity of relationships between the Father and the Son realign our understanding of the immanent reality of God (*in se*) and the economic relatedness of God to the world (*pro nobis*). The Son is constituted, as it were, in his identity and mission through his relationship to the Father. For his part, the Father is constituted in his paternal self-giving in relationship to the Son. In every aspect of the being and action of the

---

10. For an illuminating account of Holy Spirit in the immanent Trinity, drawing on Eastern and Western positions, see Gary D Badcock, *Light of Truth and Fire of Love*, 234–256.
11. For a considerable bibliography and a fuller expression of my own approach, see Anthony J Kelly, *Trinity of Love*, and *An Expanding Theology: Faith in a World of Connections* (Sydney: EJ Dwyer, 1993); 'A Trinitarian Moral Theology', in *Studia Moralia*, 39 (2001): 245–289.

Word, there is the 'verb' of the Father's timeless self-utterance and engendering, as mentioned above. The 'subsistent relationship' of the Father is revealed in his ceaseless generation of the Son, even while the identity and mission of the Son in intelligible only in his continuing coming forth from the Father, in order to reveal the primordial source of life and light.[12]

The experience of God radically destabilizes ordinary identities and relationships. God can no longer be 'kept in his place', for the Father has sent his Son into the world. For its part, the world itself has lost its self-made boundaries with what the Gospel of John calls the 'opened heaven' (Jn 1:51). Nor can Jesus be kept in his place, as he leaves this world for the Father. Even death ceases to be in place for him as an opaque impenetrable limit to human life. His dying is integral to the radiance of the love of God revealed in the self-giving of the Son. As for his disciples, though they will suffer the grief of their master's absence, his love 'to the end' demands of them an excess of mutual love that will leave them far more disturbed than any grief over his departure can cause. The reality of Jesus' absence leaves a space where no believer can ever live again in self-contained isolation: 'Just as I have loved you also should love one another' (Jn 13:34).

This interpersonal reciprocity and the mutuality of relationships described in John's Gospel led in the centuries to come to the full blown Athanasian trinitarianism of the post-Nicene doctrine.[13] A seismic displacement of meaning occurred: the culminating gift of truth (Jn 1:14) has broken open the range of human experience to the dimensions of the 'opened heaven' (Jn 1:51). The truth of God's love occurs as an upheaval in the previously imagined world. The varied responses, of incomprehension, acceptance or scandalised rejection, make the words of the poet Paul Celan especially apposite: 'A Rumbling: truth/ itself has appeared/ among humankind/ in the very thick of their/ flurrying metaphors.'[14]

---

12. On the necessity of understanding this divine reciprocity of relationships in an active and 'verbal' sense, see G Lafont, *Peut on connaître Dieu . . .*, 272–277.
13. For an excellent account of the theological development involved, see TF Torrance, *The Trinitarian Faith*, 47–75.
14. Paul Celan, *Poems*, translated by M Hamburger (Manchester: Carcanet, 1980), 202–203. (EIN DRÖHNEN: es ist/ die Wahrheit selbst/ unter die Menschen/ getreten,/ mitten ins/ Metapherngestöber. For further comment, see John Milbank, *The Word Made Strange: Theology, Language, Culture* (Oxford: Blackwell, 1997), 131.

What kind of reality is Christian faith trying to objectify out of its experience of God? How does such experience and meaning affect the Christian's experience of reality? The imagination of trinitarian faith envisages ultimate reality as intrinsically relational. Doctrinal theology, in order to avoid implying that the divine persons are three different substances, goes on to speak of the divine persons as 'subsisting relationships'. That is to say, that the divine three are understood only in relation to one another, as *for* and *in* the other. Thus, the absolute one-ness of God is concretely realised in a pure self-communication to the other. God is God by being a communion of mutual self-giving. The Be-ing of God is, therefore, a communion of self-giving and other-directed love.

God is (Father) expresses his fullness in the Word, and rejoices in its infinite excess in the Spirit. In that self-utterance and self-gift, all that God is, all that the universe is or will be, is contained. The universe, emerging in the long ages of time, is ever being called into existence by the gift of God. Consequently, the eternal Now of trinitarian life is the matrix of time, not its contradiction.[15] That relational vitality within God, which theology calls the 'divine processions' of the Word and the Spirit, creates the universe in its dynamic image. From the divine processions within God flows the 'process' of the universe.[16] This is to say that the divine processions are imaged forth in the unfolding of the cosmic process. The universe finds its ultimate coherence as the *universe* in as much as the Trinity draws it to participate in its own field of relationships. It unfolds in the light of the Word, and is energised by the power of the Spirit, just as it lives in every moment in thankfulness to the originating love of the Father. From its experience of this relational field of divine presence, Christian faith comes to confess the Trinity as the transcendent presence immanent in all existence. All instances of being, becoming and

---

15. For a rigorous examination of the theme of divine eternity, see John C Yates, *The Timelessness of God* (Lanham, Md: University Press of America, 1990).
16. I do not think this distinction is sufficiently appreciated. When it is not, 'process' becomes the ultimate reality, but not 'procession' in the trinitarian sense. There is a big difference between deifying the process and adoring the 'proceeding' divine persons. Even a survey of such towering expertise as Barbour, *Religion in an Age of Science* does not mention the relevance of the trinitarian mystery to current evolutionary and genetic understandings of reality. Remaining only with the category of process strikes me as being theologically far too timid.

life have their beginning, form and goal in the 'love-life' of God', so 'that God might be all in all' (1 Cor 15:28). The evocative language of Nicholas of Cusa returns such intense theological expressions to the world of mystical imagination: 'The Godhead is the enfolding and unfolding of everything that is. The Godhead is in all things in such a way that all things are in God.'[17]

The utterance of the Word 'in the beginning' (Jn 1:1) is the primordial self-expression of the Father. Through this communication, God is self-differentiated, the 'I' and the 'Thou', the 'I' and the 'We', the self and the Other. The universe, created in the Word (*Logos*) is a world of endlessly differentiated 'words' (*logoi*) or meanings. As Aquinas reminds us, 'created things cannot attain to the perfect image of God in a single form'. It was fitting 'that there be a multiplicity and variety in created things so that God's image be found in them perfectly in accord with their mode of being'.[18]

In the order of the creed, the third divine person is breathed forth by Father and Son. The Love that differentiated itself as Father and expressed itself in the Son and Word, becomes, in the circulation of trinitarian life, the shared ecstasy of other-directed loving. The relational dynamics of creation can therefore be understood as a participation in the unifying ecstasy of the Spirit. The Breath of God moves the differentiated, distinct, and independent realities of creation into self-transcending communion of the self with the Other. In this perspective, the cosmos lives and breathes the mystery of the original, expressive and unitive Being-in-Love at the heart of its existence.[19] If the original and ultimate reality is inherently relational, if ultimate unity is self-giving communion, trinitarian faith is a healthy disturbance of all closed little worlds of isolated independence. Defensive alienation from the other, resistance to peace and reconciliation, all deliberate disharmony or exploitation in regard to the rest of creation set us outside the trinitarian flow of life.

---

17. Quoted in Rupert Sheldrake, *The Rebirth of Nature: The Greening of Science and God* (New York: Bantam Books, 1991), 198. Noteworthy, too, is the influence of Sheldrake on the deep Trinitarian structure of Bede Griffith, *A New Vision of Reality*.
18. Aquinas, ScG, l. 2, c. 45.
19. Here I have adapted three terms taken from John Macquarrie, *Principles of Christian Theology* (London: SCM Press, London, 1977), 195–202.

Such a trinitarian conception of ultimate reality stands in contrast to a mechanistic worldview, however dominant and long entrenched. A mechanistically-modelled science has little patience with any theology, let alone any theology needlessly complicated with Trinitarian references to processions, relationships, and the plurality of the divine persons. Nonetheless, current views of the processive and relational character of the cosmos might well find some aspects of trinitarian theology quite intriguing. Contemporary paradigms of science and aspects of trinitarian thinking show signs of convergence. After all, for two thousand years, Trinitarian theology have come to regard ultimate reality as a realm of processive, interpersonal, relational life. It turns on understanding God as concretely one only in a manifold of relationships. As a more holistic science becomes aware of this trinitarian perspective, dialogue is enabled, and a collaborative exploration of what constitutes ultimate reality is set in motion.

Traditional trinitarian theology after Aquinas passes from the consideration of the processions and relationships of the divine persons *ad intra* (that is, in the eternal 'within' of God) to their presence and relationships *ad extra*, in the God-created universe. The self-communication of the Trinity to the created world, is treated under the heading of the biblical category of 'mission' or 'sending'—the way, for instance, God 'sends' the Son and Spirit into the world.[20] The processions of Word and Spirit within God are, as it were, prolonged into the world of time. Given the present evolutionary horizon, much can be gained by retrieving some aspects of the classic yrinitarian tradition.[21] In this brief remark, we are taking some liberty with traditional terminology in the hope of making it more meaningful in the present context. For example, Aquinas asks, how can a divine person be 'sent'? The problem here is to imply neither inequality in the co-equal Trinity, nor a primitive form of spatial movement from one place to another—as though God were not everywhere in the first place. In answer to this question, Aquinas makes two points: First, The divine person is sent inasmuch as the eternal procession of the Son/Spirit

---

20. For a creative treatment of the divine missions, see Robert M Doran, *The Trinity in History: A Theology of the Divine Missions* (Toronto: University of Toronto Press, 2012).
21. For an overview of Aquinas' approach to theology, see Anthony J Kelly, 'A Multidimensional Disclosure: Aquinas' Theological Intentionality', in *The Thomist* 67/3 (July 2003): 335–374.

is prolonged into time and history. In this, the divine consciousness takes in the world of time and its emerging world. Because the mission is an extension into time of the eternal procession, it means that the divine persons begin to exist in the world in a new way: 'Thus, the Son is said to have been sent by the Father into the world, even though he was already in the world, but now he begins to be in the world in a visible, incarnate way manner. The Word was made flesh . . .'[22] We can therefore understand the divine missions as the self-immersion of the Trinity in the created universe. The risk and the fragility, along with the beauty and dynamics of a temporal world, have been given a place in God's trinitarian consciousness. In this way, the world is an aspect of God's own experience. From this point of view, the missions of Word and Spirit are the Trinity's opening out to the world and to history in order to enfold creation into its communal life.

But there is a second point. Aquinas allows for two dimensions of these missions, the 'invisible' and the 'visible'. This traditional distinction, more fully understood, can prevent Christianity from being locked into a narrowness that is ill-prepared for the cosmic scope of its present challenge and responsibilities of interfaith dialogue. So, first, a word on the *invisible missions*. We begin with the recognition that God is present to everything and everyone in an absolutely fundamental manner, as sheer Be-ing, *Ipsum Esse*, the source of all being. It follows that, as the source of all being, God is present in the innermost depths of all reality. But from the depths of the ocean of Be-ing in which all exist, there comes a wave of divine freedom, of self-communicating love. God is not content, as it were, simply to be the nameless universal mystery at the heart of reality. Beyond giving ourselves to ourselves, The Trinity wishes to give itself to us, so that we can enter a new realm of selfhood and communion. This is the area of grace. By receiving this new gift we are not only God's creatures but also become God's intimates. Thus, the Trinity is present in creation in self-giving love. God acts through all creation in the nakedness, creativity and unifying power of love.

This trinitarian self-communication brings about a transformation of human consciousness—traditionally called 'sanctifying grace'. It brings about a special intimacy with the divine mystery.[23] The

---

22. *STh* I, q. 43, a. 1.
23. *STh* I, q. 43, a. 5, ad 2.

human self is 'conformed to God'. Through the experience of loving and being loved, the human person conformed is to the Spirit of love. Likewise, through the gift of faith and wisdom, believers share in the wisdom of the Word: 'because by such knowing and loving, created consciousness (*rationalis creatura*) lives actively in contact with God. The special mode of the interaction involved means not only that God is intimately present to human consciousness, but also dwells within us as in his temple' (*STh* I, q 43, a 3).[24] All time or space opens out within this horizon of God's loving presence, for the Word and Spirit are said to be 'invisibly' sent to indwell human consciousness. However unnamed, unexpressed, the depths of human consciousness are awakened to a new level of life and communion with God. The human being, however implicitly, begins to participate in the very consciousness of God's own knowledge and love. Wherever there is evidence of a consciousness lovingly alive, in reconciling wisdom and self-transcending love, it is evidence of the indwelling of God. And that is to be in the 'state of grace'. The Word of God is not some abstract form of information, but is given so as to reach the heart: 'for the Word is not any kind of word, but the Word breathing love.'[25]

This metaphor of 'mission' might give the impression of the divine Word and Spirit being sent from some kind of outer space where God dwells. On the other hand, once the spatial limits of the metaphor are recognised, the reality of the divine missions is more like a blooming or an emergence of the mystery out of the depths of existence where God is ever present. What could have appeared to be a universe of simple fact, however uncanny, now appears as a radiant field of divine consciousness and communication. God dwells in us and we dwell in God in the circulation of divine life and love.

But there is more. The divine missions are not only 'invisible' as the Word and Spirit illuminate and enkindle human consciousness within the indefinable horizon of life. They are also *visible*. The divine Word who had been invisibly present in grace, becomes incarnate. The Spirit, too, who had invisibly dwelt in the hearts of all good people, is manifested as a movement in history. The gift of the Spirit transforms lives and forms communities of faith, hope and love in an

---

24. Thomas also speaks of the Father as given and indwelling through grace, but not as 'sent'. The first divine person is present precisely as the source of all divine life and love, the Father who is 'above all and through all and in all' (Eph 4:6).
25. *STh* I, q. 43, a. 5, ad 2.

energy animating all witness and sacraments of Church. This visible dimension arises from the reality of God's self-giving as it is attuned to the embodied reality of our human being. God's self-communication takes shape in the time and space of this particular world. God is not to be found only in a transcendent realm, but more so in the flesh-and-blood of our world. Aquinas remarks,

> Now it is connatural for a human being to be guided by the visible to the invisible. Through the evidence of creatures, God has in some way manifested himself and the eternal processions of the persons. Likewise, it is right that the invisible missions of the divine persons be made manifest through visible creation. Now this occurs in one way with the Son, and in another way with the Holy Spirit: . . . the Son is visibly sent as the author of holiness; but the Spirit as the witness to that holiness.[26]

The embodied world of our existence is the natural milieu for human communication. Trinitarian communication respects this given 'ecology' of human existence in order to draw human beings into the divine life of communion. The created world, in all its differentiation, structures, relationships, and dynamics already manifests the relational and communicative reality of God. A trinitarian dynamism is originally inscribed into every element of the created world. The Trinitarian orientation of creation is intensified. The visible mission of the Word incarnate in Jesus Christ expresses in the world of human communication the transcendent mystery of God at work. And the Spirit, symbolised in the water, the wind, the air, the flame of our natural experience, opens into the field of ultimate connections.

In such a perspective, the Church is an extension of the visible missions. It can be identified as that part of the world that is expressly alive to the universal mystery of love at work. Accordingly, the community of Christian faith deals in words, signs, symbols and sacraments in order to live and manifest the trinitarian mystery. The Church belongs to the ecology of divine presence and communica-

---

26. *STh* I, q. 43, a. 1. For further treatment of the missions, Jean-Hervé Nicolas, OP, *Synthèse dogmatique: de la Trinité à la Trinité* (Paris: Beauchesne, 1985), 231–265.

tion, even if it neither represents nor limits the total scope of God's grace at work in all creation.

The invisible and visible missions arise from the Trinitarian vitality of God. Today these missions demand a re-expression in an evolutionary perspective. Both the Trinity communicating itself to the world, and the world itself, need to be understood in a vital and dynamic manner. In that regard, the invisible missions are *invisible* precisely because they energise the indefinable totality of the universe. Animated by such energies, the emergent universe can be contemplated in the light of one vast act of divine self-communication. In that horizon, the self-giving God becomes the soul, the heart, the mind of the world's emergence: 'There is . . . one God and Father of all, who is above all and through all and in all' (Eph 4:6). On the other hand, the *visibility* of the missions discloses the universe in terms of God's embodiment. The mystery of Love incarnates the Word in the body of creation as its form, structure and goal. Love, too, enters the world as the Spirit acts in all the self-transcending dynamics that characterise our human and cosmic development. And, as the Father is intimated as the source of both Word and Spirit, the world of time moves toward its absolute future in God.

In this way, the trinitarian God is 'enworlded'. The divine communal life is the relational ground of a cosmos of growing connections and relationships. The mind of the Word incarnate finds expression in the desire, 'As you, Father are in me, and I in you, may they also be in us . . . may they be one as we are one' (Jn 17:21–23). Then, there is the promise: 'When the Spirit of truth comes, he will guide you into all truth . . . and he will declare to you the things that are to come' (Jn 16:13).

Realism insistently demands an acknowledgement of the tragic world of conflicts in which we live. Whatever our eschatological hope, this is no whole world of harmonious connections or gently conducted dialogue. We must realistically bear in mind that visibility of trinitarian grace in such a world must first of all be a force for healing and reconciling, before it is simply transforming. The energy of God's gifts—indeed of divine self-giving—is marked with the intensity of self-sacrifice. The missions of the Son and the Spirit are directed to human beings locked in an apparently insuperable problem of evil. The problem and its solution reach a limit when the incarnation of the Word results in the crucifixion of the Father's beloved Son. However, the Father himself is revealed as having no self-disclosure in this world other than through the Crucified One. Similarly the Spirit of love and peace is sent into the world of self-enclosure and exclusion of the other. In that world of resistance, the Holy Spirit witnesses to no power and no truth other than that of the selfless love manifested in the Cross. This, through the visible missions, God's visibility in the world comes up against our problem of evil. In that conflict, the self-giving love of God is exposed to the alienation, failure and fragmentation of our world, but in a way that proves ever greater than the power of darkness. Its promise of transformation presumes that it is first of all a healing for the self-destructiveness manifest in n our history.[27]

This, then, is an outline of the way in which the traditional schema of processions, divine relations, invisible and visible missions can be reworked in reference to the emergent global world. God's communication is not reserved for pure spirits, but meets the vast history of human existence in its temporal, historical embodiment.[28]

A Continuing Exploration

There is nothing new in exploring the reality of God by way of analogy with created realities, nor in interpreting the world of created reality in the light of God. Augustine's 'vestige' and 'image' doctrine is a good instance.[29] In Catholic tradition, it developed into the typically Franciscan cosmic sense of all reality sacramentally manifesting God. For example, over seven hundred years ago, Robert Grosseteste, the first Chancellor of the University of Oxford, contemplating a speck of dust, to find in its existence, form and goodness a manifestation of the three divine persons.[30] Now, a speck of dust caught in the light beaming in through a medieval scholar's window is rather different from other specks we know today. For example, the earth is a mere speck in a universe of some hundred billion galaxies. Indeed, the Big Bang represents the unfolding of the cosmos through 14.7

---

27. See Kelly, *Trinity of Love*, 168f; 195–202.
28. Cf *STh* I, q. 43, a. 7; q. 88, a. 3.
29. *De Trinitate* VI; VIII-XV.
30. Servus Gieben, 'Traces of God in Nature according to Robert Grosseteste', in *Franciscan Studies* XXIV (1964): 154–6.

billion years from the infinitesimal super-compressed 'speck' of its beginnings. Theology, therefore, in continuity with its past, can contemplate the originality, the dynamic form, the wonder and beauty of cosmic reality. In so doing, a reflective faith is coming to a fuller insight into the deeper implications of its central mystery.[31]

Likewise, St Bonaventure, in his ladder of contemplation, could consider creation as implying a Trinitarian presence on three ascending rungs of intensity. First, there are 'footprints' (*vestigia*) of the Creator found in the pre-personal. Second, there is the divine 'image' in the spiritual creature with its powers of intelligence and love. Third, there is the divine similitude or 'likeness' brought about as the created spirit is transformed through grace:

> The creation of the world as a book in which the creative Trinity shines forth. It is read according to the three levels of expression, the ways of vestige, image and likeness. By these, as up a ladder's steps, the human intellect has the power to climb by stages to the supreme principle which is God.[32]

The implied metaphor of a stable ladder leading upward tends now to be replaced by the arrow of time moving forward in an evolutionary direction. The 'footprints' or traces of God now have to be tracked in the history of the billions of years of the world's emergence. And then the image of God is disclosed in terms of human consciousness emerging in such an evolutionary world so that world becomes known and appreciated as the gift of the Creator. The higher 'likeness' of God, in its turn, is revealed in the transformation of consciousness as it indwells, and is inhabited by, the primordial mystery of creative Love.

For his part, Aquinas sums up the themes of the great Greek theologians, especially Athanasius and Gregory of Nyssa, when he treats of the presence of the Trinity in the act of creation:

> [T]he divine persons are causes of the creation of things in the order of their procession, since God acts from his knowledge

---

31. For the analogical shift in our understanding of God's relationship to the world, see Carol Jean Vale, SSJ, 'Teilhard de Chardin: Ontogenesis vs. Ontology', in *Theological Studies* 53/2 (June 1992): 313–337.
32. Bonaventure, *Intinerarium Mentis in Deum* c. 3, n. 5.

> and will as a craftsman acts in regard to what he produces. The craftsman acts through a word conceived in his mind and through love in his will in reference to what is to be made. Hence the Father creates through his Word which is the Son, and through his love which is the Spirit.[33]

In such a vision, the trinitarian mystery is implicit in what it means to be a creature. Moreover, the trinitarian processions of Word and Spirit are at the foundations of the cosmic process. Indeed, Aquinas goes on to say that

> The knowledge of the divine persons is necessary for us for two reasons: in the first place, to have a right sense of the creation of things. Because we say that God created all things by his Word, the error is excluded of holding that God produced things out of the necessity of his nature. Because we hold that there is a procession of love within him, it is clear that God did not produce creatures out of some extrinsic need, but on account of love for his goodness . . . In the second place, and this is more important, [the Trinity is disclosed] that we might have a proper sense of the salvation of the human race, which is brought about by the incarnation of the Son and through the gift of the Holy Spirit.[34]

That 'right sense of creation' implies that creation is not a divine necessity. It is an act of love, a communication from the heart of God. Second, the 'salvation of the human race' results from God's self-gift to human beings within the historical and evolutionary dynamics of their world. In continuity with its traditional resources, trinitarian theology is free to exploit anew resources of language and experience to explicate the trinitarian form of creation. It must explore the variety of ways in which the presence of the trinitarian God can be discerned within a relational and evolutionary perspective.

In this regard, trinitarian theology traditionally employed an evocative technique known as 'appropriation'. The essential divine attributes common to each of the divine persons, for example, love, wisdom, union, power, are 'appropriated' to the three in such a way

---

33. *STh* I, q 45, a 6, ad 2.
34. *STh* I, q 32, a 1, ad 3.

as to bring out the distinctive character of each one. This theological technique works to personalise trinitarian faith in a certain sense by making the less-known manifest through the more-known.[35] That is not to imply that we already have an adequate knowledge of the divine attributes in question, nor that they can be considered abstracted from an explicitly trinitarian setting.[36] This is evident in the most developed form of appropriation shaped by what is generally referred to as the 'psychological analogy'. This kind of analogy relies heavily on Augustine's *de Trinitate*, especially as developed by Aquinas in the thirteenth century. By examining what is involved in the human activities of knowing and willing, the psychological analogy offers some understanding of trinitarian consciousness in its relationships and activities. The result is a fruitful understanding of the biblical and doctrinal data. Moreover, it suggests an experiential intimacy with the trinitarian mystery so that it can be subjectively 'appropriated' within the form and dynamism of our own intentional existence.

This analogical instance of enriches the cognitive content of trinitarian theology. Believers are invited to reflect on their conscious experience of their cognitive and affective activities. And this can be applied within much larger field of meaningful attributions in terms of historical developments and interfaith dialogue. This technique of appropriations is designed 'to manifest the persons'. Each is present and acting in the human heart and in history as a whole, and so contributes to 'a manifestation of the truth'.[37] The psychological analogy indicates a way of speaking of each of the divine persons in their distinctive characteristics, while connoting the essential attributes common to the three.[38] In all this, theology is forced to admit that the experience of faith is always more than even the best kind of analogical thinking. Within the trinitarian mystery there is an incalculable excess of meaning and interpersonal communication which necessarily transcend the partial understanding that the any analogy can offer. If we follow Aquinas' ordered presentation of the mystery of

---

35. *STh* I, q. 39, a. 7.
36. Jean-Pierre Torrel, *Saint Thomas d'Aquin*: The Person and his work (Washington DC: Catholic University of America Press, 2005), 208–213.
37. *STh* I, q. 39, a. 7, ad 1.
38. For a recent treatment of this topic, see Timothy L Smith, 'The Context and Character of Thomas' Theory of Appropriations', in *The Thomist* 63 (1999): 579–612.

God, we must first acknowledge the limitless space of the divine transcendence—the divine Be-ing and its attributes. We can then move forward through the psychological analogy to consider the Trinitarian processions and the relationships. But in a third phase, there is a doubling back in order to form include the whole of richness of tradition in its scriptural, mystical and liturgical dimensions. The complete, but ever developing, field of faith's experience guides the activity of appropriation. None the less, the divine reality always transcends—and expands—human conscious experience. For example, trinitarian theology has in recent times included specific attention of divine revelation related to the cross and resurrection.[39] That, in turn, has provoked an examination of how the psychological analogy works within the narrative drama of trinitarian revelation, calling into play further symbolic, aesthetic, affective and psychological dimensions of human experience as subject to the transformative action of grace.[40] The possibility of a new range of appropriations emerges. The psychological image, rather than being replaced, is notably enhanced. In any theological scheme, the divine persons are never comprehended in rigid categories, but are more vividly disclosed through the play of appropriations based in the scriptural narrative. In this regard, the divine self-revelation is always more than the sum total of theological techniques.[41] Nor should it be forgotten that the gifts of the Spirit, especially wisdom, understanding and knowledge, add an instinctive and supra-rational quality to faith's experience of the trinitarian self-communication (*STh* I–II, q 68, a 1–2).

In short, the practice of appropriation reminds theology not to lose contact with its scriptural data, it liturgical practice and mystical experience. The aim of appropriation, therefore, is to stimulate the most meaningful expression of the trinitarian shape of Christian experience. As a result, theology has growing resources in order to disclose the distinctive character of each of the divine persons. The Trinity is appreciated more fully as the central truth to be explored, as the mystery to be invoked and adored.

---

39. Anne Hunt, *The Trinity and the Paschal Mystery: A Development in Recent Catholic Theology* (Collegeville: Liturgical Press, 1997).
40. Anne Hunt, 'Psychological Analogy and the Paschal Mystery in Trinitarian Theology', in *Theological Studies*, 59 (1998): 197–218.
41. On this point, see Carl N Still, '"Gifted Knowledge": An Exception to Thomistic Epistemology?', in *The Thomist* 63 (1999): 173–190.

Particular considerations of the unity of God and of the common divine attributes are thus given a trinitarian focus. For example, power, wisdom and goodness are referred to Father, Son and Spirit respectively. Likewise, unity, equality and harmony are notions applied in order to disclose each of the divine persons in their Trinitarian order, and further triads of, say, efficient, exemplary and final causality, and so on, are similarly employed. With such a plethora of terms, Trinitarian thought tries to give some expression to the encompassing mystery of God 'ever beyond us' as Father, the all-inclusive Source and Goal; of God now 'with us', as Word and Son incarnate; of God ever 'within and between us', the Holy Spirit, the inexhaustible gift of God poured out on the world. Appropriation, a particular personal way of speaking of the divine persons goes beyond the constraints of any one theological system or synthesis, to anchor faith more creatively in prayer, liturgy and meditation on the scriptures.

Such traditional expressions anticipate a new set of trinitarian connections, drawn from 'the book of creation' but now read through modern eyes. Many writers speak of the direction of evolution in terms of increasing 'differentiation, subjectivity and communion'.[42] The initial cosmic event unfolds into a marvellous variety of particles, forces, elements, life-forms, cultures. With that differentiation, there occurs an increase of interiority and consciousness. Living, self-organising unities emerge in a growing complexity, through the nervous system to the human brain. In the human phenomenon, consciousness emerges as intelligence and freedom. Evolution becomes conscious of itself. The universe is self-aware. And in that self-awareness, the mystery of our common origins and shared destiny comes to expression. Beatrice Bruteau remarks that 'The cosmos has all the marks of the Trinity' in its unity, internal differentiation and in the dynamics of its expansion and interrelatedness.[43]

An awareness of the trinitarian dimension of human existence profoundly affects the lived sense of human selfhood. Christian theology speaks of the divine indwelling, God dwelling in us, and our dwelling in God. To search into who we are is find ourselves in the presence of God, the 'Self', as it were, in all our selves. The three clas-

---

42. For example, Thomas Berry, *The Dream of the Earth* (San Francisco: Sierra Book Club, 1988), 44–46.
43. Beatrice Bruteau, 'Eucharistic Ecology and Ecological Spirituality', in *Cross Currents* (Winter 1990): 504.

sic biblical expressions of such intimacy with the divine mystery are familiar. We are temples of the Holy Spirit, members of the Body of Christ, sons and daughters of the Father. Through this indwelling and union with the divine persons, faith possesses an inside or participative knowledge of the mystery of the Trinity. It shares in the Love-Life that God is:

> Beloved, let us love one another, because love is from God; everyone who loves is born of God and knows God . . . For God is love . . . No one has ever seen God; if we love one another, God lives in us and his love is perfected in us (1 Jn 4:7–12).

To experience God in such a way is to find oneself as a relational identity, a self-to-be-realised in relationship to the other. Adoration of God and union with the divine persons orientate the believer into a world of relationships and communion—of global, ecological, and cosmic dimensions. In that sense, the Trinity implies an agenda for conversion and transformation, for ourselves, our communities, and our global co-existence. In a world of both of complex differentiation and growing interconnectedness, Christian faith can find a new health and a new wholeness in contemplating the universe in the light of its fundamental mystery—the Trinity gathering creation to itself. In the Trinity, the universe comes home; and all the struggling emergence of time finds its absolute future. Through such trinitarian reflections our exploration into God comes to rely on God's own 'inside knowledge' as it is revealed to faith.

Brother Anthony

Poor old fellow,
angular, pinched awkward man,
taut and pink-faced,
like a preserved quince;
shrewd and sensitive despite his endless chatter:
even now, the original orphan
left at every doorstep;
Everyone hesitates to take him in,
wincing at his eagerness,
and protecting conversation
from his fantastic interruptions,
his perverse skill in missing every point.
His need is to construct the world
in every instant from the start:
recently he discovered the name of his mother,
long dead, and found some brothers,
and the strange world of blood relations . . .
Now a gush of communication
after the long legal amnesia,
he reports a big barbecue
to celebrate the discovery
of belonging after all:
the heat is off us now --
unless, of course, you take him
as a parable . . .

By Way Of Negation: Biblical and Philosophical Perspectives

Any exploration into God cannot bypass the dark or hidden character inherent in the notion of God. Thought we might be attracted to the boundless Light of God, there is the way of negation. It resides in the inherent limitation and darkness of the human mind, and finds traditional expression in 'the threefold path' of affirmation, negation, super-affirmation, an in the dynamics of analogical thinking.[1] That may sound rather foreign and philosophical when compared with the confidence of living faith, the words of scripture and the celebration of the sacraments and the liturgy. None the less, there is an inevitable darkness.

An Essential Negation

Von Balthasar makes a basic point when he speaks of the self-surrender inherent in the movement of faith. It implies a certain self-dispossession and expropriation:[2]

> In faith and through it, rather, I am made open and dispossessed of self... The important thing is the movement away from myself, the preference of what is other and greater,

---

1. A standard reference here is William J Hill, *Knowing the Unknown God* (New York: Philosophical Library, 1971), especially 163–219. For a deeply philosophical, interfaith, and historical discussion, see David B Burrell *Knowing the Unknowable God: Ibn-Sina, Maimonides, Aquinas* (Notre Dame, Indiana: University of Notre Dame Press, 1986).
2. Hans Urs von Balthasar, *The Glory of the Lord: A Theological Aesthetics: I: Seeing the Form*, translated by Erasmo Leiva-Merikakis (New York: Crossroad Publications, 1982), 228.

> and precisely the person who has been expropriated for God does not want to become fully secure with regard to this Other and Greater.³

The way of negation affects the whole person, not only the mind and its cognitive scope and ability. In this chapter, we would like to bring together a number of aspects of our notion of God and divine revelation, and its relation to human experience. The classic theological tradition insists that any theological knowledge has to be content with telling us what God is not—compared to human imagination and expectations. Divine Be-ing infinitely exceeds every mode of the being found within the immediate world of our existence. The notion of the all actual fullness of divine Be-ing functions as a kind of clearing space in which the mystery of God can be explored and affirmed, even though never to be fully known. We are like bats flitting through the sunlight, and never able to look at the source of light. But even if we find our way around like the bat through radar-like auditory signals, the beatific vision and its 'light of glory' seem an impossibility. However, God does not frustrate the human effort to know him, but respects the creaturely mode of our present existence, and the limitations to human knowledge that result.⁴ The human mind must proceed by way of analogy—of likeness and greater unlikeness.⁵ Clearly, there is a continuous play of language in the biblical witness to God. The Judaeo-Christian traditions are most familiar with references descriptions of God as 'light', 'the fountain of life', 'the Good Shepherd', and so forth. But even the most simple affirmation of the goodness of God implies three stages in its meaning. First there is the affirmation, 'God is good'. Second, this is followed by an immediate awareness of the limitations of thinking and speaking in this manner, so that God is not 'good', in the ordinary limited ways we experience what we call 'good' in things or persons of our world. And then, thirdly, after that moment of healthy hesitation, the mind can spring forward into the open free air of what God must be, even if how that is so remains unknown: God is good in a boundless, inexpressible

---

3. Von Balthasar, *The Glory of the Lord I*, 22.
4. *STh* I, q. 13, a. 7
5. See Francis Clooney, SJ, *His Hiding Place is Darkness: A Hindu-Catholic Theopoetics of Divine Absence* (Stanford, CA: Stanford University Press, 2014), especially 22–31.

manner, beyond our capacities to understand or imagine. Though present in all that is, God is not like anything in the world, and the Kingdom of God surpasses the projections of human imagination: 'No one has ever seen God' (1 Jn 4:12).

When it comes to exploring the Mystery of God, any approach must include prayer and reverence, especially when confronted with the now conventional irreverence of modern speech. The beginning and end of exploration must be more personal, engaging one's sense of life's direction and value. That self-investment offers a preliminary anticipation of 'God', the One to whom we pray. The personal 'we' is important at this point, for it implies a certain other-directed solidarity, a sense of common purposes and destiny. The great family of humanity, one way or another, faces life and death, suffering, and hope for the future, in the overwhelming contingency of its existence, with the religious conviction of a future fulfilment given in the intimacy of union with God, and finally seeing God, face to face. In a lapidary description of that experience, Lonergan writes,

> That fulfilment is not the product of our knowledge and choice. On the contrary, it dismantles and abolishes the horizon in which our knowing and choosing went on and it sets up a new horizon in which the love of God will transvalue our values and the eyes of that love will transform our knowing ... Though not a product of our knowing and choosing, it is a conscious dynamic state of love, joy and peace that manifests itself in acts of kindness, goodness, fidelity, gentleness and self-control.[6]

Jewish tradition refrained out of reverence from pronouncing the sacred name, *YHWH*.[7] Other names and titles for God were employed, such as the 'Lord', the 'Holy One', 'the Most High' and so forth. While it is true that Christian faith in the incarnation introduced into human history a new kind of familiarity with God, there is still the need for Christians to constantly refresh their sense of reverence and wonder in regard to the infinities of God's love, wisdom and power. Without such awe, religious activities become increasingly banal.

---

6. Lonergan, *Method*, 106.
7. See 'God' in the biblical Jewish tradition in Hurtado, *God in New Testament Theology*, 31–43.

The New Testament Paradox

The Bible presents privileged data from the past concerning God's self-revelation. In the experience of Abraham, of Moses, of the whole people of Israel, especially in the great prophets and sages, God was self-revealed as 'the Lord', the Holy One to be adored and loved, trusted and obeyed. The experience of John the Baptist, of Jesus himself, and in the different experiences of Mary, Peter, Paul and all the disciples and apostles numbered among the earliest followers of Jesus, and the different communities of the early Church, the One God is present in climactically personal way—loving, merciful, self-giving. Though the writings of the New Testament witnesses to the light of divine revelation, they are not afraid of the darkness in which faith and hope must operate. The resurrection of the Crucified One occurs in a world where the innocent still die, and the ways of God are beyond human comprehension. Hope must maintain itself in patience. Take the case of the earliest witnesses to Christ. After his crucifixion and death, Jesus 'had presented himself alive to them by many convincing proofs' (Acts 1:3). Yet they could still ask, 'Lord, is this the time when you will restore the kingdom to Israel?' (Acts 1:6). Jesus' answer is instructive: 'It is not for you to know the times or the periods that the Father has set by his own authority' (Acts 1:7). Judgments, calculations and desires based on the proportions of time or place or culture—that is anything less than God's transcendent freedom—are precluded, even if the disciples are to witness to Christ, 'in Jerusalem, in all Judea and Samaria, and to the ends of the earth' (Acts 1:8). There is simply no clear blueprint.[8] Let us look more closely at a number of instances of the negative style of the rhetoric of hope as we sample it in the Letters of Paul, in the Synoptic Gospels, and in the Gospel of John. Here we make a brief remark on each of these and the role of negativity in their writings.

Paul, for example, knows no hesitation in declaring that the resurrection of Jesus is the focal point of Christian existence. Nonetheless, he emphasizes the need for a patient openness in regard to what God is bringing about. In reference to Isaiah, he writes, 'Eye has not

---

8. Kevin Hart, *Kingdoms of God* (Bloomington, Indiana: Indiana University Press, 2014) is an outstanding phenomenological illustration of the different and sometimes conflicting theological and philosophical approaches to God and the Kingdom of God.

seen nor ear heard nor the heart of man conceived what God has prepared for those who love him' (1 Cor 2:9; *cf* Rom 11:33). Paul's references to the future are more like descriptions of what is being left behind. A rear-vision mirror does not map what lies ahead. The Apostle's impatient reply to a Corinthian query is noteworthy: 'How are the dead raised? With what kind of body to they come?' (1 Cor 15:35). He answers in predominantly negative terms. The risen body is contrasted to what is 'perishable, dishonourable, weak, physical' (1 Cor 15:35) in our present experience. Yet in the light of Christ's resurrection, he anticipates that the risen body of each one will become 'imperishable', 'glorious', 'powerful', 'spiritual' (1 Cor 15:42–44). Hope for a risen existence reaches beyond any capacity to determine or even to represent the future. It awaits a fulfilment in the God who, 'by the power at work within us is able to do far more abundantly than all we ask or think' (Eph 3:20). Paul contrasts the straining after a controlling knowledge of the future with surrender to the transcendence of God's wisdom. Here, he quotes both the prophet (Isa 29:14) and the psalmist (Ps 33:10) alike: 'I will destroy the wisdom of the wise and the discernment of the discerning I will thwart' (1 Cor 1:19). He goes on to say, 'For since in the wisdom of God, the world did not know God through wisdom, God decided through the foolishness of our proclamation to save those who believe' (1 Cor 1:21). The apostle points to the source of true wisdom that lies beyond all human measure and control: 'And we speak of these things in words not taught by human wisdom but taught by the Spirit, interpreting spiritual things to those who are spiritual' (1 Cor 2:13).

In this reversal of values, a certain negation or 'deconstruction' of routine expectations and desires is demanded. The ever-new gift is not a simple *datum*, a 'given', but an incalculable *donum*, a 'gift'. What God gives cannot be represented in the calculations and categories of present experience.[9] It comes from beyond the horizons formed by prevailing religious or philosophical projections. If 'the Jews demand

---

9. As Kevin Hart writes in a larger frame of reference: 'Conversion is always needed; it is a perpetual turning toward God, not away from the world but away from being enthralled by it . . . On my analysis, this turning to the *Basileia* has two moments: the first is . . . *kenosis* in which the "I" empties itself out in order to receive the Holy Spirit. But Christianity, to my mind, does not stop here . . . There is a second moment of . . . *epektasis*, in which one stretches out in the love of God and neighbour . . . (Hart, *Kingdoms of God*, 3).

signs and the Greeks desire wisdom' (1 Cor 1:22), the cross of Christ will be a stumbling block to the expectations of the traditional religion, just as it will appear to the philosophers—and to any imperial ideology—as an extravagant or subversive folly: 'For God's foolishness is wiser than human wisdom, and God's weakness is stronger than human strength' (1 Cor 1:25).

Even though Paul himself is justified in claiming the riches of the tradition of Israel as his own—'a Hebrew born of Hebrew, as to the Law, a Pharisee . . .' (Phil 3:4–6), he has come to regard all this as 'loss' (Phil 3:7; cf Mt 10) and 'refuse' (Phil 3:8), so that he might gain Christ and find justification in him alone (cf Phil 3:7–11). Hope in Christ has meant for him a 'deconstructed' life, intent on the ways of God, rather than relying on an inherited intellectual or traditionally religious assurance. When Christian hope in any age is focused on the resurrection of the Crucified as its luminous centre, something like Paul's vertiginous 'loss' of past assurances is a sign of its health and authenticity.

The Christian imagination must not be allowed to rest in any image drawn from the present sphere of human experience. In his Letter to the Romans, Paul states, 'Now hope that is seen is not hope. For who hopes for what is seen? But if we hope for what we do not see, we wait for it in patience' (Rom 8:24–25). Hope comes into its own only by yielding to what only God can bring about. Even praying for the fulfillment of hope must not be constricted to the limitations of human desire. Our desiring needs the guidance and direction of the Spirit: 'for we do not know how to pray as we ought, but the Spirit himself intercedes for us with sighs too deep for words' (Rom 8:26). An extraordinary paradox runs through the whole of Christian experience. Despite the clarity of its faith in the risen Christ, Christian hope must learn to live not only with not-understanding and not-representing, but also with a certain not-willing. It must yield its mundane desires and expectations to the incalculable dimensions of the Spirit. Thus, the mundane ego, even in its most religious expressions, is radically disturbed in its desires and projections. This is a point at which Buddhist and Christian cannot but agree—and learn from each other.[10]

---

10. See Anthony Kelly, 'Eschatological Hope: A Christian Perspective', in *Hope: A Form of Delusion? Buddhist and Christian Perspectives*, edited by Elizabeth Harris (Munich: Editions of Sankt Ottilien, 2013), 229–250.

For their part, the Synoptic Gospels do nothing to lessen the distinctive Christian sense of negativity and provisionality. Despite the evidence that the Gospel writers were dead-sure that the all-deciding event of God's action had occurred in Christ, they left plenty of room for what is yet to be revealed and further assimilated. Though Jesus preached the Kingdom of God, its growth and seasons are not in human hands, nor subject to human law or prediction (Mk 4:26–29). Moreover, the scope of God's reign allows for wild aspects of undecidability. It nets fish of all kinds and qualities (Matt 13:47–50), and permits the weeds to grow alongside good grain (Matt 13: 24–30). To enter into this Kingdom is to treasure new things and old in a proportion that remains unclear (Matt 13:51–52). For Luke especially, if one is to be included in the incalculable scope of God's mercy (Lk 6:37–42), it means refraining from judgments and the condemnation of others. The true relatives of Jesus are not those represented by blood relationships, but those who do the will of God (Lk 8:19–21). Most notably, the separation of the sheep and goats in Matthew 25 is disconcerting to all believers—and non-believers too—who have allowed a cultural form of religion to obfuscate the inclusiveness of God's reign (Matt 25:31–46).

Then there is the Johannine perspective. Even though Jesus encourages his disciples to accept his word, he allows that they cannot yet bear the full reality of what has to say: 'I still have many things to say to you, but you cannot bear them now' (Jn 16:12). His followers must go beyond their present apprehension to await an as yet incalculable future: 'When the Spirit of truth comes, he will guide you into all truth . . . and will declare to you the things that are to come' (Jn 16:13). Earlier in the Gospel, Jesus declared to the Samaritan woman that 'you will worship the Father neither on this mountain nor in Jerusalem' (Jn 4:22). The true worship of God is not tied to sacred sites marking the particularities of religion and culture, but must be conducted in the space proportioned 'in spirit and in truth' (Jn 4:23–24). Neither geographically, ethnically nor conceptually bounded, the only horizon that remains is the indefinable reality of the Father himself who is seeking out true worshipers.

Clearly, John is confident of the continuing revelatory power of the Spirit. But that confidence does not preclude his warning against believing every kind of spirit: 'Beloved, do not believe every spirit, but test the spirits to see if they are from God . . . By this you know the

Spirit of God: every spirit that confesses that Jesus Christ has come in the flesh is from God' (1 Jn 4:1–2).[11] Such a demand for discernment is not without its difficulty. When faced with the elusive and opaque human reality of 'the flesh' in which Jesus has come, discernment becomes complex. Only to a lofty Gnostic system is everything clear, pure, and untroubled by the presence of the utterly other. But true discernment points in another direction: 'We know love by this, that he laid down his life for us—and we ought lay down our lives for one another' (1 Jn 3:16). This demand is insistent: 'for those who do not love a brother or sister who they have seen, cannot love God whom they have not seen' (1 Jn 4:20). John's letter has a stark, but not altogether surprising, conclusion: 'Little children, keep yourselves from idols' (1 Jn 5:21).

Some kind of orientation beyond neat religious notions or consoling interpretations seems to have been envisaged all along: 'let us love, not in word and speech, but in truth and action' (1 Jn 3:18). This is the original emphasis of the Gospel itself. To know God is not a matter of 'seeing' the divinity in some immediate evidence. Following of the other-directed 'way' of Jesus (Jn 14:6) however, is the essential requirement, for 'no one has ever seen God; it is the only Son, who is turned toward the Father, he has made him known' (Jn 1:18). Believers are reminded not to settle for any provisional version of human identity, no matter how secure the promise of eternal life, for 'it has not yet appeared what we shall be' (1 Jn 3:2). Though Jesus is 'the resurrection and the life' (Jn 11:25), the risen Lord is never an object of matter-of-fact description. Experiences of his presence and absence interweave in the lives of these early witnesses to faith (cf Jn 20:29–31).

The great prayer of Jesus (Jn 17) strikingly expresses the dynamic of Jesus' return to the Father and his involvement with all who believe in him: 'I glorified you on earth by finishing the work you gave me to do. So now, Father, glorify me in your own presence with the glory I had in your presence before the world existed' (Jn 17:4–5). The heavens are so opened (cf Jn 1:51) as to enfold the world into that relationship that exceeds all created forms of belonging, namely the communion existing between the Father and his Son. As a result,

---

11. See Christopher Morse, *Not Every Spirit: A Dogmatics of Christian Disbelief* (Valley Forge, PN: Trinity Press International 1994).

as Jesus is going to the Father, the disciples will begin to inhabit the world in a new way—as witnesses to what God is bringing about: 'And now I am no longer in the world, but they are in the world, and I am coming to you' (Jn 17:11a). Jesus asks the Father to protect his followers so 'that they may be one as we are one' (Jn 17:11b). Because of who his disciples already are, and because of what they will later do, a new community based in the unity the Father and the Son comes into being (Jn 17:20–21). Jesus prays that the disciples given to him by the Father will be transported into a new sphere of existence—to be where he is and to share in his vision and glory (Jn 17:24a).

This prayer in the Gospel of John is not dealing with some distant existence in the future, but has immediate impact on Christian consciousness. By ascending to the Father and leaving the familiar world of his disciples, Jesus has in effect relocated them. Their world is changed. They live now in the heavenly realm of life and communion to which Christ has ascended, breathing the atmosphere of the Father's house of many dwelling places (Jn 14:2–3). The Father's original love for Jesus is now overflowing to those identified with him: 'that the love with which you have loved me may be in them, and I in them' (Jn 17:26b). United with Jesus in his return to the Father, the disciples are drawn into the universe of mutual love and self-giving communion (Jn 13:34–35; 15:12, 17). It follows that not only is Jesus ascended, but also the disciples themselves are in a profound sense now 'ascended' with him, and share in his communion with the Father. By ascending to 'my Father and your Father, to my God and your God' (Jn 20:17), the ascended and glorified Jesus transcends all worldly realities, categories and previous conceptions. He now belongs to his followers in the deepest intimacy of his relationship to the Father.

Nonetheless, the invisibility of God remains, along with the impossibility of reducing the divine to an object or a particular factor within the world. Though the Johannine writings speak in strikingly intimate terms of our coming to know God (Jn 17:3; 1 Jn 4:7), being born of God (1:13; 1 Jn 3:9) and dwelling in God (1 Jn 4:16), there is a certain reserve when it comes to speaking about 'seeing God'. In fact, the Gospel states the opposite (for example, 1:18; 1 Jn 4:12).[12] Aquinas

---

12. Though 3 Jn 1:11b does associate doing good with 'seeing God', it is most likely that the author is speaking in reference to God's revelation in Christ.

continues this tradition by speaking of being joined to God as to one radically unknown, who always transcends limited human knowledge. God is known only through the contemplation of the "effects" of his action. In other words, God is known in what he does, not directly, and never comprehensively.[13] Still, loving familiarity with God is possible, since love for God can go further than knowledge,[14] to 'join' us to what always exceeds our knowing.[15]

The prologue of the Gospel ends by directing its readers from the gift to the giver. If God has uttered his Word in the flesh, if the Father has sent his only Son, if God is so unreserved in giving, how are we to imagine the God who is the source of such grace? The answer is to be found in the gift: 'No one has ever seen God; the only Son, who is turned toward the Father, he has made him known' (Jn 1:18). The invisible mystery of God the giver is made known in the flesh of history. By initially focusing on the Word, the prologue suggests that God is to be heard, rather than seen. Even though faith rejoices in 'gazing' on the glory of the only Son, the visibility in question is of the Son *from* the Father (Jn 1:14cd). God is invisible and the Father inexpressible—save by becoming visible and expressible through his Word and Son. Because Jesus Christ alone is turned toward God as the Word (Jn 1:1), and turned toward the Father as the only Son (1:18), he embodies the gift of the truth and unfolds the character of the Father.

The remarkably direct denial of any human capacity to see God, with which the prologue concludes, is not only an affront to the Jewish piety of the day. It also undercuts prevalent gnostic pretensions of knowing the absolute 'One and the True'. Yet the negativity of this denial serves the positive plenitude of God's self-revelation in Jesus Christ. The negation works in the believer to inspire a sense of

---

13. *STh*, 1, 12, 13 ad 1; *Summa contra Gentiles*, 3, 48. For his extended comment on John 1:18, see *In Evangelium B Johannis*, c.1, lect 9.
14. *STh*, 1–2, 27, 2 ad 2.
15. As an explicitation of the Johannine experience of God ('everyone who loves is born of God and knows God' [1 John 4:7b]', this medieval position is far from irrelevant, as will be seen--especially when linked to the Thomist analyses of grace as an 'interior instinct' (*In Evangelium B Johannis*, c 6, lect 5, n 3), as a conformity to the divine persons (*Summa Theol.*, 1, 43, 3–6, of charity as a participation in God's own love (2–2, 24, 2), and of the rules for the discernment of the state of grace (1–2, 112, 5).

receptivity and surrender to the mystery of the Father and his will. Faith brings no controlling knowledge of God. What it does bring is a relationship to Jesus Christ—soon to be revealed as the way, the truth and the life (cf Jn 14:6). To know him is to know the Father (Jn 14:7, 9–11). In his 'heart to heart', Father-ward relationship (Jn 1:18), the only Son is unreservedly receptive to the divine will, and to all that God is, and is doing in the world. The eternal character of Jesus' identity as Word is thereby acted out in a relationship extended in time through his whole historical existence. Through this, dialogical relationship the Father will be revealed; and his love for the world (Jn 3:16) will be enacted and expressed in the events that make up the Gospel story.

The Gospel prologue has not aimed primarily to teach a new idea on God, but to introduce a story leading to an all-surpassing new experience of God—who is yet to be disclosed in the glory of Jesus. Thereby, it stands as declaration demanding to be countersigned by innumerable generations of others in their experience of the life, the light and the love that has come to them.

This is to say that, though the Word does not reduce human speech to silence, it does affect human powers of expression with a kind of unrelenting negation in the light of the excess that marks the glory to be revealed. It subverts any overconfident pretensions to knowledge on the part of the disciples (cf Jn 1:41, 45; 3:2, 9–10; 5:37b, etc), and is always outside the horizon of human anticipation and experience. Until there is the hearing and seeing of faith, all lesser levels of hearing and seeing are radically called into question. On the other hand, neither previous revelation nor the original coherence of all things in the Word, are negated. The great positives remain. Jesus will still be numbered among 'the Jews [from whom] comes salvation' (Jn 4:22). The Word he embodies and communicates is still the fulfillment of the Scriptures (Jn 1:23; 6:45; 17:12; 19:24, 36). The world continues to be the object of God's love (Jn 3:16). Even with his historical departure, Jesus is still present to 'the advantage' of his disciples, in the gift of the Spirit (Jn 16:7), and in the blood and water of the sacraments (Jn 19:34–35). Above all, the original glory which was proper to the Son 'before the foundation of the world' (Jn 7:24) breaks on that world in final hour of fulfillment. And the genesis of all creation in the Word is climaxed in his exultant cry, 'It is finished' (Jn 19:30).

The Revelation Effect

There is a multidimensional impact of each of these revelatory aspects of the Christian mystery on the life and imagination of the Church. An overbrimming excess of the images, symbols, narratives and interpretations of the Christ-event finds expression in the New Testament. His ascension is at once a looking back and a looking forward. It looks back in order to amplify faith's comprehension of the meaning of Jesus' life, mission, death and resurrection. However, it also looks forward. The disciples are not left impotently gazing into the heavens, but looking outward into the life and mission of the Church in its outreach to all peoples and all ages. As a result, Christian existence, retrospectively and prospectively, is deeply marked with the character of surrender, waiting and hope. Jesus has gone before us. But in the present time, the faith of his followers must now wait, longing for his return as the Lord and judge of all. Though no longer in the world as he was before, he is neither absent nor disengaged from it. The numinous cloud accompanies his departure and his promised return (Acts 1:9–11). But he is carried upward to this divine realm with arms extended in blessing (Lk 24:50–53)—a gesture of effective solidarity with all who will follow him (*cf* Lk 22:42–43). It does not represent Jesus turning away from the community of faith, but rather an all-embracing turning to them from the height, depth and breadth of the mystery of God.

Necessarily, all believers follow Paul's directive words, whatever their respective situations: 'Forgetting what lies behind and straining forward, I press on toward the goal for the prize of the upward call of God in Christ Jesus' (Phil 3:13–14). Today, however, anyone sharing the Apostle's eagerness 'to press on toward the goal' cannot but be affected by the mood of hesitation and disillusionment characteristic of this present historical period. It is often referred to as a 'postmodern' era—a suitable tag to evoke the disconcerting fluidity in the ways of thinking and living in an increasingly complex world. 'Postmodern' obviously means a period coming after what is assumed to be the solid style and clear certainties of the lengthy 'modern' era. In this regard, it suggests a slippage from the classical forms of philosophy, theology, art, and even social and political organization. The classic forms which shaped the formative traditions informing the modern world up to the present were held in place by implicit philosophical commitments. There were shared assumptions concerning the nature of reality, the human person, the human capacity to know, the existence of God, values of religion, beauty and virtue. But a great change has taken place. Opinions may well differ in describing the present situation or in diagnosing its problems. But all agree that this is a changing world. Consequently, the Church, being part of that world, is not spared exposure to the seismic shifts that have occurred in human and historical experience.

In this postmodern context, faith, though it knows a deeper darkness, is spurred into a fresh creativity—to be bolder and more confident in its commitment to the distinctive character of Christian revelation—including the sense of reality it communicates and the moral conduct it inspires. When the shape of reality in all its guises has become so fluid, it is a good time to rise to the challenge of witnessing to the singular reality of the God revealed in the Christ-Event, and to explore it in the largest hermeneutical and contemplative space—cosmic, ecumenical, interfaith and eschatological. To that degree, all this is a stimulus toward a more creative catholicity.

A new focus on the singularity of the Christian phenomenon brings its own costs. When faith is concentrated on the concrete and the singular, it can lose the universal connotation of the more philosophical abstract outlook. On the other hand, a clear sense of the distinctive and singular character of Christian reality and the particularity of its revelation must be critically cherished. There is a singularity to be respected—the divine, freely chosen economy of God's self-revelation in this particular manner. It could have been otherwise—but this is how divine wisdom determined it—as enacted in Christ, and in his life, death, resurrection, ascension, in the outpouring of his Spirit, and in the promise of his return at the end of time.

By defending the singularity of Christian revelation against the abstract universals of religion, spirituality, universal revelation and so forth, a deeper negativity and darkness can result. The Word became flesh and, it can seem, be left out of the general, ever-fluid and inconclusive exchanges of the human conversation. Christian belief in the incarnation does not mean a contradiction of the human, but a new appreciation of humanity and a new way of belonging to it. It is here that some philosophical aspects of phenomenology can throw light on the negative-positive character of theological statements.

A critically elaborated account of the radically 'given' but paradoxically hidden quality of what is disclosed is found, for instance, in Jean-Luc Marion's influential trilogy, *Reduction and Givenness*, *Being Given*, and *In Excess*.[16] In a way that combines the negative and positive aspects of revelation, Marion speaks of a 'saturated e phenomenon'. In the experience of revelation, the overbrimming or 'saturated' significance the phenomenon imposes itself on the subject. It is given to such an extent that the subject is more like a witness to an event rather than an agent of its construction.[17] The believer is a recipient, more passive than active. In this respect, the gift of God's revelation is expressed most of all in the grammar of the dative case, for the gift is given *to* the believer. Revealed truth is not simply 'there' to be inspected or possessed, as something taken for granted. It is, rather as aspect of the divine self-giving, and self-communication to the receiving subjects, to re-constitute them in a new awareness: 'for those who are in Christ, there is a new creation' (2 Cor 5:17). In this instance, what is given is primary—not the conditions laid down by our rational capacities. 'Positive' revelation demands the negation of rationalistic presuppositions and conditions. To think truly is to be aware of the how thinking begins in response to something given. It is less thinking 'about' something, and more thinking from *within* what is given, by responding to it, and by allowing to appear what is arrestingly 'other'. This phenomenological return to the given provokes a kind of theological conversion in method and style so that a theology of revelation is beholden, humbly and reverently, to what is given. It is marked by contemplative receptivity to the data of faith as disclosing the mystery of God and divine self-revelation. True, there is the danger of collapsing everything into a fideistic subjectivism

---

16. Jean-Luc Marion's influential trilogy, *Reduction and Givenness: Investigations of Husserl, Heidegger, and Phenomenology*, translated by Thomas A Carlson (Evanston, IL: Northwestern University Press (1998); *Being Given: Toward a Phenomenology of Givenness*, translated by Jeffrey L Kosky (Stanford. CA: Stanford University Press, 2002); *In Excess: Studies of Saturated Phenomena*, translated by Robyn Horner and Vincent Barraud (New York: Fordham University Press, 2002). For further elaboration and background, see *God Without Being: Hors-Texte*, translated by Thomas A Carlson (Chicago, IL: Chicago University Press, 1991); 'Le possible et la revelation', in *Eros and Eris: Contribution to a Hermeneutical Phenomenology: Liber Amicorum for Adriann Peperzak*, edited by P van Tongeren, P Sars, C Bremmer and K Boey (Dordrecht: Kluwer Academic, 1992), 217–231; 'The Saturated Phenomenon', in *Philosophy Today*, 40 (1996): 103–124.
17. Marion, *Being Given*, 216.

which would be an obstacle to the full development of the theological intelligence and wisdom. At the other extreme, some may be rightly wary of an objectivism that overwhelms the role of the believing and thinking subject. But the biggest problem for theology is to think that the believing subject is already established before anything is given. When phenomenological style puts the emphasis on the self-giving 'object', any activity on the part of the subject is marked by receptivity and responsiveness to what is given so that rationalistic pretensions no longer occupy centre-stage. What is radically precluded is a notion of the subject as a detached, all-knowing monad projecting itself onto what is other.[18] For the subject is the one who is 'subjected' to what is overwhelmingly other, by witnessing to it and being stripped of all pretensions to comprehend or constitute what is given.[19] The healthy negativity here implied in this receptive role makes the mind of the believer into a luminous indicator of what is given.[20] Paradoxically, the sight of faith finds is focus in disclosing the 'visibility' of what has been given from beyond its vision.

Yet intelligence and further exploration are not thereby put to sleep, and left in the dark. Take, for example, the phenomenon of one's own birth. A response of gratitude is called forth for whatever it was, and whatever it led to. It occasions an endless effort of interpretation of the personal and communal meaning of such an unobjectifiable event.[21] It provokes an exploration of both the past that preceded it, the time in which it happened, its outcome in the present as it occurs, and of the future it gives rise to—even though the event of my 'being born' fits into no prior project on my part—and perhaps not on the part of my parents!

The subject-object polarity inevitably shapes discussion, despite the extremes of both objectivism and subjectivism being spurious totalities. Rigid polar categorisations are incapable of appreciating what is given or the manners in which it provokes the response of thought or action. An approach to the given can be so overloaded by preconceptions and concerns that it is immediately subjected to one's own interests. In that case, the given experience would be merely raw material to be reduced to an acceptable conceptual and

---

18. Marion, *Being Given*, 261.
19. Marion, *Being Given*, 216–217.
20. Marion, *Being Given*, 264–265.
21. Marion, *Being Given*, 289; *In Excess*, 33, 42.

rational form by the self-contained subject. However, in the sense of Marion and others, the phenomenon is 'saturated', not by one's prior attitudes, notions and tastes, but in its overbrimming significance. Its inexhaustible freshness leaves thought ever at a loss to objectify what has so disclosed itself. The excess of the 'saturated phenomenon' calls into question any prior limitation to the event of the self-revelation of God. In that light, all else is darkness.

As a phenomenon of revelation, the incarnation represents a culminating moment in the self-revelation of God. As an event it saturates in its intensity and expansiveness our sense of God, our view of the world and of the universe itself. As the manifestation of divine beauty, the incarnation contests the world made ugly by despair and evil. In the flesh of the risen One, our own enfleshed or incarnate lives have already entered the realm of an eternal life of communion with God. On the face of the Jesus, we discern, in a clouded way, God's glory and our true selves. The Word incarnate in Christ Jesus is a phenomenon that saturates our perceptions. Admittedly, a phenomenology restricted to clearly determined philosophical limits will contest this theological extension of what are otherwise regarded as mundane phenomena. On the other hand, the Church is a phenomenon in world history, and it would seem unrealistic not to appreciate it as such, and to explore its manifold influences. Further, a theology, more habituated to a propositional and systematic exposition, may find this exposition too primitive. Yet what is at stake is not only the distinctiveness of the focal Christian phenomenon but also the play of light and darkness inherent in it. There is no intention of bypassing the critical demands of systematic theology and its ordered explorations of the meaning of God, but to awaken such theology to a new freshness.

Inevitably, the more phenomenologically specific and concrete Christian faith is in its singularity, the more it is likely to experience itself as the 'foolishness' that Paul speaks of (1 Cor 1:18–25). The erudite 'scribe' or the rationalist 'debator of this age' (v 20) will find that the actuality or possibility of the event of Christ crucified cannot be rationally entertained. But a genuine Christian sense of God does not apologise for the particularity of what has been given to faith. Nor must it concede that it is 'irrational'—when it is only such to a 'rationality' that cannot allow God to exist and to act in this particular way, as in the scandalous bodiliness of raising the crucified Jesus from the dead.

Transcendent Mystery

The category of saturated phenomenon attempts to appreciate the complex play and many-sided character of the Christian experience of God. It is, therefore, is not unrelated to the polyvalent and originally biblical word, 'mystery'. In current common usage, it refers to a puzzling phenomenon that demands investigation even though leaving us in the dark; and, for the adept investigator, the anticipation of detecting an eventual solution. Then, the mystery is solved, all questions are answered, and the plot ends when the 'mystery' is no more. In contrast, Paul can speak of 'the mystery that has been hidden throughout the ages and generations but has now been revealed to his [God's] saints . . . Christ in you, the hope of glory' (Col 1:26–27). The language of Christian doctrine refers to the 'mysteries of faith'—the Trinity, incarnation, grace and the beatific vision. These are the revealed objects of faith, for reason unaided could not deduce them. On a more devotional level, there are the 'mysteries' of the life of Jesus, for example, the once fifteen and now twenty mysteries of the Rosary, as various aspects of Christian revelation are become the subject of contemplation. On a more theological plane, say in the theology of Karl Rahner, 'mystery' is fundamental notion expressive of God's self-communication to the human spirit.[22] In this sense, the mystery is not something to be solved, but something so given, so self-giving in its power to attract and fulfil the human heart that it constitutes the basic horizon of life and existence itself. The many 'mysteries' of faith are aspects of the one self-giving mystery of God, which even as it communicates itself in the Word and Spirit, remains ever beyond any finite grasp. Human destiny culminates in the 'beatific vision', God seen in a face-to-face vision, and yet in the inexhaustible infinities of the divine reality. Even though the blessed participate in the life of God, the divine mystery is not lessened, but more positively appreciated in its boundless excess.

Why not speak more simply, then, of the 'mystery' of the revealed God rather than make this phenomenological detour? Would not that word say more than any quasi-philosophical term could suggest and say it better? In response, I would simply suggest that the

---

22. For a seminal article, see Karl Rahner, 'The Concept of Mystery in Catholic Theology', in *Theological Investigations* IV, translated by Kevin Smyth (Baltimore, MD: Helicon Press, 1966), 36–73.

term 'mystery' and its specific Christian and theological meaning is best recovered, and even intensified, by appreciating it as a saturated phenomenon. To the degree we treat the phenomenonality of divine revelation in this manner, there will be less likelihood of reducing a particular truth of faith to the ambit of the rationally acceptable. It is one way of locating the events of revelation outside the consciousness of the believer/ theologian by making it an object of some kind to be inspected at will and assigned a place in some larger scheme of interpretation. In this sense, a genuine phenomenological approach restores a sense of mystery, and more so, in the instance of saturated phenomena, but most of all in the event of God's self-revelation.

The chiaroscuro of our knowledge is intensified in what we previously referred to as 'limit situations or experiences'.[23] Any effort to speak of God is earthed in fundamental human experiences of limits and frontiers—the limit of our capacity to understand or express, and the frontier of something given from beyond the horizon of our experience.[24] This kind of experience of excess is so fundamental in fact that without them we could not speak of God at all. Touched by the altogether Other, we human beings experience limitation. Not only do we confront out own mortality, but also all other limitations to our existence in mind or in action, and in all the ways we might experience human fragility and sinfulness. Great simple words, such as love, joy, peace, beauty, and insight, try to convey a certain range of elemental experiences. At the other extreme, there are moments or states when the words like guilt, powerlessness, suffering, despair, and absurdity resonate as more honest expressions. These expressive words indicate the positive or negative situations in which, one way or another, we are taken to the limit, to the edge . . . We are brought to the frontier of something else and something quite 'other'—to touch the fringe of inexpressible mystery. It is to touch on 'another world' as when one is entranced by great art or struck with the goodness, beauty or wisdom of another person. Ordinary horizons suddenly expand to new dimensions in the presence of what cannot be contained, an inexpressible something or Someone. Quietly or dramatically, life draws us to such limits, to the beyond. Such experiences

---

23. See John F Haught, *Christianity and Science: Toward a Theology of Nature* (Maryknoll, NY: Orbis,2007), 24–29.
24. Lonergan, *Method*, 131, 235–237.

refresh what the word, 'God' can mean. Whether such occurrences are felt as unsettling edges of this world or as the frontier of another world, they are 'God events' and direct mind and heart into the darkness of the inexpressible. They are windows both into what God has meant in the past, and what God can mean now. This experience of limits shapes our deepest selves and make us face into the dark. The ecstatic self is ever moving on, out, and toward what is Other. Exposure to other religions, spiritual traditions and cultures intensifies the darkness of the human search. Our experience of struggling and hoping and loving, of living and dying, puts us in fruitful contact with all witnesses to God, as they experienced the holy mystery in different ways and know the darkness and light in which it is wrapped.

Though faith enlists its own range of images, it employs them precisely *as* images, not as idols or as mere fabrications of human sentiment. To that degree, the images of faith are not idols but *icons*—precisely designed to let the mystery disclose itself on its own terms. The images of faith shine with a light from beyond, evoking the infinity of the mystery that has expressed itself in our world. The images employed by faith are not projections onto the blank screen of human aspiration, but in the darkness of human existence they are back-lit, as it were, by the revelation of a love not of this world. In short, an authentic faith is intent on letting God be God!—in the scandal of the Cross; in a humble invocation of the Spirit; in the shared celebration and witness of those who make up the People of God, saints and sinners alike.

A purified faith can refresh the notion of God, even in what appears to be a post-religious and 'godless' phase of culture. The myth, not the science, of evolution tended to undermine human dignity and to rob the world itself of its mysterious depth within God's creation. As naive notions of how God acts in nature are surpassed, faith is free to explore how God is ever creative, the great attractor drawing the immense, groaning, manifold totality of the world towards its goal.

In this respect, Israel's invocation of the Lord as *YHWH*, was a kind of gracious riddle. God gave his name as 'I will be who I will be' (*cf* Ex 3:14). Subsequent generations of faith have invoked God named in such terms, and then to find faith in God self-revealed in Christ and the Spirit. However unreserved God's gracious communication, it can be received only through the gift and in the receptivity of faith. The word of God is spoken from a great silence, so to provoke an attitude of listening in the human heart. The attentive mind is ever searching for words, the better to serve the truth revealed. The Word of God and the Spirit of God cannot be contained or constricted, nor reduced to anything less than God's own self-communication. With the prophet, Elijah, all believers must struggle against the false gods, to know the one, true God only in humble self-surrender to the 'sound of sheer silence' (1 Kgs 19:12). Such is the awesome silence of the mystery within which the whole world groans, hopes and prays for fulfilment (*cf* Rom 8:18–27).

In the silence and darkness of the mystery, God is experienced as 'No-thing'—for God is not like anything else occurring within the horizon of human experience or knowing. God is beyond the range of our words, and outstrips all ideas and concepts. Gregory of Nyssa, one of the great mystical doctors of the Church, wrote long ago, 'The unlimited divine nature cannot be accurately contained by a name.'[25] However intimately present to the heart of faith, God infinitely surpasses all human capacities of understanding and expression. Speech about God, therefore, must always favour the language of analogy, as was mentioned above. The scope of religious expression shuffles between what is known within our experience, on the one hand, and the unknowable, inexpressible reality of God, on the other. All our words lead into the divine silence, just as the holy darkness surrounds what little clarity our ideas might have. In comparison, therefore, with the clearly defined world of particular realities, God is 'No-thing' and 'No-where', never contained within any category or concept or image. Although the creed certainly intends to affirm the true reality of God, it does not disclose it, but directs faith to the full dimensions of the mystery. Every profession of faith, every formula of belief, all alike fall short, and await the evidence that only God can give. The mystery eludes all human language and does not encourage religious chatter. Nonetheless, the words of faith reach forward in adoration and love: 'Beloved, let us love one another, because love is from God; everyone who loves is born of God and knows God, for God is love' (1 Jn 4:7f). To have faith is to be plunged into the depths of the Mystery which we can never objectify nor stand back from. To exist, to live, and finally,

---

25. Gregory of Nyssa, *Commentary on the Song of Songs*, Chapter 1, v 3, translated by C McCambley (Brookline Mass: Hellenic College Press, 1987), 53.

to love, is to be drawn into the homeland our hearts immediately recognised as more real than the air we breathe.

While the way of negation is a theoretically subversive and demanding way of knowing, a larger context is always to be borne in mind. All worthwhile knowing has, in some way, a negative dimension because it is personal and participative in self-involving manner. As mentioned before, a couple cannot look up the meaning of their marriage in a textbook, for it is found only in the living and the loving. A work of art is not produced by simply following a book of instructions. Artists know what they have to offer only by doing it. The greater the reality, it would seem, the more our knowledge is tacit, and the more we feel our way forward. It means living on the inside of experience, and being content with a participative knowledge that we can never stand back from.

Still, it is possible to have the meaning—understood as a series of concepts or logical formulations—and yet to miss the experience. Unless the distinctive experience of God that the Gospels invite us to is appropriated, theological language must appear abstract and general. What was once universally unquestioned, namely the existence of God and the spiritual dimension of human being, is now widely problematical. When 'the truths of faith' drift free from traditional moorings, a sea of relativity seems to be the only option, while the question of meaning is endlessly deferred.[26]

Moreover, many predict that future Christianity will be increasingly in spiritual dialogue with the great religions of the East.[27] In a key article,[28] Rahner emphasises the importance of the experiential grounding of faith. He writes,

> Today it is becoming clearer, and that too within Christianity at the doctrinal and institutional level, that this experience of God . . . really constitutes the very heart and center of

---

26. With regard to the range of problems—and challenges—associated with postmodernity and the "deconstructive" methods associated with it, see *The Post-Modern God: A Theological Reader*, edited by Graham Ward (Oxford: Blackwell, 1997): the Editor's 'Introduction' is particularly stimulating (xv-xlvii).
27. The need to be attuned to the experiential dimensions of Christian truth is challengingly brought out by Joseph O'Leary, *La vérité chrétienne à l'âge du pluralisme religieux* (Paris: Cerf, 1994).
28. Karl Rahner, 'The Experience of God Today', in *Theological Investigations XI*, translated by David Bourke (London: Darton, Longman and Todd, 1974), 149–165.

> Christianity itself and also the ever living source of that conscious manifestation which we call 'revelation'.[29]

It will be necessary to reclaim the Christian experience of God as it is documented in the New Testament. Without a reclamation of the God-ward movement of conversion inscribed in the singularity of that experience, the formulations and doctrines of faith cannot but appear abstract and exotic, while theology will look like a more or less sophisticated distraction from the singular personal form which the Gospel witnesses to. The evangelists were not intent on providing material for conciliar definitions; nor were Jesus and his disciples theologians giving seminars. In their respective ways, they were witnessing to the all-transforming gift of God. The more believers are refreshed in their experience of God, the more doctrines of faith will be seen as signposts pointing into the inexpressible mysteries they are meant to serve; and the more theology will be continually re-invigorated in its exploration of what has been historically revealed.

To conclude: this note on 'the way of negation' in both its biblical and philosophical versions is meant to amplify, in a positive manner, the inevitable and desirable component of negativity in referring to God. There is no negativity in the Light that God is, in the divine intelligence and intelligibility. But the human mind unaided cannot in this life be exposed to the light, but is rather bat-like in its experience and understanding of the divine light. It is well to keep both these polarities in mind.

---

29. Rahner, 'The Experience of God Today', 164.

Strange Universe

The evil is too much
of course,
beyond all measure.
But of late—
was it the winter sun this Melbourne afternoon?
Or that old fellow helping
a long-haired crippled girl,
Or the lilied tranquillity
and the bell-birds
of the Yarra billabong
Exploding in the laughter of two kookaburras? --
I have begun to take
great pleasure
in this strange universe.

The Exegete and The Theologian: Is Collaboration Possible?[1]

My specialisation, in the context of interdisciplinary studies, is what is unsatisfactorily termed 'systematic theology'. Some years ago, I collaborated with the distinguished Johannine scholar, Francis J Moloney, SDB, in producing the book, *Experiencing of God in the Gospel of John*.[2] These methodological reflections owe much to the experience of that collaboration.

The Methodological Context

Bernard Lonergan's *Method in Theology*[3] has addressed the question of how the ever-pullulating specialisations of modern scholarship might find common cause—but without each losing its own integrity, or pretending to a totalitarian self-sufficiency. Lonergan identified some eight 'functional specialties'[4] in his concern to present a 'framework of collaborative creativity'.[5] His method was designed to serve particular specialisation, and yet to be sufficiently flexible to enable researchers, exegetes, historians dealing with the past to share in one collaborative enterprise with those who are more future-directed,

---

1. This is a revision of a longer version of 'Dimensions of Meaning: Theology and Exegesis', in *Transcending Boundaries. Contemporary Readings of the New Testament*, edited by Rekha M Chennattu and Mary M Coloe (Rome: LAS, 2005), 41–56.
2. Anthony J Kelly, CSsR and Francis J Moloney, SDB, *Experiencing God in the Gospel of John* (New York: Paulist, 2003).
3. Bernard JF Lonergan, SJ, *Method in Theology* (London: Darton, Longman and Todd, 1971).
4. Lonergan, *Method*, 125–148.
5. Lonergan, *Method*, xi.

that is, those facing the demands and possibilities of transforming culture in the interests of a larger appropriation of the Gospel. Lonergan's methodological framework does not clamp a philosophical, epistemological or doctrinal rigidity onto the creativity of theology. It appeals to something much closer to home by inviting scholars, whatever their specific concerns, to take notice of the workings of their own minds in their coming to know anything at all. While in its Christian specification theology finds its focus on Christian experience and tradition, it is firmly based on an anthropological datum, namely, the self-transcendence of the conscious subject that each of us is.[6] In this regard, human consciousness unfolds through the four inter-related levels of experience, understanding, judgment and decision, none of which is irrelevant to the work of exegetes or theologians, above all if they wish to collaborate in any project.[7]

The Proximate Context: Meaning

While such methodological matters are largely implicit in an interdisciplinary work such as *Experiencing God*, the notion of meaning is crucial in such kinds of collaboration.[8] The nature of meaning, though a pervasive category in the human sciences, may seem so obvious and general to the exegete as to scarcely merit attention. Yet, just as obviously, the Gospel of John is a textual field of meaning. It emerges from the past, witnessing to a once lived and still living, field of meaning which is shaped by singular events and encounters. The biblical writer had once to ask not only what does all this mean, but also, how to mean and communicate it to future generations of faith.

In some striking sense, Jesus Christ 'meant the world' to the early community of believers. 'In the beginning was the Word' (Jn 1:1), and this creative, enlivening and enlightening Word (Jn 1:3–4) 'became flesh and dwelt among us' (Jn 1:14). That is to say the Word entered

---

6. Lonergan, *Method*, 6–19.
7. For other possibilities, especially regarding history, see Ben F Meyer, *Reality and Illusion in New Testament Scholarship: A Primer in Critical Realist Hermeneutics* (Collegeville: Liturgical Press, 1994) and Anthony J Kelly, 'The Historical Jesus and Human Subjectivity: A Response to a Recent Suggestions', in *Australian Lonergan Workshop II*, edited by Matthew C Ogilvie and William J Danaher (Drummoyne, NSW: Novum Organum Press, 2002), 151–179.
8. Kelly and Moloney, *Experiencing God*, 55–60; 92–96;136–140; 395–405.

into the world of human meaning. In the course of the Gospel narrative, the meaning of the Word incarnate is expressed linguistically as, say, a question (Jn 1:38), a conversation (for example, Jn 1:47–51), a command (for example, Jn 13:34), a judgment (for example, Jn 5:27) and a prayer (for example, Jn 17). It is carried in symbols such as light (Jn 8:12), bread (Jn 6:35), the good shepherd (Jn 10:11), the true vine (Jn 15:1), to name but some. It is dramatically instanced in works of healing as with the man born blind (Jn 9:13–39) and in interpersonal gestures such as Jesus washing the disciples' feet (Jn 13:1–11). It generates its own art as in the prologue to the Gospel and the discerning arrangement of Gospel narrative itself. This complex of meaning culminates in the subversive glory of the Cross, for it incarnates the meanings of all the words, gestures, relationships and symbols that anticipated it.

Four Dimensions of Meaning

The Johannine writings richly evoke the manifold character of the experience from which they arise. But when the phrase 'experiencing God' appears in the title of the book referred to above, the critical reader must be immediately suspicious of the elusive term, 'experience'. Can the interpreter express anything more than what the Johannine writings say *about* God—for example, about how Jesus is related to the Father, how the Spirit is related to them both, how consequent answers and even formal doctrines were formulated and received by various groups. Nonetheless, we should be careful at this point not to presume a too abstract a notion of experience, as though it were detachable from meaning in some elemental way. Experience is always potentially or actually meaningful—otherwise we would have no questions to ask and nothing to understand. Experience, therefore, provokes questions of meaning; the fact and content of experience is recognised by meaning and shaped by it into intelligible forms. Without meaning, the experience could not be registered, known or spoken of. On the other hand, to reduce the data of the Johannine experience merely to catalogue of objective statements or to the articulation of a number of new doctrines about God, would be jejune. There are, for instance, elements of personal transformation and qualities of consciousness to be found, along with new imperatives toward community, and new values and new forms of ethical conduct inherent in what we might call the Johannine 'experience'.

Following Lonergan's sketch of some four dimensions of meaning,[9] I suggest that such a manifold of inter-related dimensions of meaning can be a useful tool in elaborating the compact experience of the truth of God as found, in this instance, in the Johannine writings. Different dimensions of meaning shape the density of the experience of the Johannine community in the past. Alertness to such dimensions of meaning can suggest ways in which that experience in the past it can be now personally appropriated in this far distant time. It can then be productively transposed, at once to challenge and also to meet the needs of the present situation.

For the Word to become flesh was to enter into the world of human meaning, with its questions, answers, conflicts, fears, failures and hopes. Given the variety of human conflicts inspired by the conflict of desires and impulses that move the human heart, it is notable that the first words of the Word in the Gospel are a question: 'What are you looking for?' (Jn 1:38). That question provokes four inter-related ways of answering it in our search for answers regarding:

- The ultimate truth that summons and judges us in the chiaroscuro of our experience of the world. There is an objectively *cognitive* meaning of the Gospel, set in contrast to lies and ignorance;
- The truth of who we are as it informs our authentic identity as conscious subjects. This *constitutive* meaning of faith in Christ contrasts with other identities formed in the pursuit of idols, or as the result of other filiations and paternties;
- The truth of how we can and should belong together in mutual responsibility. This is *communicative* meaning of the Word—in contrast to self-enclosed alienation, from God and our neighbour;
- Truth in action, in its world-transforming power. Here, the *effective* meaning of the Gospel contrasts with the fear and despair resulting from lip-service and timidity.

---

9. Lonergan, *Method in Theology*, 76–81. See also his 'Dimensions of Meaning', *Collection: Collected Works of Bernard Lonergan*, Volume 4, edited by Frederick E Crowe and Robert M Doran (Toronto: University of Toronto Press, 1993), 232–243.

Cognitive Meaning

While not implying any temporal ordering of these dimensions of meaning, we first treat the most obvious dimension of meaning, namely, the *cognitive*. The adult no longer lives in a child's world of immediacy. What is real is not reducible to what is already out there to be seen and touched. Reality is known through the actuation of all our capacities to experience, imagine, understand, reflect and judge. Knowing is, therefore, a compound of activities, including but going beyond what our senses, imagination, feelings and their various projections can deliver. The cognitive dimension of meaning implies a definable content grasped in an objective judgment. It is inherent in faith's answer to the questions, Who is the one true God? How is this God revealed? How is the divine will to be discerned? In this cognitive dimension, the Word enters our experience as an objective *datum*, provoking questions, and demanding an assent to the reality of the God so revealed. In this regard, we can recognise things known that were previously unknown (for example, Jn 16:29), and come to the realisation of the need for further illumination (Jn 16:12-14; 1 Jn 3:2).

As the Gospel leads its readers further into the depth and breadth of the Christian experience of God, it moves along lines shaped by the disconcerting otherness that Jesus brings into the situation. It looks back and upward—to his origin with the Father; and out—to the scope of what the Father is bringing about. The experience of God gives rise to an enriched *cognitive* sense of the God of Christian faith. Take one example drawn from John 5: Though the one God of Israel is working in all that happens, the singularity of Jesus' witness to this one God discloses a unique form of communication and communion between the Father and the Son. It presumes a reciprocity of consciousness between the Father who unceasingly works, and the Son who also works. Not unexpectedly, such an implication provoked theological outrage (Jn 5:17). Undifferentiated monotheism allows for no self-communication, either within the divine realm, or beyond it to the world. The presumption had been that God is not only one, but also ultimately alone. To the degree such a presupposition goes unquestioned, Jesus' filial experience of God is a scandal. As a result, 'the Jews' see him not only as a breaker of the Sabbath law, but also as blasphemously making himself God's equal by 'calling God his own Father' (Jn 5:18).

This charge occasions the expression of a cognitively rich and nuanced theology on the part of the Johannine author. His frame of reference always includes the utterly 'Father-ward' relationality of Jesus' existence and action (Jn 5:19, 30, 43). And yet the Father's 'Son-ward' communication is stated in various ways: 'The Father loves the Son and shows him all he himself is doing' (Jn 5:20). The Father's 'showing' to the Son includes the 'work' of raising the dead, and giving life 'to whom he will' (Jn 5:21, 26. Still, it is not only a matter of the Father's *showing*, but *giving* to the Son. This paternal giving to the Son includes the gifts of 'all judgment' (Jn 5:22), of having 'life in himself' (Jn 5:26), and the 'authority to execute judgment' (Jn 5:27), along with 'the works' that are his to accomplish (Jn 5:36). While Jesus bears witness to the Father from whom he comes, the Father both sends the Son into the world and bears witness to him (Jn 5:37). Even though he receives all from the Father and is unreservedly surrendered to the Father's will, Jesus remains a free agent; and his relationship to the Father is acted out in freedom (Jn 5:17). In one respect, the Father 'rests' while the Son 'works', for 'the Father judges no one, but has given all judgment to the Son' (Jn 5:22). In this regard, the Father not only gives, but yields, to the Son the properly divine activity of judging. In so yielding and giving over judgment to the Son, the divine purpose is 'that all may honor the Son, even as they honor the Father' (Jn 5:23).

The intentional reciprocity and the mutuality of relationships here described will give rise, in the centuries to come, to a full blown trinitarianism of the post-Nicene doctrine. Here it is sufficient to observe the striking cognitive development in John's presentation. Jesus' personal action and authority cannot be considered apart from the Father who sends, loves, reveals, gives and even yields to the Son. In this, the Gospel transforms former religious and philosophical notions of undifferentiated divine unity.

Constitutive Meaning

Second, meaning functions in a *constitutive* manner. The meaning of the Word affects the experience of human identity. In this dimension, the Word of God 'informs' the sense of self. It not only speaks about God, but forms a 'Godly identity'. This dimension of meaning 'constitutes' believers in an awareness of being 'the children of

God' and recipients of the gift of the truth. The believer thus enters into the divine meaning to find a new self in the light of God's truth. The horizon of Christian existence is radically affected. By living this identity-shaping dimension of meaning, we can read the Gospel with the question: 'What new identity do we have as believers in the light of the God who is self-revealed in Jesus Christ?'

Although the Spirit will come as gift, witness and guide to serve the Father's communication to the world, the disciples still have to contend with their own confusions and sorrow. With the work of God still in progress, they have little sense of the unity and direction of the divine purpose and the phases of its timing (Jn 16:15–19). Their experience is determined by the opaque finality of death—the silence, darkness, defeat, and terminal separation from the Jesus who is leaving them by going to the Father. Still outside of the Father's house and lacking the benefit of the Spirit's guidance, they interpret any promised 'little time' as the long time of death—when the dead stay dead, and human fate is wrapped in dread and obscurity. They have no eyes to look forward into the future and to that visibility of the glorified Jesus which will result from his going to the Father. The disciples cannot comprehend how his promised return will be a source of life from beyond the limits of death. In the history of faith, they are not the last to express the limitations of both their vision and their patience: 'we do not know what he means' (Jn 16:18b).

The dispirited sadness of the disciples is met with the assurance of Jesus as he moves toward his goal. At the depths of apparent defeat, and in the face of the world's celebration of victory, a great transformation will take place. The glorification of Jesus will mean a transformation of the consciousness and very imagination of his disciples: 'Amen, amen I say to you will weep and lament, but the world will rejoice; you will be sorrowful, but your sorrow will turn into joy' (Jn 16:20). A world-transforming birth is about to occur. In the hour determined by the Father, new life is being brought forth. Genuine believers, modeling their faith on the Mother of Jesus (Jn 2:4–5), will participate in a joyous birth. Their present sorrows are not symptoms of a terminal distress, but are, rather, signs of the travail inherent in the experience of being born from above to abundant life (Jn 10:10). Despite the inevitable darkness of history, the true light will bring its joyous evidence. The cross will reveal the glory of God; and the life that streams from the Crucified will lead to its consummation in perfect joy. The followers of Jesus will experience their lives unfolding in the sight of Jesus—'I will see you again' (Jn 16:22)—in a kind of eye-to-eye contact unclouded by the darkness of death and failure. But the experience of joy is not moved indefinitely into the future. The journey of faith in time, whatever its conflicts, will unfold in the presence of the gracious Father. Believers will no longer experience themselves as outsiders to the communion existing between the Father and the Son, and so needing to address Jesus in order to contact the Father. The Gospel promises that, through Jesus, his followers will be drawn into an immediate relationship with the Father, 'for the Father himself loves you' (Jn 16:27). In Jesus, and in his victory over the world, they will have peace (Jn 16:33). Christian identity thus derives from intimacy with God—and implies sharing in the joy and peace of Jesus. In the joy of that life that has been revealed, believers will come to know themselves as involved in the conversation of heaven, as when Jesus prays to the Father, 'They are yours and you gave them to me' (Jn 17:6).

Communicative Meaning

Third, the meaning of the Word is *communicative*. A community of common experience, conviction and identity is the outcome of communication of the ultimately meaningful. The followers of Christ are 'meant' into a co-existence founded on their shared experience of God. The communicative dimension of meaning is clearly of prime importance in all the New Testament, as well as in the Johannine writings. The very choice of the name, 'the Word', in the first verse of the prologue of the Gospel underlines the communicative meaning pervading the Gospel right to its end (Jn 20:31). At a moment of climactic intensity, Jesus asks the Father that the disciples and their successors be one as he and the Father are one (Jn 17:20–24).

The communicative dimension of meaning is elaborated even further in the First Letter of John. It witnesses to a communion, a *koinonia*, which unites present believers with the witnesses of the past, '. . . from the beginning' (1 Jn 1:1; 3:11), with communities in other places (2 and 3 Jn), and, most of all, with the Father and the Son (1 Jn 2:23–24). The field of communication in question has historical,[10]

---

10. Cf 1 Jn 1:1–3; 2:1, 7, 8, 12, 21, 26; 4:6; 5:13.

geographical,[11] interpersonal,[12] inter-generational,[13] transcendent,[14] and cosmic[15] dimensions. The communicative meaning of divine revelation in 1 John includes past witnesses, present relationships with those both near and far, communion with the Father and the Son, and, more implicitly, a relationship with the world itself.

Effective Meaning

Last, the meaning of the Word is *effective*. Jesus Christ, and the God revealed through him, means Christians to transform the world in new and hopeful ways. The Word of God is effectively expressed in the supreme example of Jesus washing the feet of his disciples (Jn 13:1–11), and in the new commandment to love as he loved (Jn 13:34). The effective meaning of the Word of God entails following him who is 'the way' (Jn 14:6), as it affects every aspect of existence. So central to the Johannine experience of God is this effective dimension that the three other dimensions of divine meaning would collapse if the meaning of faith is not effective. To pretend to love God while hating a member of the community is to be in darkness (1 Jn 2:9, 11). We cannot love the invisible God without loving the all-too visible human other (1 Jn 4:20). Hence, the exhortation, 'Let us love one another, because love is from God. Everyone who loves is born of God and knows God' (1 Jn 4:7). Believers must walk in the light (1 Jn 1:7), confess their sins (1 Jn 1:9), obey the commandments (1 Jn 2:3; 5:2–3) and do the Father's will (1 Jn 2:17).

All this is to suggest that these classic texts of Christian faith 'word' the experience of God in accord with these four dimensions. They are interwoven and interpenetrate in a holographic manner within the density of faith's experience of divine life, love and communication. To ignore this manifold meaning would result in being locked into a literalism of an extreme kind. On the other hand, a consideration of these four dimensions can prove to be a valuable tool in interpreting

---

11. Cf 2 Jn: 1:10–11; 3 Jn 1:5–8.
12. As in 1 Jn 1:7; 4:20.
13. 1 Jn 2:12–14.
14. See 1 Jn 1:3; 2:23–24; 5:11–12.
15. Cf Jn 3:16; 1 Jn 2:2; 4:9, 14; 5:4–5.

the experience of God in the Johannine writings and for structuring collaboration between the theologian and the exegete.

Conclusion

But there larger question remains. How can this rich and manifold fund of meaning be transposed into the present context of Church and world? The cognitive context has been immeasurably extended when compared to the world of the past. Our knowledge of the world, for instance, has now to include data pointing to the nearly fifteen billion years of cosmic emergence, and the three and half billion year evolution of life on this planet. Planet Earth circles the sun, a medium-sized star in a galaxy of some hundred billion such stars are said to shine, in a cosmos of perhaps a hundred billion galaxies. Moreover, our known world includes religions and spiritual paths beyond the imagination of the Johannine world. When Mt Gerizim in Samaria and the Temple of Jerusalem were significant markers in the religious topography of the Gospel, what now of Benares or Mecca or Nairobi or Kyoto or New York, or the forty-thousand year history of Aboriginal inhabitation of this country? How, in this far larger spiritual context, is the Johannine *Logos* the all-creative, enlightening and life-giving utterance of God? How does it dwell among us when 'we' are an inexpressibly larger community?

Then, the constitutive meaning of Christian identity, with its characteristics of peace, joy, life and communion with God, has moved into a new context. Once Darwin, Marx, Nietzsche, Freud and evolutionary biology have had their say and communicated their respective 'suspicions', in what does our deepest identity reside? Given the phenomenon of the 'unemployed self' within the technological world of our experience, where does 'the Father' find those worshipers in 'spirit and truth' (Jn 4:23) he is seeking out?

The evidence suggests that those early Johannine communities suffered a special grief, and felt beleaguered and isolated, at enmity with the world—which, however hostile, was still understood to be the object of God's love. Those small, fragile communities have now died into the Great Church, which, in turn, is located in an unimaginably greater world—of both promise and threat. How does light and truth of the Gospel continue to communicate, inspiring—and risking—modes of communication and solidarity in ways that would have been beyond the horizon of those early Christian generations?

Finally, the inescapable imperatives of Christian love which are such a striking aspect of the way of life witnessed to in the Johannine writings, have now to develop into a much broader effectiveness. Loving one's fellow believers must meet not only the (more Synoptic) challenge of loving one's suffering neighbour, but also of loving the 'neighbourhood' in this time of threatened ecology and pressing environmental concern.

In an expanding theology,[16] each of the dimensions of meaning can be productively applied not only to the Johannine writings, but also to all our Biblical texts in ways that can supplement the splendid achievement of scripture scholars, and assist in a fruitful collaboration between them and theologians.

---

16. See Anthony J Kelly, *An Expanding Theology: Faith in a World of Connections* (Sydney: EJ Dwyer, 1993), and revised (November 2003) Web version: http://dlibrary.acu.edu.au/staffhome/ankelly/

Derrida at Monash

For KH

The tanned fresh-wise face under a white brush --
a small Algerian Frenchman, Paris-dapper now,
Jewishly insistent, not wanting to sit,
a challenge to the chair of this-or any- meeting:
By invitation only; in fact, a visitation:
In a playful lack of gravity,
He rises not to the occasion
But to the questions,
a playful lack of gravity
disappointing Newton's solemn law . . .
Not really our style, the papers say,
this intellectual fidget,
In the land of images and regulations
Where truth is of little interest:
the African sun, like ours, should have cured him:
of making a profession of interrogation:
his faith B without conditions –
in this human condition
so implicated in conditions,
that he is prepared to wait for grace:
Looking the gift horse in the mouth,
He detects weak lungs.
Nothing can really be taken for granted,
unless of course, it is all for granted—
Despite the alien economy,
Against prevailing calculation,
With the giving, and, possibly, forgiving,
He goes with the gift . . .
To be given away, and away –
satisfaction deferred, you might say.

Refreshing Experience: The Christ-Event As Fact, Classic and Phenomenon

The exploration of faith is an ongoing activity, ideally refreshing itself in every age, and communicating the authentic meaning of faith as a gift and a responsibility to the culture in which it moves. Theology's grounding in the realities of experience is wide and deep, but most of this is subterranean, tacit and never fully objectifiable. The interpersonal community of faith, its corporate consciousness, institutional forms, charismatic persons, saints, martyrs, wisdom figures, and so forth, together with its symbols and sacraments, inspired writings and key doctrines, its art and overall 'philosophy constitute an immense, historic and largely undifferentiated current of experience in which theology lives.

But there are difficulties—a loss of this sense of reality from within, and the resistance of the culture from without. With the success of the methods of empirical science and the cultural dominance of a scientific mentality, theology began to suffer a long-term crisis. Traditional and originally philosophical notions such as 'being', 'presence', 'essence' and 'nature', so basic to Catholic doctrines, lost their metaphysical assurance in the world of modern science, and then were further dislocated in the shifting sands of the postmodern world. Consequently, the capacity of theology to attend to the data of experience, either in the realm of faith or in contemporary culture, was diminished. A renewed receptivity to the 'what' and the 'how' of Christian revelation as it is registered in human consciousness is now called for.

Whatever the explanation of how theology lost its experiential grounding, part of the problem lay in the often unnoticed limitations of exploring the data of faith with a consciousness already shaped, explicitly or not, by an ossified metaphysical structure. When a venerable array of concepts and definitions are already in possession, there is an ideological obstacle to theological creativity sensitive to the experience of the Church, the diverse expressions of culture, and the history of the world in which Christian communities exist.

Bernard Lonergan's *Method in Theology*[1] was an outstanding contribution to the reintegration of theological activities which had grown apart in the face of the complex data with which theology had to deal. Appearing some forty years ago, its vital ingredient was the regulatory role of conscious experience in regard to the theological development and employment of metaphysical terms. He writes,

> The point to making metaphysical terms and relations not basic but derived is that a critical metaphysics results. For every term and relation there will exist a corresponding element in intentional consciousness. Accordingly, empty or misleading terms and relationships can be eliminated, while valid ones can be elucidated by the conscious intention from which they are derived. The importance of such a critical control will be evident to anyone familiar with the vast arid wastes of theological controversy.[2]

Lonergan's familiarity with 'vast arid wastes of theological controversy' is shared by numerous others who had grown weary of abstractly rational procedures. His phenomenology of the love of the Holy Spirit flooding Christian consciousness in its self-transcending dynamism was of fundamental importance for theology developing in an ecumenical and interfaith context. However, the phenomenon of self-transcending love still needed to be correlated to the phenomenon of the Christ-event if the interests of a distinctive Christian theology were to be served.[3]

In what follows, I sketch a way in which three perceptions of this Christ Event—termed here, 'the Fact', 'the Classic' and 'the Phenomenon'—arise out of the one experience of faith, and figure in theological and Christian communication. We aim here to promote a distinctive

---

1. Bernard Lonergan, *Method in Theology* (London: DLT, 1972).
2. Lonergan, *Method*, 343.
3. Anthony Kelly, 'Be Attentive: Theological Method and the Christian Phenomenon', in *Fifty Years of* Insight, edited by Neil Ormerod, Robin Koning and David Braithwaite (Adelaide: ATF Press, 2011), 93–109.

realism in theology based firmly in a 'thick' sense of experience. Any such effort must begin with the recognition that reality reveals itself in different ways to different minds, at different times, and in different levels and registers of experience. A book, for example, can lie on a desk as an empirical object, perhaps to be weighed and sent by mail; or it may be taken up and read, and so becomes a source of, say, aesthetic, intellectual or moral enrichment. Conversely, there are many modes of receptivity corresponding to the manifold richness of reality,[4] as different as looking at a book, admiring its dustcover, throwing it to the floor—or, reading it, underlining particular passages, re-reading some of its more striking sections, and engaging others in discussion of its content, style, usefulness, potential impact, or assessing its suitability as a gift to a colleague. Such a manifold of potential experience is pre-eminently the case when thinking focuses on the figure of Christ and the larger notion of the Christ-event. But first, let us begin with the most general and diffuse of the three perceptions, the empirical *Fact* of Christian reality.

The Christian Fact

Clearly, the Christ-event is an historic fact in the narrative of civilization—originally in the Mediterranean world, then in the West, but now in an increasingly global manner. Christianity may wax or wane, but Christ remains a commanding personal symbol, immeasurably enriching the moral and religious imagination of human beings. The story of his birth, life, moral teaching, death, resurrection and ascension is woven into the history of individuals, peoples and nations in ways that are impossible to deny—even if it can be questioned whether all such instances, in all their occasions and degrees, are authentic manifestations of who he was, what he stood for, and what is entailed in following him.

The Christian Fact[5] is so elemental, so empirically saturated and pervasive that, when subjected to analysis, it appears daunting in its

---

4. See Jean-Yves Lacoste, *La Phénoménalité de Dieu: Neuf études* (Paris: Cerf, 2008), 134.
5. See Jaroslav Pelikan, *Jesus through the Centuries: His Place in the History of Culture* (New York: Harper and Row, 1987), 1–8. On a much larger scale, see Diarmaid Maculloch, *Christianity: The First Three Thousand Years* (New York: Viking Penguin, 2010).

complexity and objectified with great difficulty. It includes in its range endless particular topics, which, like Russian dolls, contain a number of successively smaller shapes: moral inspiration, liturgical celebrations, festive occasions, multiple aesthetic forms—music, literature, painting, architecture, and even film in which 'Christ figures' is an established category. Apart from religious and moral considerations, the Christian Fact has been a prodigious aesthetic and literary event. In this variety of embodiments and influences, the Fact of Jesus Christ has permeated the world of human meanings and values in a unique manner. For the two billion Christians of the world, he is the focus and exemplar of the spiritual and moral life. In a penumbra of relationships to other religious traditions, he is, sometimes unsettlingly but nonetheless inescapably, a factor. For non-Christians, it is impossible to escape the multiple associations of his presence in images, writings, institutions, works of art, holidays and feasts and so much else, all inspired by what and who he was. The dating of the calendar, the structure of the week and the year, the biblical references that are part of the language itself, the holdings of art galleries, the repertoire of classical music, and Christian witness in all ages and cultures, create a complex of content and influence so as to constitute an immense *Fact*. At very least, theology is called on to explain the intrinsic meaning, value and implications of this factual phenomenon, even in the less propitious times of contemporary secularism.

The Christian Fact is a massive presence, whether encountered from without or lived from within. In this regard, theology is not first of all defending an idea or expounding a theory, but a reflection on an immense, empirical, historical, social, cultural and religious reality. Though critics may well reject the idea of 'Christianity' or the authority of Christian teachers, or the moral tone of Christian practice, they cannot deny this Christian Fact, whether admired or detested, and that it has massively shaped world-history. It is public, multivalent, ever emerging, not as an idea to be justified, but an objective and event confronting reality. It is a continuing and unfinished event as an institution and a global community. It witnesses to what is 'otherwise', however familiar and sedimented its expression may have become.

To register this Fact in any positive sense is to be drawn toward the classic expressions associated with it, along with the phenomenon of the originating experience in which it occurred. The Fact, of itself, is publicly accessible in the empirical world. Christian classics—

pre-eminently the writings of the New Testament—are intrinsic to this Fact, even though expressing an excess of meaning that eludes objectification. We pass, then, to a consideration of what 'the classic' entails.

The Christian Classic

Before the writings of notable French phenomenologists such as Jean-Luc Marion, Michel Henry and Jean-Yves Lacoste were well known in the English-speaking world, David Tracy's *The Analogical Imagination*,[6] with his extended treatment of 'the classic', was covering much of the same ground, and for much the same reasons—that is, to recover the distinctive sense of Christian reality and the experience of self-disclosure or 'revelation' intrinsic to it.

Though an adequate summary of Tracy's prodigiously documented chapters treating of the classic is beyond our scope,[7] we may usefully draw attention first of all to the capacity of the classic to refresh and revitalise any area of tradition or thought—and especially in regard to theology.[8]

The Classic in General

Particular instances of classics are found in every domain of human culture. They are commandingly *there* in an elemental, incontrovertible way—in art, science, philosophy, religion, history. In his preliminary general description of the classic, Tracy contends that the 'naming certain texts, events, symbols, rituals, images, persons'

---

6. David Tracy, *The Analogical Imagination* (New York: Crossroad, 1981).
7. Tracy, *The Analogical Imagination*. The exposition of the meaning and interpretation of the religious classic (99–230) is followed by a major section dealing with the Christian classic (233–338).
8. For a profound theological background reflection, surveying both the subjective and objective perspectives, see Hans Urs von Balthasar, *The Glory of the Lord I: Seeing the Form* (Edinburgh: T&T Clark, Edinburgh, 1982). Referring to the primal (or classic) phenomenon, von Balthasar warns in his Introduction,

> Whoever insists that he can neither see it or read it, or whoever cannot accept it, but rather seeks to 'break it up' critically into supposed prior components, that person falls into the void and, what is worse, he falls into what is opposed to the true and the good (20).

as classic suggests that the culture is recognising 'nothing less than the disclosure of a reality we cannot but name truth'.[9] The classic expresses an excess of meaning, and so discloses a fresh, and even a transformative, sense of reality. Through it we glimpse what is 'the essential' in life, just as we are summoned to ever further learning and appreciation.[10] To that degree, familiarity with the classic inspires a wholesome humility and a more refined receptivity in regard to all reality. It gives intelligence a quality of tact,[11] for there are realities that can only be received, contemplated, beheld—but never mastered or fully analysed. Lonergan, anticipating a theological application of this notion, writes that, 'the classics . . . not only are beyond the initial horizon of their interpreters but also may demand an intellectual, moral, religious conversion of the interpreter over and above the broadening of his horizon.'[12] Consequently, the special impact of the classic lies in its ability to reshape horizons, and to provoke a conversion to something higher or deeper or broader than the projections and routines of previous outlooks.[13] The classic's special provocative power, in both its artistic and other forms, is strikingly expressed by George Steiner as follows:

> In a wholly fundamental, pragmatic sense, the poem, the statue, the sonata are not so much read, viewed or heard as they are *lived*. The encounter with the aesthetic is, together with certain modes of religious and metaphysical experience, the most 'ingressive', transformative summons available to human experiencing . . . the shorthand image is that of an Annunciation, of 'a terrible beauty' or gravity breaking into the small house of our cautionary being. If we have heard rightly the wing-beat and the provocation of that visit, the house is no longer habitable in quite the same way as before. A mastering intrusion has shifted the light.[14]

---

9. Tracy, *The Analogical Imagination*, 108–10.
10. Tracy, *The Analogical Imagination*, 108–12.
11. George Steiner, *Real Presences* (Chicago: The University of Chicago Press, 1989), 147–149.
12. Lonergan, *Method*, 161. He quotes Friedrich Schlegel words, a few paragraphs later: 'A classic is a writing that is never fully understood. But those who are educated and educate themselves must always want to learn more from it'.
13. Steiner, *Real Presences*, 147.
14. Steiner, *Real Presences*, 143.

'The classic provocatively intimates dimensions of human existence in the face of dehumanising pressures.[15] It is an 'annunciation' of larger mystery, despite the postmodern reduction of sensibility to the banal.[16] It offers a radical refreshment to the routines of experience with an implication of something more.

The Religious Classic

The communication of an excess of meaning is characteristic of the religious classic. True, making hard and fast distinctions, say, between an artistic or religious classic, is problematic, given the elusive, provocative and overbrimming significance of a classic in any area. Nonetheless, Tracy helpfully indicates some quasi-specific features of the religious classic. It can be appreciated as a revelatory event in that it meets the limits of human existence with the disclosure of a fullness, a wholeness, and a healing that comes from beyond—'a radical and finally gracious mystery'. This disclosure comes with its own originality, but it also presupposes an antecedent willingness receptive to what is offered.[17] Keeping in mind some instance of the persons, texts or events that have attained classic status in a religious tradition helps clarify certain features of the religious classic. Here we make three remarks:

First, religious classics express surprising possibilities at the limits of human existence. There are, indeed, the dark limits of guilt, death, suffering, powerlessness. But these are met with the positive experiences of forgiveness, being loved, and being able to love in return, along with the gifts of enlightenment, wonder, joy, hope, and gratitude. The light shines in the darkness, and the darkness does not conquer. The routine world is typically 'at a loss for words' when its familiar boundaries are breached.

Second, while the religious classic never simply conveys the whole meaning of life, it does radiate a certain sense of wholeness, of 'what it is all about'. Mind and imagination are drawn into a radical unknowing. In contrast to the familiar, the calculable, the manageable, the intimations of the religious classic conceal even as they reveal. Con-

---

15. Steiner, *Real Presences*, 224–6.
16. Steiner, *Real Presences*, 96.
17. Tracy, *The Analogical Imagination*, 163.

ventional categories and routine perceptions are no longer enough. Language is silenced before an ineffable gift. There is a luminous excess inviting the spirit to expand, and to leave unsaid what cannot be spoken. The presence of 'No-Thing' within one's world subverts all limited categories. It makes space for the 'Nowhere' which appears as a true homeland, the *patria*, the place where the promise of life is kept.

Thirdly, the revelatory impact of a religious classic presupposes a willingness to reflect on the ultimate bearing of existence. If searching and questioning are suppressed, the intimations of the religious classic will be felt as too threatening, fatiguing, too obvious—or otherwise, too alien. There is a disturbance in that too much is revealed—and provoked. Anyone searching into the origin, the direction, the goal of this universe, cannot afford to reject out of hand what the inspired classic brings to expression. It offers an arresting glimpse of the ultimate in the world. To reject *that* would be to deny what is most ecstatic and inspiring in human history, and to be cut off from what human beings most treasure in their humanity.

The Christian Classic

What then of the story of the life, teaching, and death and resurrection of Christ? He is unavoidably a presence in a world of classics figures, but he also affects human culture more specifically as a unique religious classic. Through him, the Word is incarnate, summoning consciousness to a specific sense of God's relationship to the world and to human destiny. Christians may well feel in the interpersonal intimacy of faith that Christ is more than *a* religious classic, but he is certainly not less than that.

Tracy describes the peculiar ability of the religious classic to evoke an ultimate mystery communicating itself at the frontiers of life. Even though it is given through human witness—word, sacrament, deed—it is not primarily a human production. There is the quality of inspiration, not so much as information 'about' a transcendent something, but as an intimation of the 'Other' in a quite original sense. To that degree, the religious classis the character of a free and personal self-revelation. The 'Other' is experienced as a 'Who'—as is manifestly the case in the Abrahamitic religions. In the Christian experience and its interpretative tradition, the 'Who' is the culmination of God's self-revelation in Jesus Christ, the *Yes* to all God's promises and the *Amen* to all our prayers (cf 2 Cor 1:20). The Christ event is mediated through an immense complex of symbols, images, institutional forms, doctrines, writings, events, communities and persons (apostles, confessors, martyrs and pastors) as God's own self-manifestation.

Despite this profusion, the Christian classic has some seven irreplaceable features which structure the New Testament narrative and various versions of the Creed:

- There is the originating love of the Father;
- divine self-giving in the Son;
- unconditional love revealed on the Cross;
- the triumph of God's action in the resurrection;
- the Spirit as the inexhaustible communication of the gift of God;
- Church as the sacrament and witness of God's saving will in history;
- eschatological consummation in 'the life of the world to come'.[18]

With the coming of Christ, the believer's sense of self, of the universe and of God, are all alike called into question. Traditional notions are expanded, provoked, revised, drawn beyond any provisional interpretation. The past words, deeds, life and death of Jesus are continually present, for, as the Risen Lord, he breathes his Spirit into the Church and the world in each moment. Christ is a question resonating on all levels of culture. In the above-cited words of Steiner, he embodies something 'grave and constant' in the human condition, to incarnate a 'terrible and disturbing beauty'. His parables, his crucified corpse, his return to his disciples in a life beyond death, penetrate into the meaning of our humanity and its ultimate hopes. The classic force of the New Testament is found in the radical confession of Jesus as 'the Christ', 'the Lord', 'the Alpha and Omega', 'the resurrection and the life', and so on. Yet there is a startling dynamic of negation in such confessions, extending to the 'invisibility' of God (Jn 1:18), to Christ also (1 Pet 1:8), to the selfhood of the believer (1 Jn 3:2), and to the

---

18. For a pastoral experiment in communicating the classic form of Christianity, see Anthony J Kelly, *'God is Love': The Heart of Christian Faith* (Collegeville: The Liturgical Press, 2012).

times of fulfilment (Acts 1:7).[19] To that degree, the original Christian classic engenders an experience of a holy darkness. Each canonical expression of revealed truth draws the believer into ever-deeper and broader dimensions of wonder, searching and self-surrender.

In terms of Christian realism, the Classic possesses the communicability of the Christian Fact. It attracts the beholder into an inside knowledge of what has empirically taken shape in historical experience. Now we move from the Fact and the Classic to the Christian Phenomenon, and the manner in which it is experienced.

The Christian Phenomenon

Compared to the Christian Classic, there is a deeper level in the phenomenon of Christian revelation out of which arise the various classic expressions. Appreciation of this Phenomenon requires a disciplined receptivity to what has been given, and continues to be given, in the consciousness of Christian faith. What is routinely 'taken for granted' in theological discourse must a deeper receptivity so as to be taken precisely as granted or given.[20] What is the nature of this receptivity in relation to the specific character of the Christian Phenomenon.

Receptivity to the Given

Max Scheler, one of the earliest and most formative of philosophers in the field of phenomenology, wrote on the need for an appropriately open, unbiased and refined phenomenological receptivity:

> [T]here is nothing more disastrous for all epistemology than to establish at the beginning of one's methodological procedure a too narrow, restrictive concept of 'experience', to equate the whole of experience with one particular kind of experience and with that mental attitude that is conducive [only[to it, and then to refuse to recognize as 'primordially

---

19. For the pervasive 'negative theology' of the New Testament, see Kelly, *The Resurrection Effect*, 53–60.
20. For the following remarks, I am especially indebted to Anthony J Steinbock, *Phenomenology and Mysticism: The Verticality of Religious Experience* (Bloomington and Indianapolis: Indiana University Press, 2009), 1–27.

given' anything that cannot be reduced to this one kind of experience.[21]

A phenomenological approach calls into question the naïveté of the narrow band of everyday experiences, just as it holds in suspension habitual convictions about the 'real world' interwoven into routine and partial perspectives. First, we must throw some light on the question of how meaning arises and the elemental experiences basic to it, but without either collapsing everything into monodimensional horizontalism, or getting snagged on predetermined notions of subjectivity or objectivity. A phenomenological implies an intense and disciplined act of recollection so as to allow consciousness to be freshly 'struck', as it were, by what is given from beyond the self and its self-interest. This attitude is behind the phenomenological vocabulary of 'active openness', 'conversion to the given', *epoché* or 'reduction', and so forth. In this respect, phenomenology is never purely descriptive, for it intends to illumine experience so as 'to point us further to the radical bases of our lives'.[22] As a result, a phenomenological attentiveness can enrich experience with new awareness of the self, and of the depth and breadth of what is given and registered in human consciousness.

Theology remains indebted to Husserl's seminal influence in phenomenology. Steinbock quotes with approval an observation from the Husserl Archives which, in some sense at least, presumes collaboration between philosophical phenomenology and theology:

> I want what the churches want: to lead humanity to *Aeternitas*. My task is to try to do this through philosophy. Everything I have written up to now is only preparatory; it is only a development [*Aufstellen*] of methods. In the course of one's life, one unfortunately does not arrive at the core, at what is essential. It is important for philosophy to be led out of liberalism and rationalism, and to be led once more to what is essential, to *truth*. The question concerning ultimate reality,

---

21. Max Scheler, *Vom Ewigen im Menschen, Gessamelte Werke*, Volume 5 edited by Maria Scheler (Bern: Franke), 250—cited in Steinbock, *Phenomenology and Mysticism*, 6.
22. Steinbock, *Phenomenology and Mysticism*, 27.

truth, must be the object of every true philosophy. This is my life's work.²³

The founding-father of phenomenology sought therefore to call into question the abstractions of conceptually inflated systems, along with their accompanying rationalistic, ego-centred mentality. Accordingly, he proposed a renewed concentration on 'the things themselves' (*zu den Sachen selbst*). He thus reacted to an Enlightenment intellectuality which presumed a situation in which an already-constituted rational self anticipated and treated the data to be understood only within the reductive horizon of pre-established possibilities. But when attention is focused on the phenomenon—consciously experienced, appreciated in its own right and in the conditions of its disclosure—reality begins to be experienced in its arresting and particular otherness. A concrete surplus of significance earths the abstraction of concepts, systems and theoretical methods; and provokes attentiveness to what is given, and the mode of its appearance. In a theological perspective, the *data* derive from the God-given *donum*, while that gift comes from a giving and a giver beyond any worldly horizon.

The Christian Phenomenon

Recent writers, such as Marion, Henry, Lacoste and Steinbock, have insisted on extending the range of phenomenology to include religious phenomena. The religious dimension had ceased to be of intrinsic significance for a philosophy confined to horizontal analysis at the expense of the vertical dimensions of the heights and depths of experience.²⁴ But this 'other dimension' cannot be reduced to the level of purely empirical or intellectual presentation. There occurs a disruption in mundane experience and an irruption into it. This mode of given-ness, in traditional religious rhetoric, is termed 'revelation' and 'epiphany', and suggests a vertical rather than an exclusively horizontal perspective.²⁵ The verticality of experience

---

23. Steinbock, *Phenomenology*, 28: his translation of Ms E III 11, 1934, 3b, Husserl-Archief, Leuven, Belgium (with permission).
24. Steinbock, *Phenomenology*, 9.
25. Steinbock, *Phenomenology*, 9–10).

moves within a vector of surprise and grace as the gift and action of God. For its part, the horizontal is largely what it is within one's reach and under one's control—at least within the ambit of a given culture.[26]

The varied types of experience and the diversity of data manifest in each situation require different levels and types of receptivity, as the Scholastic adage has it, *quidquid reciptur recipitur per modum recipientis*. That is to say that the degree of receptivity is affected by different mentalities, capacities, attitudes, moods, preoccupations and perspectives of the recipient. A plurality of possibilities affects not only an endless variety of individuals and communities, but also cultures, societies, historical epochs, and successive ages in the Church itself. Consequently, a refined, properly buoyant and receptive theological attitude contest any conception of the revealed *donum* as an uncarved block of reality, already-out-there-now, complete, immediately accessible to intuition and contained in conceptual formulation. For, thus possessed, articulated and routinely comprehended, the sediment of religious consciousness is communicated in a stock array of signs, ideas and definitions. In contrast, revelation is an ever-original event of self-communication on God's part, given into history as it unfolds 'for us and our salvation'.

The receptivity of faith to the self-revelation of God is not (usually) the property of a subversive individual. Rather, dynamics of receptivity presuppose the interpersonal experience of a community faith formed by an animating tradition containing sacred texts, doctrines, symbols, sacraments, and examples of holiness.[27] The Christ-event introduces a new horizon in which the transformative act of God's love affects every dimension of consciousness. It transvalues values, and engenders new dimensions of meaning in ideas of God, our selves, and our world. What took place in this originating event was not contained within the previous horizon of expectation, but rather disrupted it. There occurred an excess, attractive and demanding, in what is given within the experience of faith.

---

26. Steinbock, *Phenomenology*, 14.
27. Edward Farley, *Ecclesial Man: A Social Phenomenology of Faith and Reality* (Philadelphia, MD: Fortress Press,1975) is still a valuable exposition of the phenomenology of the corporate Christian reality.

Jean-Luc Marion's fertile reflections in this area[28] show an appreciation of the overbrimming or 'saturated' character of the Christian phenomenon. It permeates the receptive consciousness of faith. It makes the believer a witness to what is given rather than an agent of its production.[29] Though the grace of Christ is freely offered, it is not simply 'there' to be inspected, possessed, and taken for granted. In the words of St Thomas, one is conscious of the radical gift of grace only *coniecturaliter per aliqua signa*—'by way of conjecture/discernment 'through various signs',[30] amongst which are the peace of a good conscience and surrender to God. Whether subtly or dramatically, consciousness as affected by the Christ-Event expands in a new horizon, or, as St Paul would say, 'for those who are in Christ, there is a new creation' (2 Cor 5:17). In this regard, a phenomenological theology is less thinking *about* some object of Christian belief, and more a form of thinking from *within* the experience of what is given, by allowing it to appear in its arresting 'other-ness' and provocative power. There is, therefore, a 'eucharistic' moment at the heart of theological thinking, such that, to use a Heideggerian wordplay, 'thanking' and 'thinking' interweave. Inscribed into theological activity traditionally described as *fides quaerens intellectum*, there is the moment of *fides recipiens donum Dei appropriandum*—faith open to receive and appropriate the Gift of God as it is offered.

A phenomenological attitude does not presume that the Christ-event and the grace of God are phenomena in the same way as, say, a human face, a work of art or an historic event can be. Collapsing everything into a fideistic subjectivism might appear to be the danger. That would be at one extreme, whereas, at the other, we may be rightly wary of a revelational 'objectivism' that overwhelms the role of the believing and thinking subject. Admittedly, a theology of dis-

---

28. See Jean-Luc Marion, *Reduction and Givenness: Investigations of Husserl, Heidegger, and Phenomenology*, translated by Thomas A Carlson (Evanston, IL: Northwestern University Press (1998); *Being Given: Toward a Phenomenology of Givenness*, trans. Jeffrey L Kosky (Stanford, CA: Stanford University Press, 2002); *In Excess: Studies of Saturated Phenomena*, translated by Robyn Horner and Vincent Barraud (New York: Fordham University Press, 2002). For further elaboration and background, see Marion's *God Without Being: Hors-Texte*, translated by Thomas A Carlson (Chicago, IL: Chicago University Press, 1991). (Paris: Grasset, 2003).
29. Marion, *Being Given*, 216.
30. Thomas Aquinas, *STh* 1-2, q 112, a 5.

closure, that we have been here suggesting, inverts those habitual patterns of thinking which routinely presume that the subject is already self-constituted and given, already 'self-possessed', before anything else is given or appears to it. In contrast, a phenomenological attitude puts the emphasis on the uncanny given-ness of the *what* and *who* of 'the other'. As a result, any activity on the part of the subject, as well as its mode of self-awareness, is radically affected by a fundamental receptivity to what is given, in its transcendent otherness. In the receptivity of faith, therefore, the rational, all-critical ego no longer occupies centre-stage. It does not act as a self-contained monad projecting itself onto what is other and external to it, thus 'subjecting' everything to its powers of reason.[31] In the phenomenological and theological case, the subject is one who is 'subjected' to what is graciously and provocatively disclosed to it. As a result, it is forearmed against all pretensions to exhaust or constitute the gift.[32] Through its receptivity, the subject witnesses to what is originally given.[33]

Regarding receptivity to the phenomena, Marion refers to five instances of what he terms, 'saturated phenomena': an event, a work of art, the flesh/body, the face, and, in a way that tends to combine all four, revelation.[34] In theological terms, the *event* that makes all the difference, which calls on the believer to participate in its unfolding, is Christ's death and resurrection. In the light of faith, the community of believers is beholden to a light and a *beauty* not of this world. In its celebration of the Eucharist, the Church lives out a new sense of incarnate existence as the *Body* of Christ.[35] Through the conversion of faith, believers encounter the *face* of the One who sees them, and indeed, 'sees through them'.[36] The lived communal sense of the gift of God-given truth grounds the appreciation of what God's self-*revelation* might mean. All five such instances share a sense of a primordial self-giving.[37] None of them is constituted by the subject, but each appears in its original and self-imposing impact. Thus, the believing

---

31. Marion, *Being Given*, 261.
32. Marion, *Being Given*, 216–217.
33. Marion, *Being Given*, 264–265.
34. Marion, *Being Given*, 234–236.
35. See Anthony J Kelly, "'The Body of Christ. Amen!': The Expanding Event of the Incarnation', in *Theological Studies* 71 (2010): 792–816
36. See Rev 1:17–3:22.
37. See Kelly, *The Resurrection Effect*, 29–42.

subject comes to itself in a new consciousness only through self-giving otherness of the phenomenon concerned.

Theology can be only enriched by a more phenomenological attentiveness.[38] And, in its turn, theology is able to extend the range of phenomenology to the singularity of positive revelation.[39] Still, the general phenomenological principle stands. The saturated phenomenon shows itself by giving itself; and this takes place in a more intense and overwhelming manner in the case of the faith seeking to understand what it has received as gift and revelation.[40] At no point is it implied that the phenomenon of revelation is so overwhelming as to incapacitate the intelligence, responsibility and imagination of the believer. Rather, what is so given in revelation inspires its own tradition of rationality in which faith, phenomenology and critical realism play their respective parts.[41] On the one hand, the multi-faceted creativity of Christian intelligence can never be reduced to its experiential basis. Nor, on the other hand, must a self-sufficient rationality be allowed to remain undisturbed in its ideological isolation from the reasons of the heart that reason itself cannot know, and so, cut off from the love that recognises no limits as it 'bears all things, hopes all things, endures all things' (1 Cor 13:7–8).

Interconnections

The three topics presented in this sketch—the Fact, the Classic and the Phenomenon—at least point in the right direction, whether as converging considerations, as complementary viewpoints, or as different levels of perception. Within the Christian Fact are found both the refreshing power of the Classic and the revelatory power of the Phenomenon. From some angles, it is true, the empirical Fact, the Classic and the overbrimming Phenomenon are not easily distinguishable. There are phenomenological dimensions of the classics

---

38. For a critical appreciation of Marion's contribution, see Brian Robinette, 'A Gift to Theology? Jean-Luc Marion's "Saturated Phenomenon" in Christological Perspective', in *Heythrop Journal* 48/1 (January, 2007): 86–108.
39. Marion, 'Le possible et la révélation', 231; *Being Given*, 242.
40. Marion, *Being Given*, 367.
41. Neil Ormerod, *Meaning, Method and Revelation: The Meaning and Function of Revelation in Bernard Lonergan's Method in Theology* (Lanham: University of America Press, 2000), 217–219.

and their place in cultural history. Likewise, a particular classic, in its own right, is a phenomenon within a particular cultural development. For its part, the Fact is simply 'there' with a certain diffuse, unavoidable obviousness. It is accessible to empirical observation and investigation from any number of perspectives—demographic, economic, political and so forth. In contrast, an appreciation of the classic is inherently more demanding. Exposure to it may require personal development amounting to some level of intellectual, moral, and religious conversion, as Lonergan noted.[42] Further, even though the Fact has a wide cultural and even global impact, its recognition requires no particular phenomenological or hermeneutical attitude or method, beyond the ability to register empirical data—that is, 'the facts', welcome or not. None the less, this Christian Fact may invite an appreciation of the classic articulations of the Christ-Event, and a deeper searching into the phenomenon of Christian experience.

The Classic, on the other hand, is a commanding instance of making sense of the Christian Fact. Each Gospel, for instance, is an expression of the whole revealed truth; it works, as Tracy suggests, with the power of the whole. It emerges from a community of faith and for the Church in every age. There is a sense of excess and originality despite the obvious human and historical origins of the writings concerned. For such texts are received as 'sacred'. That is, they both witness to the culmination of revelation in Christ and derive from the living witness of the apostles and evangelists in the early Church. The community of faith has discerned in them, not only an authentic expression of the Word of God in terms of content and reference, but also as also a quality of 'inspiration', that is, as given in the power of a self-giving, self-revealing agent, the Holy Spirit. These 'sacred' and 'inspired' writings exceed all mundane categories and agencies in their capacity to express and carry forward the meaning of what has been given from beyond the world.

This sense of transcendent given-ness—from beyond, yet, at the same time, exceeding, the capacities of human agency, carries over to affect the Christian phenomenology, both in terms of content and the way such content is disclosed and communicated.

---

42. Lonergan, *Method*, 106.

Conclusion

To refer to Christian experience in terms of Fact, Classic and Phenomenon is not without risk. It might suggest a collage of Christian images or a range of scattered impressions lacking any critical controls. They may appear merely as projections, reflecting back to society, at a particular stage of its history, a range of self-serving expressions of, say, power, national or cultural superiority, aesthetic enjoyment or even ethical righteousness. How can such an approach pretend to escape the parameters of a world of consumption, self-assertion and control. There is, however, another possibility within the 'thick' description of aspects of Christian experience offered here. Theological expression is not necessarily idolic, as if a pattern of projections on to the blank screen of human aspiration. In contrast, theology works in a more iconic fashion—not therefore by constructing mirror images of the self, but by shaping windows in order to allow the light of another world to enter. If that is the case, the phenomenon of Christian revelation can be appreciated as a vertical, horizon-changing irruption. It can summon to conversion, of mind, heart and imagination; and thus be a creative source of new understanding and greater freedom in the light of what the self-revealing 'Other' (*cf* 2 Cor 3:18).

With the aim of enriching theological intentionality with a sense of greater realism, we have exploited the three notions of Fact, Classic and Phenomenon in a blend of empirical, critical and contemplative awareness. Admittedly, there is a certain circularity involved, despite the order of exposition followed here. After all, what, in the broadest sense of the word, is more a 'phenomenon' and a continuing 'event' than the Christian Fact? And yet the Fact would dissolve into a cloud of contradictory impressions if there were no Classic to hold it together with a sense of the whole and capacity to express its intrinsic meaning. However, the Classic would come from nowhere and find no reception in the corporate mind of the Church if there were no fertile depth of experience given in the Christian Phenomenon. From this, the Classic form arises, and serves to focus the understanding of the Christ Event, in its content, origin and end.

The ways in which the mystery of Jesus Christ—the Christ-event—is in its totality, registered in human consciousness are manifold and diffuse. The ambition to develop a theological method entirely adequate to Christian revelation and its relevance to all times and cultural contexts will inevitably encounter problems, such as the lack of cultural, spiritual, academic resources, etc. Communicating a creative and critical sense of the Christian reality, aware of the promise and the distortions inherent in the contemporary culture, is not so much doomed to defeat, but remains an ongoing task requiring the best energies of Christian believers in every age.

If the Fact imposes itself on empirical consciousness, if the Classic inspires a critical attention to what has been uncannily revealed, the Phenomenon requires a form of focused recollection within the consciousness of the Christian community. At a time when Church leaders call for a 'New Evangelisation', it is appropriate for theology to make a contribution by refreshing the sense of the Christian experience from which the mission of the Church arises; and to which it returns for endless inspiration and energy.

Lost Art

*Even in these lovely lands
you must rise with open hands
to let all you held be free,
to find its own and fly away:
let all your doves and eagles
have the freedom of the sky.
The wise ones will always say
that suddenly, on a summer day,
the returning eagle will look with eyes
alight with the span of heaven --
where all is healed and forgiven:
and wink knowingly, an angel in disguise.
And the doves? Take this one here:
Look, now she has no fear!-
In the surrounding darkness no longer lost,
she was the one I was missing most . . .
Perhaps she is the Holy Ghost?
An other holds a splinter in its beak,
plucked from once sightless eyes:
that is what she flew off to seek.
Now blind eyes see, for the dove is wise.
She comes to hand . . . but I set her free . . .
whispering, `Love, go! . . . bring back the branch
of the olive tree.'*

Mary: Icon of Trinitarian Love

The Marian presence in Christian life is a manifold phenomenon—in scripture, liturgy, doctrine, devotion, art, spirituality,[1] personal witness and theological traditions, not to mention apparitions and special places of pilgrimage. In Catholic parlance, this compact, multifaceted and intensely personal presence is often referred to as the 'mystery of Mary' in the life of the Church. It cannot be separated from what Paul speaks of as 'the mystery that has been hidden throughout the ages and generations but has now been revealed to his [God's] saints . . . Christ in you, the hope of glory' (Col 1:26–27). Doctrinal language refers to the 'mysteries of faith'—the Trinity, incarnation, grace and the beatific vision. These are the revealed objects of faith, since reason unaided could not deduce them. On a more devotional level, there are the 'mysteries' of the life of our Lord. Various aspects of Christian revelation become the subject of contemplation—as in the once fifteen, and now twenty, 'mysteries of the Rosary'.[2] On a more theological plane, say in the theology of Karl Rahner, 'mystery' is fundamental notion expressive of God's self-communication to the human

---

1. The number of male and female religious orders/ congregations is a massive phenomenon in its own right. Examples are close at hand: the Marists (the different Societies of Fathers, Brothers, and Sisters), The Institute of the Blessed Virgin Mary, The Presentation Sisters, the Sisters of Mercy, the Oblates of Mary Immaculate, the Servites—where do we stop, since practically every known religious order/congregation boasts of a Marian inspiration?
2. John Paul II, *Rosarium Virginis Mariae*, <http://www.vatican.va/holy_father/john_paul_ii/apost_letters/documents/hf_jp-ii_apl_20021016_rosarium-virginis-mariae_en.html>

spirit.[3] The mystery in this sense is not something to be solved, but something so given, and so radically self-giving, that it constitutes the basic horizon of life and existence itself. Consequently, all the 'mysteries' of faith are aspects of the one self-giving mystery of God which, even as it communicates itself in the Word and Spirit, remains ever beyond any finite grasp. Even in the beatific vision of God face-to-face, the inexhaustible infinities of the divine reality are not comprehended. In that final vision, the divine mystery is not lessened in the life of the blessed, but more positively appreciated in its boundless excess.

In this perspective, the mystery of Mary in the life of the People of God can be helpfully appreciated as 'saturated phenomenon' (Jean-Luc Marion). It so permeates Christian consciousness as to demand a special kind of receptivity appropriate to the gift of revelation itself. Christian theology, through it is 'faith seeking understanding', can get lost in refined conceptualism and systematic control unless it is phenomenologically grounded in a 'faith receptive to the distinctiveness of what has been so given'. There is an 'excess' of the divine self-giving that overflows and disrupts the mundane routines of human experience and rational control.

In line with such a phenomenological perspective, this article is presented in four main sections:

1. A phenomenologically attuned theology of Mary;[4]
2. Doctrinal Development: The Marian Catalyst;
3. Key Terms in the Marian phenomenon;
4. Seven evocative correlations.

A Phenomenologically Attuned Theology of Mary

Fundamental to a phenomenological approach is receptivity to what is given on its own terms. It must be allowed to impose itself on the

---

3. For a seminal article, see Karl Rahner, 'The Concept of Mystery in Catholic Theology', in *Theological Investigations IV*, translated by Kevin Smyth (Baltimore, MD: Helicon Press, 1966), 36–73.
4. In have treated these points more extensively in *The Resurrection Effect: Transforming Christian Life and Thought* (Maryknoll, NY: Orbis, 2008). As the title implies, the book was primarily focused on the phenomenon of the Resurrection of the Crucified One, but the 'effect' permeates all Christian life and thought. See especially, chapter 2, 'A Phenomenological Approach to the Resurrection', 24–43.

consciousness of faith in its own singularity. Whether it is the Christian phenomenon as a whole, or the place of Mary within it, what has been *so* given, must be allowed to disclose itself in its own way. That is to say that the phenomenon, least of all in the realm of faith, does not show itself as already circumscribed by the abstract, systematic generalizations of the rational ego that are already in place. Neither human nor divine possibilities are so pre-established. In the teeming, elusive relativities of the postmodern world, there is an opportunity for Christian faith to show not only the courage of its own convictions, but also to act with a fresh receptivity to the distinctiveness of revelation, and so witness to the prodigal excess of the gift from which it is born.[5]

What has been so given constitutes the *data* for Christian intelligence. More deeply, it is received as the *donum*, the gift, flowing forth from the inexhaustible and ever-continuing self-giving of God in Christ. This prodigality of self-giving saturates every dimension of Christian life. In the light of the resurrection, Christ gives himself as incarnate among us, present in the gift of the Spirit, and in the word of the inspired Scriptures, in the sacraments of the ecclesial community; and, indeed, through the entire universe transformed in him. This manifold self-giving of Christ contains a particular dimension. He gives his Mother to the Church represented by the Beloved Disciple at the foot of the Cross (Jn 19:26–27).

For the moment, we observe simply that the phenomenality of Mary in the life of the Church is saturated with the singularity of the Christ-event in which she stands. In that horizon of grace, Mary is not an idolic or mythological projection of religious sensibilities. She appears, rather, as an iconic 're-presentation' of the Christocentric focus of Christian existence. Her presence is back-lit, as it were, by the 'light from light', to use the phrase from the Nicene Creed. Her singu-

---

5. Jean-Luc Marion's influential trilogy, *Reduction and Givenness: Investigations of Husserl, Heidegger, and Phenomenology*, translated by Thomas A Carlson (Evanston, IL: Northwestern University Press, 1998), *Being Given: Toward a Phenomenology of Givenness*, translated by Jeffrey L Kosky (Stanford, CA: Stanford University Press, 2002), *In Excess: Studies of Saturated Phenomena*, translated by Robyn Horner and Vincent Barraud (New York: Fordham University Press, 2002). For further elaboration and background, see *God Without Being: Hors-Texte*, translated by Thomas A Carlson (Chicago, IL: Chicago University Press, 1991).

lar place in the event of God's self-giving love affects faith's perception of the truth that is revealed, of the identity it confers, of the community it forms, and of world-renewing praxis it inspires. When the Christian community contemplates the Marian phenomenon in all its dimensions, faith is not distracted from the realm of light inaccessible (1 Tim 6:16). Nor does it turn from the light that shines through the face of Christ (2 Cor 4:6). Rather, the figure of Mary gestures toward the source of light itself. She represents the intentionality of faith in its receptivity to the Christ-event. In the words of Elizabeth's greeting, 'Blessed is she who believed that there would be a fulfilment of what was spoken to her by the Lord' (Lk 1:45). Mary has surrendered to the incalculable significance of what is being revealed, and yielded to its unfolding in time. In her maternal receptivity to God's self-involvement in the world, 'Mary treasured all these words and pondered them in her heart' (Lk 2:19), for 'his mother treasured all these things in her heart' (Lk 2:51). She embodies the heart of faith surrendering to the God for whom 'nothing will be impossible' (Lk 1:37).

For Mary, the mystery is not only in her heart and mind; for she is also *in* it in the wholeness of her being. She is caught up in excess of what is taking place, within the event itself, and participating in its unfolding in history. Given to faith in the saturated phenomenon of Christ, she is 'in Christ' in her uniqueness. She pre-figures the transformatively new: 'if anyone is in Christ, there is a new creation: everything old has passed away; see, everything has become new' (2 Cor 5:17). As the Virgin Mother of Jesus, as Mother of the Church, already possessed by the Holy Spirit, she intimately belongs to this 'new creation'. Though what we shall be is not yet revealed (1 Jn 3:2), the destined transformation of all is anticipated in Mary. As Mother of Christ, head and members, she witnesses to the incalculable rebirth of all in the Spirit. She represents in her person that such a world-changing event is not a time-conditioned *fait accompli*, but an ongoing drama for human freedom. In this regard, she represents the adventure of the Christian vocation, in the deepest meaning of the word, *ad venturum*, literally, 'toward the one who will come'. She stands at the point where human existence has been made open to the imaginable future of 'God all in all' (1 Cor 15:28). She stands, therefore, within the event of God's self-revelation as its servant and witness.[6] In this measure, the event of God's entry into human his-

---

6. See Kelly, *The Resurrection Effect*, 29–42 as it calls on Marion, *Being Given*, 234–236.

tory shows its 'anarchic', irreducibly original character in the Virgin Mother. She proclaims the grace she has received, witnessing to the God who 'scatters the proud in the thoughts of their hearts', who brings down the powerful from their thrones, exalting the lowly, and filling the hungry with good things (*cf* Lk 1:48–53).

As the history of Christian art testifies, Mary has inspired the deepest feelings for the beautiful, to give faith's dim apprehension of the glory to be revealed a focus and embodiment. In the divine beauty that plays on her, the mundane house of human experience must be arranged to let in new possibilities. The aesthetic character of God's self-disclosure has provoked refined responses in theological phenomenology.[7] God enters the human world by appealing to the intimations of beauty and longing that stir the human heart. Speaking of art more generally, a noted critic, George Steiner, makes a telling point. To appreciate any work of art, be it a poem, a painting, a sculpture or a great piece of music, we must enter wholly into it and breathe the sense of life it evokes. We do not behold it from the outside, but give ourselves over to entering into the world it depicts. Art transforms consciousness. It reorients our existence by inspiring sensitivities to what has previously been hidden or overlooked. Beauty enacted in art evokes a deeper awareness of the mystery of being and the depths of experience. It has a transformative impact, even as it witnesses to the transcendent. Steiner, a European intellectual of Jewish background, finds in the image of the Annunciation an evocation of aesthetic dimensions usually bracketed out of our routine experience:

> the shorthand image is that of the Annunciation, of 'a terrible beauty' or gravity breaking into the small house of our cautionary being. If we have heard rightly the wing-beat and the provocation of that visit, the house is no longer habitable in quite the same way as before. A mastering intrusion has shifted the light . . .[8]

---

7. Hans Urs von Balthasar, *The Glory of the Lord. A Theological Aesthetics I: Seeing the Form*, translated by Erasmo Leiva-Merikakis, edited by Joseph Fessio, SJ and John Riches (Edinburgh: T&T Clark, 1982); David Bentley Hart, *The Beauty of the Infinite: The Aesthetics of Christian* Truth (Grand Rapids, MI: Eerdmans, 2003).
8. George Steiner, *Real Presences* (Chicago: Chicago University Press, 1996), 143.

To use Steiner's image, Mary stands at the point where the light shifts, and a larger horizon opens up. When the Angel Gabriel is sent to Mary to announce that she is to be the mother of Jesus, the Messiah, the measure of 'the small house' of our humanly-bounded existence is made open to another presence—the One she is to conceive. Around her gathers the 'terrible beauty' and 'gravity' of God's self-revelation with its 'transformative summons'.

As the Mother of Christ, she is now related to the Church as a unique member of his transformed body of Christ. For from her flesh, Christ was born; and in her flesh, she is united with him in his glory.[9] Her 'body' or 'flesh' is saturated with a special sense of immediacy and unobjectifiable intimacy with her Son, a field communication with God, in mutual indwelling and self-disclosure. Her whole bodily being has been re-experienced in the flesh of Christ,[10] to incarnate the form of self-giving love for those who are 'members, one of another' (Eph 4:25), 'for no one ever hates his own flesh, but he nourishes and tenderly care for it, just as Christ does for the church, because we are members of his body' (Eph 5:30). The Letter to the Ephesians does not hesitate to appeal to the most intimate, ecstatic and generative human experience of the body in sponsal love to express Christ's relationship to the ecclesial body. Just as man and woman become "one flesh" (Gn 2:23; Mt 19:6; Mk 10:8), the risen One is one flesh with the community of believers. As the human mother of Jesus, she is 'one flesh' with her son. In the realm of the new creation, she is now 'one flesh' with him in a nuptial sense (*cf* Gen 2:23; Mt 19:6; Mk 10:8)—for Christ has 'made her holy' (Eph 5:26) and presented her 'to himself in splendour, without spot or wrinkle' (v 27).

When the face of Mary is turned toward the Church, her features reveal something of the invisible totality of Christ, the son she holds

---

9. John Paul II, *Redemptoris Mater*:

    Mary, as the Mother of Christ, is in a particular way united with the Church, 'which the Lord established as his own body'... It is significant that the conciliar text places this truth about the Church as the Body of Christ... in close proximity to the truth that the Son of God 'through the power of the Holy Spirit was born of the Virgin Mary'. The reality of the Incarnation finds a sort of extension in the mystery of the Church-the Body of Christ. And one cannot think of the reality of the Incarnation without referring to Mary, the Mother of the Incarnate Word (No 5). <http://www.vatican.va/holy_father/john_paul_ii/encyclicals/documents/hf_jp-ii_enc_25031987_redemptoris-mater_en.html>

10. Marion, *Le phénomène érotique*, 185.

within her. Her gaze makes its own demands: 'Do whatever he tells you' (Jn 2:5). Her face is not a mirror reflecting back our own image, but more a window through which the light of an arresting otherness breaks through. Paul speaks expansively of Christ, 'the image of the invisible God' (Col 1:15). It calls forth prayer, adoration and self-surrender. The *eikon* of Christ inspires a waiting and longing for his final appearance, typified in the earliest recorded Christian prayer, Maranatha, 'Come, Lord!' (1 Cor 16:22; Rev 22:20).[11] Mary thus turns to the faithful with the features of one who been found among those who 'look upon the one whom they have pierced' (Jn 19:37). She is an anticipation of the promised 'face to face' vision (1 Cor 13:12), for already the God of light has shone in her heart 'to give the light of the knowledge of the glory of God in the face of Christ' (2 Cor 4:6).

These brief evocations of the 'saturated phenomenon' of Mary in the life of the Church—in relation to the event, the radiance, the flesh, and the face of Christ—have a certain equivalent expression in the Anglican-Roman Catholic document, *Mary: Grace and Hope in Christ* (2004).[12] She is "the pattern" of grace and hope. She belongs to the 'celebration of important aspects of our common Christian heritage', as the 'exemplar of faithful obedience', the expression of 'grace-filled response' to the divine intention to unite all in the 'body of Christ'. As such, she is 'the figure of the Church' as open in 'receptivity' to the Spirit—a point of 'convergence' in the worship of 'a vast community of love and prayer'.[13] The document looks back to common Chris-

---

11. Marion, *In Excess*, 124.
12. <http://www.vatican.va/roman_curia/pontifical_councils/chrstuni/angl-comm-docs/rc_pc_chrstuni_doc_20050516_mary-grace-hope-christ_en.html>
13. From *Mary: Grace and Hope in Christ*, Introduction:

> Our Agreed Statement concerning the Blessed Virgin Mary as *pattern* of grace and hope is a powerful reflection of our efforts to seek out what we hold in common and celebrates important aspects of our common heritage. Mary, the mother of our Lord Jesus Christ, *stands before us as an exemplar* of faithful obedience, and her 'Be it to me according to your word' is the grace-filled **response** each of us is called to make to God, both personally and communally, as the Church, the **body** of Christ. It is as *figure* of the Church, her arms uplifted in prayer and praise, her hands open in *receptivity* and availability to the outpouring of the Holy Spirit, that we are one with Mary as she magnifies the Lord. 'Surely', Mary declares in her song recorded in the Gospel of Luke, 'from this day all generations will call me blessed.' [my emphasis]

tian traditions and the Trinitarian and ecclesial dimensions implied.[14] Inherent in such common traditions is the forward-looking 'eschatological' significance of Mary for Christian faith and hope.[15] All such considerations figure in a 're-reception' of Marian doctrine in the interests of a deeper ecumenical consensus. Since this would imply, along with the necessary historical and theological studies, a greater attentiveness to the experiential roots of faith at the level of mind, heart, feeling, imagination and responsibility, I have reflected first on a fresh 'receptivity' to the Marian phenomenon, the better to enable a re-reception on the level of doctrine.

A freshly 'receptive' re-reception becomes necessary when previous forms have become too narrow and ossified. Fundamentalisms, of either devotional or intellectual kinds, bring forth their own kinds of ideological projections and polarisations. The older self-contained Mariology of dogmatic theology can no longer be simply retrieved. It is a matter of finding a new focus within a fresh horizon, expansive enough to allow for the convergence of scriptural witness, doctrinal traditions, liturgy, art and devotion in ecclesial faith.

Though attempting a more phenomenological approach to figure of Mary, I am not stopping short at some form of purely aesthetic appreciation of the impact of Mary on Christian consciousness. Hence, the importance of emphasizing that, from beginning to end, Mary is situated within the summons of Christian conversion to the reign of God as Christ proclaimed it. She stands therefore within the salvific economy of God's self-revelation. Within this theocentric focus, a fresh receptivity to the Marian phenomenon will work as a *reprise* and a 're-presentation' of the theological themes embedded in Christian story of grace and salvation, in the particular manner in which she receives and gives. Within this 'trajectory of grace and hope', the entire sweep of salvation history comes into focus: cre-

---

14. *Mary: Grace and Hope in Christ*:

> This tradition has at its core the proclamation of the Trinitarian 'economy of salvation', grounding the life and faith of the Church in the divine communion of Father, Son and Spirit. We have sought to understand Mary's person and role in the history of salvation and the life of the Church in the light of a theology of divine grace and hope. Such a theology is deeply rooted in the enduring experience of Christian worship and devotion (No 4).

15. *Mary: Grace and Hope in Christ*, No 52.

ation, the election of the Chosen People, the incarnation, ministry, death, resurrection and ascension of Christ, the gift of the Spirit in the Church, all leading to eternal life and creation transformed.[16] If Christ is the Yes to all God's promises, and the Amen to all our prayers (2 Cor 1:18–20),[17] Mary appears in the radiance of the divine affirmation of our humanity, just as her *fiat*, 'Be it done unto me according to your word', (Lk 1:38), is a radical endorsement of the Amen of the human surrender to the ways of God.

Doctrinal Development: The Marian Catalyst

While a more refined receptivity to the Marian phenomenon means more than a synthesis of the Church's Marian doctrines, the figure of Mary cannot be abstracted from doctrinal developments and the intertwining of Trinitarian, Christological and ecclesial questions.[18] It was not until the fifth century, in the Council of Ephesus (431), that Mary was declared to be *Theotokos*, the 'God-bearer', the Mother of God.[19] A huge doctrinal development had been in progress over those five centuries, as is evidenced in the early councils of Nicaea (325), Ephesus (431) and Chalcedon (451). The issue turned on the distinctive truth of Christian faith. How were Christians to speak of the divine reality itself? Was God personally revealed in the incarnation? Was the incarnate Word truly and personally human, or merely gesturing in a figurative humanity? In fact, Christian thinkers, in their various attempts to answer such questions, went some of the way with the great pagan philosophers who had formed the culture in which Christian theology operated. Both Christian theologians and pagan philosophers had one common concern. Both wanted to lay to rest the lurid, polytheistic extravagances of ancient mythologies, and so to concentrate on the one, true, good ultimate reality from which everything came. But the intelligence of faith could not rest there. It had to account for the distinctive reality of what had been revealed;

---

16. *Mary: Grace and Hope in Christ*, No 6.
17. *Mary: Grace and Hope in Christ*, No 5.
18. For a critical evaluation of the emergence of early devotion or 'cult' of the Virgin Mary, a valuable collection of articles is found in *The Origins of the Cult of the Virgin Mary*, edited by Chris Maunder (London: Burns and Oates, 2008).
19. See Richard M Price, 'The *Theotokos* and the Council of Ephesus', in Maunder, *The Origins of the Cult of the Virgin Mary*, 89–104.

and, to that degree, to go beyond what even the best of what Greek philosophy had to offer. The faith, that through these early centuries had prayed, celebrated, suffered and pondered its mysteries, led to an understanding of God in completely un-Greek terms. Not only was God the creative source of the universe, but lovingly related to the world. There was indeed only one God. However, that one God was never solitary in perfection, but existed in the life of Trinitarian communion, three divine persons inter-related in an eternal vitality. This divine Trinity not only freely created the world, but had lovingly reached into the world in order to draw it into God's own life—so that God would be 'all in all' (1 Cor 15:28). [20] Furthermore, if the revealed God were so self-giving, as Father, Son and Holy Spirit, how must faith speak of the 'self' that God had to give? In the light of Christ's resurrection, everything about God, our world and our humanity—and about Mary—had to be re-evaluated and re-imagined. Indeed, unless Christ had risen from the dead, there would be no New Testament, no Church, no Trinitarian doctrines, and no Marian presence to Christian faith and hope.[21]

The confession of Mary as *Theotokos* occurred at a vital juncture in the development of Church teaching of the one person of Christ, true God and true man.[22] His humanity was not an apparent or 'docetic' humanity, for he was truly born of a human mother—'consubstantial with the Father according to his divinity, and consubstantial with us according to his humanity' (Chalcedon, 451).[23] At the same time, her virginal conception by the Holy Spirit[24] pointed to the divinity of her son—and the unique dignity of Mary's role in the incarnation. Because Christ is one person, Mary was not merely the mother of his humanity, but truly the mother of the divine person who had entered human history: she was the mother of the Word incarnate.[25] In the words of Chalcedon, 'One and the same Son . . . was begotten

---

20. See Anthony J Kelly, 'Mystery and Definition', in *The Trinity of Love. A Theology of the Christian God* (Wilmington, Del: Michael Glazier, 1989), 59–64.
21. See Kelly, *The Resurrection Effect*, 44–78.
22. *Mary: Grace and Hope in Christ*, No 31.
23. *The Christian Faith in the Doctrinal Documents of the Catholic Church* (revised edition), edited by J Neuner SJ and J Dupuis SJ (London: Collins, 1982), No 614–615.
24. *Mary: Grace and Hope in Christ*, No 33.
25. *Mary: Grace and Hope in Christ*, No 34.

from the Father before the ages as to the divinity and in the latter days for us and our salvation was born as to the humanity from Mary the Virgin Mother of God'.[26] In this doctrinal development, Mary, as the Virgin-Mother of the Incarnate Word, was understood not as a mythological regression, but as the focal point in the elaboration of the reality of the incarnation.[27]

The confession of Mary as *Theotokos*, as the virginal God-bearer, was both the stimulus and the product of intense theological efforts to clarify what the Church actually believed and meant in its fundamental Trinitarian and Christological faith. In reference to her, the great poem of Christian faith found a doctrinal vocabulary consistent enough to enable it to break free from pagan myths and traditional philosophy. There could be no going back to the goddess-worship that Israel had rejected when it encountered the fertility goddesses and the practices of ritual prostitution of its surrounding regions.[28] In New Testament times, Paul's preaching had provoked fierce reaction in Ephesus (Acts 19:23–41). His preaching of the Gospel threatened the cult of Artemis (or Diana as she was called in Rome). Demetrius, the silversmith who had a piece of the roaring trade in statuettes of the goddess, denounced Paul and his associates for undermining the local temple worship—and so for posing a threat to his profits: 'Great is Artemis of the Ephesians!' (Acts 19:34) was the indignant slogan. But the Christian veneration of Mary, emerging as it did from the

---

26. *The Christian Faith...*, No 624.
27. By the end of the fifth century, commemoration of Mary as 'God-bearer' had become practically universal in the liturgies of East and West. The earliest prayer to Mary dates from the mid third century: *Sub tuum praesidium, sancta Dei Genetrix*, while the doctrinal developments of Ephesus and Chalcedon found an enduring prayerful expression in the Akathist hymn to 'Our Lady the God-bearer and Virgin Mother'. By the end of the fourth century, churches began to be dedicated to Mary and a variety of feasts celebrated in the liturgy. See *Mary: Grace and Hope in Christ*, No 39–40. On a more theological level, see Antonia Antanossova, 'Did Cyril of Alexandria Invent Mariology?', in Maunder, *The Origins of the Cult of the Virgin Mary*, 105–126.
28. See the informative section of George Tavard, *The Thousand Faces of the Virgin Mary* (Collegeville, MN: Liturgical Press, 1996), 221–247: Canaan and Syria had Anath, Astarte and Asherah; the Balylonians venerated Ishtar, while Phrygia had Cybele, the Great Mother; whereas Egypt revered quite a pantheon of female deities (Hathor, Matit, Medfet, Wadjet, and the goddess of learning, Nekhbit, and, above all, Isis.

texts of the New Testament itself, did not regard her as a new temple goddess, nor as female substitute for the deity.[29]

In short, Mary is an icon of the divine, one in whom the light of God shines through; and so, not as an idolic projection of human fabrication. She belonged to a different order of reality. In the unfolding of revelation, she had her own place. It was never doubted that she was a finite, human being. She was an historical woman. Though she, along with everyone else, was redeemed, she occupied a unique position in God's saving design. She stood at the point where the light shifted. As the theology of God developed, so did a theological understanding of Mary and its consequent devotional affectivity find its centre and personal focus.

But with the Reformation in the sixteenth century, Marian doctrines and devotions became a source of division, despite Luther's keen theological appreciation of Mary and his inspiring commentary on the *Magnificat*. The besetting problem, of course, was what was perceived as devotional excesses taking away from the sole mediation of Christ. Later still, the snag was Catholic ecclesiology as the Magisterium proceeded to define as solemn doctrines of the Immaculate Conception (1854) and the Assumption (1950)—which, to the Protestant mind, had no clear scriptural basis. A more theological and ecumenical shift in the Catholic receptivity to the Marian phenomenon occurred in efforts to integrate the mystery of Mary into the life of the Church, as in chapter 8 of the Constitution on the Church, *Lumen Gentium*.[30] Paul VI sought to remove any implication of diminishing the role of Mary soon after the end of Vatican II, and to place Mary in the larger context of grace, Christ and the Church, with his Apostolic Exhortation, *Marialis Cultus* in 1974.[31] John Paul II,

---

29. See John Mc Guckin, 'The Early Cult of Mary and Inter-Religious Contexts in the Fifth Century Church', in Maunder, *The Origins of the Cult of the Virgin Mary*, 1–22, for a comprehensive and incisive overview.
30. The aim was 'to explain carefully both the role of the Blessed Virgin in the mystery of the Word Incarnate and of the Mystical Body, as well as the duties of the redeemed human race towards the God-bearer, mother of Christ and mother of humanity, especially of the faithful' (*Lumen Gentium*, #54). This more patristic emphasis on the Christological and ecclesial placed Mary in the broader context of Church life and faith (#68–69) as a sign of hope and encouragement for the pilgrim People of God.
31. Paul VI, *Marialis Cultus*, (AAS 66 (1974) 113–168). Note also the preceding documents, the Encyclical Letter, *Christi Matri* (AAS 58 (1966) 745–749), and the Apostolic Exhortation, *Signum Magnum* (AAS 59 (1967) 465–475).

intensely Marian in his spirituality (cf. the Marian significance of his motto, *totus tuus*), in his *Redemptoris Mater* (1987),[32] offered a deeply contemplative exposition of the both conciliar teaching in relation to a wide field of biblical data, and voiced the ecumenical significance of the role of Mary for Christian faith. One fruit of this new receptivity was the ARCIC document, *Mary: Grace and Hope in Christ*.

Key Terms in the Marian phenomenon

In this respect, the Marian phenomenon occurs as the matrix of four converging perspectives. Mary is given to faith:

- in her relation to the *dramatis personae*, the Father, Son and Holy Spirit, of God's Trinitarian self-revelation;
- as participating in the paschal enactment in the death and resurrection of Christ;
- as belonging to the sacramental actualisation in the Church throughout history;
- as anticipating the eschatological realisation of God's design.

Seven evocative (and irreplaceable, even if equivalent) theological terms interplay within the language of faith: Father, Son, Cross, Resurrection, Spirit, Church, and eschatological fulfilment.[33] These, in turn, can be related to the Johannine 'short formula', 'God is love' (1 Jn 4:8, 16).[34] What is expressed thereby is the conviction that the love of God is the source, form and end of all existence. The revelation of God's self-giving love was the matrix from which the doctrine of the Trinity emerged within the consciousness of the Church. The doctrinal challenge suggested above consisted in articulating as accurately as possible the meaning of the Johannine statement: 'Everyone who loves is born of God and knows God. Whoever does not love does not

---

32. John Paul II, *Redemptoris Mater*
33. I have chosen this particular order for present purposes, while acknowledging that any of them can be the starting point with a different ordering as a result. I would emphasise, however, that no one of these terms (or its equivalent) can be omitted from any account of Christian faith, without causing a serious distortion.
34. Bernard Sesboüé, 'Le Groupe des Dombes: Marie dans le dessein de Dieu', *Etudes*, No 3884, Avril 1998, 513–519.

know God, for God is love' (1 Jn 4:8).³⁵ It invites an active participation in the revealed mystery with profound epistemological consequences: 'Beloved, let us love one another, because love is from God; everyone who loves is born of God and knows God' (1 Jn 4:7)

Thus, the theological impact of the Marian phenomenon is manifested in the excess of love implied in:

1. the primordial initiative of the *Father*;
2. the self-giving represented in the *Son*;
3. the unconditional love of the *Cross*;
4. the transformative power of the *Resurrection*;
5. the gift of the *Spirit*, communicated throughout history;
6. the historical and sacramental form of the *Church*;
7. the *eschatological* consummation of the divine design.

Each of these seven terms is evocative of the holographic event of God's self-revelation as it saturates Christian consciousness. Each of these seven 'flash points' in the Christian narrative invites faith to reflect how Mary 'shifts the light', so to speak, and embodies the 'transformative summons' that Steiner spoke of. In each case, Mary acts and reveals because she has first received.

Seven Evocative Correlations

Father

The New Testament's naming of God as *Father* suggests that 'God is love' in an utterly original way.³⁶ The source of all creation is God's eternal and primordial begetting of divine Word, the only-begotten Son. Through the Son, the Father freely conceives of the whole universe, and calls it into existence. In his Word and Spirit, the Father loves everything into being:³⁷ 'In this is love, not that we loved God, but that he loved us, and sent his Son to be the atoning sacrifice for

---

35. See Kelly, *The Trinity of Love*, 141–173.
36. See Anthony J Kelly and Francis J Moloney, *The Experience of God in the Gospel of John* (New York: Paulist, 2003), 389–394.
37. Note, of course, the sheer gifted quality of God's love: it presupposes nothing, so that 'the love of God is ever creating and inpouring the goodness of things' (*amor Dei est creans et infundens bonitatem in rebus*). See Aquinas, *STh* 1, q. 20, a. 2).

our sins' (1 Jn 4:10). From this first divine person comes the initiative more original than any human effort and preceding all created possibilities of responding or believing. In this regard, God's primal love is more original than any original sin. It comes before any consideration of human merit or guilt. God's free grace is determined by no human worth or good work (Ps 139:13–16; Jer 1:4–5; Rom 8:28–30; 2 Tim 1:9)

In relation to God as Father, how is Mary a living icon of God's love? How does the motherhood of Mary affect the Christian understanding of the Fatherhood of God? In the long history of Catholic and Orthodox liturgical and spiritual traditions, an answer is found only on a lived, implicit level. However further articulated, it is ever the case that Mary receives. Through what Catholics have come to call her 'Immaculate Conception', Mary uniquely embodies humanity under the antecedent sway of grace—to be freed from all stain of original sin. The God-ordained destiny of all is eminently expressed in her special giftedness. As St Paul exultantly prays,

> Blessed by the God and Father of our Lord Jesus Christ, who has blessed us in Christ with every spiritual blessing in the heavenly places, just as he chose us in Christ before the foundation of the world to be holy and blameless before him in love (Eph 1:3–4).

The perverse 'originality' of sin consisted in its power to infect human history with murderous violence and enmity (Gen 4:1–16). To be preserved free from such complicity in evil means that Mary has nothing within her to close her against others. She is uninfected by the bias of evil and pride. She is originally open to the all-inclusive totality of God's saving will. Her vocation is to be a purely generative influence in human history. Grace, God's original and unstinted gift, has destined her to be the New Eve, 'the mother of all the living' (Gen 3:20). In Christian terms, she is the Mother of the whole Christ, head and members.

Though gifted with a singular destiny, she is in no sense divine. Every element of her being is God-given; all her grace has been received. As the Mother of Christ, she is creation at its most generative, 'Blessed among women'. She is 'full of grace' and freed from sin as the chosen associate of the eternally generative Father. Thus, in the fullness of time, she becomes the human Mother of his Son: 'For the Mighty One has done great things for me . . .' (Lk 1:49). Her receptivity to God is the foundation of her gracious relationship to all.

Her receptivity to the Father results in a unique role. To her alone it is given to be the Mother of God, *Theotokos*, the 'God-bearer'. To confess her as the Mother of *God* means to acknowledge her as the human mother of the Word made flesh. A distorted, minimalist view of Mary's motherhood would see her as only the mother of the body or human nature of Christ in the Nestorian sense. But no mother is ever simply a producer of a nature or a body. The physical and generative aspects of motherhood occur within the world of persons. Because motherhood is interpersonal, Mary is personally related to her son, to the person he is, in his radical identity as 'God from God, Light from Light'. The genesis of the universe has needed fifteen billion years. Life has emerged from primitive matter and reaches a luminous peak in human consciousness. The religious searching of Israel's faith in God at work in all things culminates in her consent to be the mother of Jesus. The One who was in the beginning, within the eternal procession of the Son from the Father, now has a new beginning in the fabric and history of the created cosmos. The eternally begotten Son is really brought forth in her. Through her, he is born into the world of creation, subjected to it. 'Born of a woman' (Gal 4:4), he would know poverty, live in surrender to the Father's will, enter into the risk of living for the Kingdom of God—and suffer the consequences. By having this human mother, the divine Son is not posturing in humanity. He is incarnate, enfleshed, born as the divine Word, into the pain, darkness and joy of human existence. In the womb of Mary, the world holds a divine reality within it: the Mother of Jesus is the Mother of God.

In her bringing forth the Christ in the power of the Spirit, Mary receives and reveals—as an icon of the Father. Through her Immaculate Conception she is located in that realm of mercy in which 'God so loved the world' (Jn 3:16). She gives her consent at the Annunciation to be the Mother of 'the holy one' (Lk 1:38). She takes the initiative in visiting Elizabeth and witnesses to the overturning power of God in her *Magnificat*. She brings forth her child and ponders the mysteries of God in her heart (Lk 2:19). Simeon foretells the sword that will pierce her heart (Lk 2:35) if she consent to the transcendent divine purpose to be accomplished through her son. In such ways she is participating in the generative love of the Father. The Father will declare in the moment of the Transfiguration, 'This is my beloved Son, listen to him' (Mk 9:7). This divine declaration is echoed in her command at the marriage feast of Cana: "Do whatever he tells you' (Jn 2:5).[38] Her radical surrender to the self-giving love of God will lead her finally to the Cross. There she stands with the Beloved Disciple. Now that the 'hour' of Jesus has come, he gives his disciple to his Mother, and presents her, in turn, to him (Jn 19:25–27).[39] Suggesting her mediating role amongst the earliest followers and blood relatives of Jesus, Luke locates in the community awaiting the outpouring of the Spirit (Acts 1:14). The Holy Spirit who will come from above onto the early Church is the same Spirit that came upon her to enable her to conceive Jesus at the beginning of his human life.

These luminous New Testament perspectives bring Mary into focus as the woman on whom the play of light shifts and intensifies. A light not of this world makes this woman an icon of the generative, life-giving love of the Father. For all the generations that call her blessed, and hear the words of Jesus, 'Behold, your mother' (Jn 20:27) and take her to themselves,[40] she expresses in a unique manner the tenderness of God, and invitation to 'the perfect love that casts out fear' (1 Jn 4:18). Just as the Father has given what is most intimately his own for the salvation of the world, she has entered into such unreserved self-giving. She brings into the world the One whom the Father eternally begets. In time and place, she gives what the Father has given and in the way that God gives, to offer this Son of the Father and her child for the world's salvation: 'God's love was revealed among us in this way. God sent his only Son into the world that we might live through him' (1 Jn 4:9). Thus, Mary figures in the drama of the divine self-giving love intent on bringing life to the world.

Mary's maternal love is the historical human manifestation of the Father's generative love. She is not an idol fabricated by human projections, but a woman in whom the Light shines through. As an icon of the Father in this way, she subverts the religious imagination that would see the ultimate origin in rigidly masculine terms. When the generative, self-giving love of the Father is disclosed in history

---

38. Kelly and Moloney, *The Experience of God*, 69–70.
39. Kelly and Moloney, *The Experience of God*, 364–368.
40. Kelly and Moloney, *The Experience of God*, 365–366.

through the love of this mother, there are consequences. In the interactions of faith and culture, the whole play of human language and symbolism must be deployed in expressing the infinities of God's life and love. She is 'perfect' as 'your Heavenly Father' is (Matt 5:48; Lk 6:36). No particular invocation of God, even under the name of 'Father', can be so absolutised as to curtail the play of the expressiveness of faith and human experience. The name of God who lives in unapproachable light is hallowed neither by dead metaphors, nor by jaded ideologies. The language of faith must be restlessly imaginative. In the current critical task of exploring the meaning of God as Father,[41] theology finds a resource, at once simple and evocative: the motherhood of Mary is a symbol of the Fatherhood of God.

Son

In the invocation of Christ as the *Son*, the affirmation, 'God is love', resonates as an expression of God's unique self-utterance and self-giving. The incarnation in all its aspects is the climactic divine self-involvement in creation. God does not simply intervene by doing something *for* us—'for us and our salvation'—but becomes personally someone *with* us in the sphere of creation. Christ is *Emmanuel*, 'God-with-us' (Matt 1:23). The Word is made flesh (Jn 1:14). The generative love that is the source of all creation gives into the flesh of our existence its most intimate self-expression: 'This is my beloved Son: hear him!' (Mk 9:7).

The magi in the Gospel of Matthew (Matt 2:11) and the shepherds in that of Luke (Lk 2:16) find Jesus with his mother. And as the Mother of Jesus she embodies the self-giving character of God's love. Yet she gives because she has first received. As the first of the redeemed, she receives all from her Son, for the Word is given into the faith and flesh of her existence. In this receptivity—for apart from him, she, like all believers, can do nothing (Jn 15:5)—she is drawn into the most intimate association with her Son's mission. The Father's 'listen to him!' (*cf* Mk 9:7) echoes in her instruction to the servants at Cana, 'Do whatever he tells you' (Jn 2:5). The words of Jesus are verified in her: 'My Father is glorified by this, that you bear much fruit and become

---

41. Anthony J Kelly, '"Come to the Father": A Theology of the Fatherhood of God', in *The Australasian Catholic Record* lxxvii/3 (July 1999): 281–291.

my disciples' (John 15:8). She indeed bears 'much fruit'. She becomes the Mother of Christ, and the mother of all the faithful. Jesus on the cross instructs her, 'Woman, behold, your son!' (Jn 19:26). The 'son' here is the Beloved Disciple, the embodiment of immediate and unreserved faith. She is now not simply his sister in the new family of God, but his mother: 'Behold, your Mother' (Jn 20:27).

Cross

The revelation that 'God is love' cannot be separated from the dramatic event of the *Cross*. God's love is disclosed as unconditional and without reserve. It keeps on being love even when exposed to the deepest darkness of the world's evil. At the point where human malice is most manifest in crucifying the Son, the love that God is, keeps on being love as limitless mercy: 'Father, forgive them for they do not know what they are doing' (Lk 23:34). Love at once unmasks and subverts the desperate violence of the loveless.[42]

Here, too, Mary gives as she has received. Greeted by Gabriel as the woman uniquely favoured by God (Lk 1:28, 30), she follows her Son in his mission, and suffers the piercing of soul that Simeon foretold (Lk 2:35). She has been given the Beloved Disciple by the dying Jesus (Jn 20:26). On her, and on this disciple, amongst those gathered at the foot of the cross as representatives of the new community of faith, the Spirit of Jesus has been given: 'Then he bowed his head and handed over the Spirit' (Jn 19:30). A new community of Christ-like selfless love has been born. It must stand against the violently idolatrous self-promotion of this world and its 'ruler' (Jn 14:30; 16:11), by witnessing to another form of community and life.

In that community of faith, Mary is invoked as the Mother of Mercy. She represents the gentle, ever-persistent presence of the Reign of God, that other kingdom that owes nothing to the inhuman rule of violence and hatred. When challenged by Pilate, Jesus had answered, 'My kingdom is not from here . . For this was I born, and for this I came into the world, to testify to the truth. Everyone who belongs to the truth listens to my voice' (Jn 19:36–37). Jesus' refers to the realm opposed to the murderous self-justifications of power and

---

42. On this theme, following the thought of René Girard, Gil Bailie, *Violence Unveiled. Humanity at the Crossroads* (New York: Crossroad, 1997).

pride. Pilate's unease is evident in his response, 'What is truth?' (Jn 19:38). The self-glorifying power of the world relegates the kingdom of the true God to the unreal. The 'real world' is constructed on the self-serving ambitions of ruthless power. Its political vocabulary dare not include words such as compassion, forgiveness, humility, obedience to God, self-sacrificing love . . . The Beatitudes leave it tongue-tied. It has no time for such 'useless'—and dangerous—notions.

But Mary belongs to the truth and has heard its voice. There are those who pray to her, 'Holy Mary, Mother of God, pray for us sinners, now and at the hour of our death'. Their prayer arises from an awareness of the seductive power of evil and the fragility of human freedom. In such a world, love is a scarce resource. If it exists, it is a pact amongst those who in effect reject others outside their circle. But to love as God loves, is to love without conditions or calculations. It is to be vulnerable—in a love that finds its source, support and true measure only in God. In this respect, Mary witnesses to the truth of the love revealed in her Son. By standing before the stark truth of the Cross, she stands against the loveless lie that drives a world of self-enclosure and the exclusion of the powerless. To the degree a culture is permeated by the seven deadly sins,[43] she is something of a threat. Her prayer expresses praise of the God who scatters 'the proud in the thoughts of their hearts'. For her, God is the One who brings down 'the powerful from their thrones' (Lk 1:51–52). In all these ways, Mary at the foot of the cross is a subversive presence.[44]

Resurrection

Only in the light of her Son's resurrection is Mary known to faith. 'God is love' in a divinely transformative event. Though love is never reduced to the level of worldly power, it is not ineffective. It is not defeated by the powers that crucified Jesus. Love has raised him from the tomb to be the form and source of the life in a new creation. Lifted up from the earth, the crucified Son draws all to himself (Jn 11:52; 12:32). He is the ultimate embodiment of the 'love that bears

---

43. Traditionally listed as pride, covetousness, lust, anger, gluttony, envy and sloth.
44. See René Coste, *The Magnificat. The Revolution of God* (Quezon City: Claretian Publications, 1987).

all things, believes all things, hopes all things, endures all things' (1 Cor 13:4-8).

How does the resurrection affect our perception of Mary? Paul wrote to his Corinthian audience: 'Now if Christ is proclaimed as raised from the dead, how can some of you say there is no resurrection from the dead? If there is no resurrection from the dead, then Christ has not been raised, then our proclamation has been in vain and your faith has been in vain' (1 Cor 15:12-15). By celebrating Mary's assumption into heaven, faith in the resurrection of the Lord finds a correlative symbol. The power of the resurrection has flowed into the existence of this pre-eminent believer, to transform her whole being and to perfect her mission. In terms of Paul's indirect description of risen existence (1 Cor 15:42-58), Mary is no longer subject to the rule of death, nor to the dishonour inevitable in the realm of worldly glory, nor to the weakness that worldly power consigns it. Her transformed existence is no long enclosed in the spiritless materialism of a world undisturbed by the creative imagination of God's Spirit. In her union with her Son, 'the resurrection and the life' (Jn 11:25), she exemplifies faith in its radical, defiant and universal hope: 'If for this life only we have hoped in Christ, we are of all people most to be pitied. But in fact Christ has been raised from the dead, the first fruits of those who have died' (1 Cor 15:19).

In the power of her Son's resurrection, Mary now lives and acts: 'Surely, from now on, all the generations will call me blessed' (Lk 1:48). God is not the God of the dead, but of the living (Matt 22:32). She lives, acts, and continues to act, from the heart of God's transforming love through intercessory prayer and compassionate involvement in the great travail of creation (Rom 8:22). Invoked as Our Lady Help of Christians, as the Mother of Mercy and of Grace, as the Mother of Perpetual Help—indeed, in all the invocations of the Litany of Loreto—she is related to all in the communion of saints. She anchors faith, inspires hope, and exemplifies the 'love [that] never ends' (1 Cor 13:8). Assumed into heaven, she collaborates with the New Adam as the New Eve in a maternal relationship with all believers.

Mary of Nazareth is the name of an historical person. Yet history has no record of her except through the documents of faith, above all the Gospels of the New Testament, and in what has been written in the hearts of believers through the ages. She is known to faith through its awareness of the universal transformation anticipated in the resurrection of her Son. She stands where the light has shifted in human hope; where the power of death and evil has been overcome.

Spirit

'God is love' by communicating the gift of the *Spirit* to every age. The love that originated in the Father, that is incarnate in the life, death and resurrection of the Son, is breathed into history as a liberating life-force. The Breath of God is the divine atmosphere invigorating the life of believers in every time and place. In the Spirit, 'the Lord and giver of life', Christ was conceived, the Church brought into being, and all creation moves in a new energy toward its fulfilment (Rom 8:26).

How is Mary linked to this gift of the Spirit? Through the Spirit, the Father begets the Son in eternity. Through the Spirit acting in Virgin Mary, the Father begets his only Son in time. In the words of Gabriel, 'The Holy Spirit will come upon you, and the power of the Most High will overshadow you' (Lk 1:35). God's self-giving love is not restricted or conditioned by what creation can produce in terms of human reproduction or generation. Her virginal maternity discloses the incalculable initiative of the Spirit in regard to all the children of God, 'who were born, not of blood or the will of the flesh or the will of man, but of God' (Jn 1:13). In confessing her precisely as the *Virgin* Mary, faith acts in adoration of the imaginative power of God to bring forth the new. It culminates in the reality of God-with-us—definitively in the Word made flesh, derivatively in everyone who 'is born of the Spirit' (Jn 3:8). Where the Breath of the Spirit plays, it transforms all it touches, including this Jewish woman, Mariam. She receives the Spirit, yet acts in the power of this divine Gift, for she has been chosen to be the created human collaborator in the incarnation itself. Her virginal maternity is a unique 'manifestation of the Spirit for the common good' (1 Cor 12:7). By the power of the Spirit, Jesus is conceived, to be born of the Virgin Mary. Under the inspiration of the Spirit, faith defines her being: she is pure receptivity to the Spirit, pure attention to the Word, pure adoration of the Father: 'My soul magnifies the Lord . . .' (Lk 1:40). She is defined in no other way, by no other relationship—neither by a human partner, nor by social expectations, nor by human ambition, nor even by the common religious notions of her time or ours. What determines her existence is solely what God can be and what God can do. She is the woman who most intimately knows that 'for God nothing is impossible' (Lk 1:37). Yet, in her Spirit-formed existence, divine freedom collaborates communicates with a created freedom. Divine Love calls forth a human love to be its partner in the world's transformation.[45]

In the horizon that refuses to impose any limits on the Spirit and the divine imagination, the Blessed Virgin Mary is invoked in the faith of the Church. In this she stands at the point where the new covenant promised by the prophets of Israel is realised: 'This is the covenant which I will make with the house of Israel after those days, says the Lord: I will put my law within them, and I will write it upon their hearts; and I will be their God, and they shall be my people' (Jer 31:33. *Cf* also, Ezek 36:25–28).

Her virginal maternity has its meaning only within the universe of grace. At this point, faith must learn its own reserve. There is no place for any form of theological voyeurism. All efforts to reduce God's 'impossible ways' to the humanly familiar are in vain. Her identity is disclosed only in the light of the resurrection of her Son and in the consequent outpouring of the Spirit. She is named only in the vocabulary of a new language speaking, with defiant hope, of the world's transformation in Christ. She belongs to the realm where love is revealed as the power at work to make all things new.

When faith turns to Mary, it recognises her unique role in God's self-communication to the world. The Spirit, active in all creation and throughout the 'all generations', brings the world and its history to a unique point of freedom in this woman. She consents on behalf of creation to receive into itself the mystery from which all existence derives. In her free consent to what God is to bring about, she is the world's overture to the power of the Holy Spirit. All the faithfulness of generations before her and after her, all their waiting on God and their yielding to the Spirit, are condensed in her act of self-surrender: 'Be it done unto me according to your Word' (Lk 1:38).

In this 'Virgin Daughter of Sion', all the hopes and faith of her people are condensed. Elizabeth, summing up the Old Testament praise of the faithful, proclaims, 'Blessed is she who believed that there would be a fulfilment of what was spoken to her by the Lord'

---

45. See Anthony J Kelly, *An Expanding Theology. Faith in a World of Connections* (Sydney: EJ Dwyer, 1993), 171–2.

(Lk 1:45). She stands both at the culminating point of the past history of divine promises, and at the beginning of their unheard-of fulfilment. Through her unconditional yielding to what the Spirit alone can accomplish, the Word adored in her faith is conceived in her womb. Henceforth, her whole life and destiny are bound up with her Son and his mission. The virginal motherhood of Mary expresses two essential and related aspects of divine action. First, the Holy Spirit is not reducible to any created power; and, secondly, God acts within the powers and freedom of creation. The incarnation of the eternal Word comes about from beyond, and yet it occurs from within the realm of creation through human cooperation. Precisely because the divine power so transcends the created order, it can work so intimately within to it. Though the Son is incarnate by the power of the Spirit, he is still truly 'born of the Virgin Mary'.

Church

'God is love' looks to an historical and identifiable embodiment from generation to generation in the *Church*. In the pilgrim, sacramental reality of Church, the saving mystery is celebrated and offered to the world. As it mediates Christ to the world, the ecclesial community is an open circle. It lives from, and witnesses to, the grace at work in all lives. It can be considered as that part of world which has woken to the superabundance of God's love.

Standing at the foot of the cross, Mary stands at the foundation of the Church. In the revelatory event of the Cross the figures of the Eve, Church, Mary and Christian discipleship interweave. The first woman was taken from Adam's 'rib' (Gen 2:22, *pleura* LXX) and became the mother of all the living (Gen 3:20). So, too, is Mary in the new community of the Church is the mother of all who receive the gift of eternal life from the water and blood flowing from the pierced side (again, *pleura*, literally 'rib') of the Crucified Jesus (Jn 19:34), and from the Spirit he breathes forth (Jn 19:30, 20:22, *cf* 1 Jn 5:8). In this Johannine perspective, Mary is both the archetype and first realization of the Church.[46] Her unconditional Yes to the design of God takes her to the Cross, and to her place in the community of the disciples, as they await the outpouring of the Spirit that had so pos-

---

46. *Mary: Grace and Hope in Christ*, No 27.

sessed her from the beginning (Acts 1:18). She is a personal symbol of the Church's corporate identity.

Mary is a luminous presence in the 'cloud of witnesses' (Heb 12:1) permeating the atmosphere of faith, a focal presence in the great 'communion of saints' gathered in praising he God of all gifts (*cf* Rev 6:9–11; 7; 8:3–4). In her, the Church finds its paradigm and exemplar of what it is called to be, 'So that she may be holy and without blemish' (*cf* Eph 5:25–27). In union with the Mother of the Redeemer, 'Mother Church' contends with the antagonistic powers of the world. The history of evil, of the Antichrist, contends with 'a great portent in the heaven: a woman clothed with the sun, with the moon under her feet, and on her head a crown of twelve stars. She is pregnant and crying out in birth-pangs in the agony of giving birth' (Rev 12:1–2). A new creation is being born.

Despite the jumbled ambiguity of the actual community of saints and sinners, the Church possesses an unfailing generative holiness: 'Holy Mother Church'. Like Mary, and in union with her, the Church is holy only because God is holy, because the Body of Christ is holy, and because the all-creative Spirit is holy. In the depths of its life, the Church inhales the Holy Spirit. Such holiness does not fail. The inexhaustible source of the Church's holiness is already realised in Mary and the 'holy ones', the saints and the great company of the apostles, martyrs and faithful witnesses in every age. Their influence precedes and accompanies, sustains and blesses the often sorry efforts of the Church in any era.

In all that she has received, in all that she is now for us, Mary is the living, acting embodiment of the God-given holiness of the Church. Whatever the sins of us Christians, individual, political or social, whatever the failings of our institutional leaders, it is only in the Church that we first met Christ, heard the Gospel and celebrated the Eucharist. Mary invites us in every age, even in the face of scandals of all kinds, to be open to the whole reality of the Church. It is always a temptation to become so censoriously fixated in some distorted fragment of the ecclesiastical reality that the holiness of the Church drops out of consideration. Scandal can be a convenient excuse for not being involved in the flesh-and-blood history of faith—with all its demands, risks and ambiguities—by hiding behind our own projections of unliveable excellence. It is possible to become all too anorexic in our appreciation of the Body of Christ in history. The temptation is to invent a self-justifying private religious 'purity', isolated from, and even against, the corporate, pilgrim existence as the Church. A Marian sense of the Church helps faith to keep a sense of proportion. Its confession of the 'holy Church' confronts believers with the grace of God far more humanly incarnate in our midst than any kind of precious, irritated moralism can perceive. Mary is not a compensation for a lack of holiness, but a living invitation to conversion, for she already embodies the holiness to which are called.

Eternal Life

Finally, 'God is love' as gathering believers through Christ and the Spirit into 'the life of the world to come'. Love is at work to bring creation to its fulfilment. The creative source of all that is has made time for the emergence of the world and for the enactment of the whole drama of human freedom. The self-giving love of God is pulsing in every moment of the world's history. It has been active in every event and human agent. It has guided the complex dynamics of this emerging cosmos. All along, God's love has been intent on that final moment of fulfilment in order 'that God may be all in all' (1 Cor 15:28). God is love, therefore, as the first and last word on the divine destiny of all creation, moving towards its final consummation and unveiling. Christ is risen, and 'behold, the new has come' (2 Cor 5:17).

Ambrose of Milan sums up the cosmic scope of what has taken place: 'In Christ's resurrection the world arose. In Christ's resurrection, the heavens arose; in Christ's resurrection the earth itself arose.'[47] In this eschatological perspective, Mary's Assumption is the realisation of her full-bodied possession of eternal life. Here, as in all else, Mary receives from Christ. In anticipation of this universal transformation, Mary, 'assumed body and soul into heaven', is already taken up into the glory of Christ. As with all the grace of Mary, the Assumption is not an exclusively Marian privilege, but the anticipation of transfigured creation and the destiny of the Spirit-charged world.[48] She is the paradigm instance of creation surrendered to the

---

47. *De excessu fratris sui*, bk 1. PL 16, 1354.
48. See Karl Rahner, 'The Interpretation of the Dogma of the Assumption', *Theological Investigations I*, translated by C Ernst (London: Darton, Longman and Todd, 1961), 215–227.

God who transforms all in Christ. Both the generativity and the destiny of God's creation are revealed in her for, as the Advent antiphon has it, 'the earth has been opened to bud forth the Saviour'.

The seer of the Apocalypse invites faith into the vision of 'the holy city, the new Jerusalem, coming down out of heaven from God, prepared as a bride adorned for her husband' (Rev 21:1–3). As the Spirit descended on Mary to make her the Mother of Christ and Mother of the Church, and as she is assumed into glory, the great cosmic marriage is begun. The Spirit has formed in her the particular beauty of creation in the sight of God. In her consent to be the Mother of Christ, history has reached its age of consent—in surrender to the transcendent love for which it was destined (*cf* Eph 5:21–33; Rev 21:9). Out of such a union, the whole Christ of a transfigured creation is born.

Conclusion

By reflecting briefly on seven evocative and irreplaceable terms (*Father, Son Cross, Resurrection, Spirit, Church and eternal life*), we have attempted evoke something of the 'saturated' character of Mary's presence to the Church. In the matrix of this manifold phenomenon, we have suggested something of the meaning of Marian doctrines and symbols guided by the most fundamental of all Christian affirmations, 'God is Love'. While the focus of Christian hope is on Christ's death and resurrection, in Mary it has both a *reprise* and 're-presentation' in anticipation of what is to come. In her, hope celebrates the grace of God, given, received, and working its transformation. In their communion with Mary, Christians become more deeply receptive to the sweep and scope of the unfolding of mystery of mercy 'from age to age to those who revere him' (Lk 1:50).

Messiah

The century dies
with too many deaths . . .
I survived, I think --
though a refugee
from successive grey Utopias,
now hesitantly naturalised
in this present place.
Still, you learn something
from the crash-course of history;
-- mostly irony --
after being always wrong,
ill-prepared and late.
But what now makes me hesitate
beyond clear borders of love and hate,
is a gentle Jew.

Faith Seeking Fantasy: Tolkien on Fairy-Stories

JK Rowling's *The Adventures of Harry Potter* and JRR Tolkien's *The Lord of the Rings* have made their way from the books into films. Given the extraordinary ongoing influence of these rich products of literary imagination, any theology concerned to relate the Gospel to popular culture might well consider the significance of this phenomenon. At the same time, a deeper appreciation of the role of imagination in this kind of literature will well serve both theology and biblical hermeneutics. True, theology in the age of the great demythologisers is nervous about going too far in this direction, lest it appear to be losing its critical edge. There are plenty of cultured despisers of religion or new-age spiritual guides who would readily reduce the incarnation to one more instance of the gods visiting the earth, while the death and resurrection of Christ is listed alongside any number of nature myths dealing with the cycle of the seasons. 'Faith seeking understanding', yes; faith seeking its ethical priorities in the culture of the day—by all means; but 'faith seeking its proper form of fantasy'? A hesitation, perhaps.

Wary of the mythological imagination, theology opts for 'objective reality', established according to the criteria of critical historical judgment, and aligned to modern scientific method, thus transcending the exuberant creativities of the fantasy. On the other hand, the yield of objectively established fact may be very thin gruel when it comes to feeding that imagination starved for centuries of its imaginative symbolic and narrative forms. Besides, the Gospel itself remains a story exhibiting unique varieties of imagination. It has passed through the minds of early Christian believers in a variety of situations; it has been shaped too by the literary imagination of the evangelists—while both of these types of imagination are ever beholden to the striking parabolic imagination of Jesus himself: 'These are my words that I spoke to you while I was still with you—that everything written about me in the law of Moses, the prophets and the psalms must be fulfilled' (Lk 24:44).

Given the stark alternative between theoretically established objective truth characteristic of the Enlightenment on the one hand, and the exuberant allegorising evident in the patristic and medieval church, to say nothing of the art of the Renaissance, one wonders whether rationality could ever exist in a pure form as far as Christian faith is concerned. Is there a sense in which the incarnation, for instance, is the redemption of the mythological imagination, with its expression of desire and hope? Is there a sense in which the resurrection of the Crucified is the reality which redeems and transforms the most inspired fantasies (in a sense to be explained) of the human heart, seeking life beyond the realm of death and defeat of all that it is best?

Tolkien's Answer

Pondering on the way such questions might be answered, I here present one approach which, however condensed and untechnical in its expression, might throw some light on the multi-dimensional discourse of faith, and the creativity called for if the Gospel is to be communicated with the tang of reality and in the full radiance of its truth. In this note I propose to leave the doings of Master Potter to more expert analysis and concentrate on Tolkien (1892–1973), though some comparison would ideally be in order. There is an advantage in this option: Tolkien, in the midst of his vast literary and scholarly productions, has left an intriguing essay, entitled simply 'On Fairy Stories'.[1] It is written with his typical erudition and lightness of touch, though not without critical acuity when required. Significantly, it is quite evidently a theological statement, with a specifically Christian focus. Moreover it was written at the very time he was bringing *The Lord of the Rings* to completion at the outbreak of the Second World

---

1. JRR Tolkien, *Tree and Leaf* (London: Unwin, 1964), 11–70. This was originally the Andrew Lang Lecture of 1938, given at the University of St Andrews. Since I will be referring frequently to this essay, I will place the page number in brackets in the body of this article.

War, and gives an indication of how his understanding of what he was doing progressed from the time he wrote *The Hobbit* to the years when his story-telling art blossomed to its maturity and highest spiritual seriousness.[2] I propose, therefore, to present the tenor of his argument with fairly generous citation from the essay concerned, and gloss it with my own remarks; and then present a brief conclusion on the role of fantasy and imagination in the life of faith.

The Realm of Faërie

Tolkien, the Rawlinson Professor of Anglo-Saxon at Oxford, begins by addressing what turns out to be a surprisingly complex question: What is a fairy-story? There is little to be gained by working with solemn dictionary definitions referring to the supposed size or magical powers of fairies, the incredibility of their accomplishments—or to the historical unreality or falsehood of what is narrated. In Tolkien's maturer view, these stories are not primarily about the variety of fairies or elves and so on, but about *Faërie*—'the realm or state in which fairies have their being' (15). It is a realm of enchantment including and, in its way, transmuting our sense of reality. Such a realm

> . . . contains many things besides elves and fays, and besides dwarfs, witches, trolls, giants, or dragons: it holds the seas, the sun, the moon, the sky; and the earth, and all things in it: tree and bird, water and stone, wine and bread, and ourselves, mortal men, when we are enchanted (16).

Fairy-stories deal with a special realm of enchantment: the magic of *Faërie* is not an end in itself, its virtue is in its operations: among these are the satisfaction of certain primordial human desires. One of these desires is to survey the depths of space and time. Another is . . . to hold communion with other living things' (18). That is his first valuable point: this realm of imaginative artistry both registers and in some fashion satisfies, 'certain primordial desires'. He gives two examples, namely, to survey 'the depths of space and time', and to be 'in communion with other living things'. We might speak today

---

2. See Randel Helms, *Tolkien's World* (London: Thames and Hudson, 1974), 9–27.

of a 'holistic sense' of universal history; and, allied to this, of the human relationship with all life, and of the inter-relationship existing between all its forms. Note here the efforts of imaginative writers such as Brian Swimme and Thomas Berry who attempt to deck out their version of a scientific account of the emergence of the cosmos in a quasi-mythological narrative guise.[3] Though the result may not be entirely satisfactory with its overlay of allegorical didacticism and clumsy literary form, it does suggest that something is missing from a purely rational scientific approach to the universe—namely an imaginative sense of the whole and all the interrelationships it comprises.

If the genuine fairy-story is not limited to the reality of a dream, but intends a wondrous depth of reality 'independent of the conceiving mind', the question of its truth necessarily arises. Tolkien would claim that, rightly understood, the fairy-story should be presented as 'true', even if such a claim requires further explanation. Are their more paths to the truth than that of rationally based judgments? In a telling article, Peter Phan addresses the question of other kinds of knowing in the age of postmodernity.[4] He accepts that there is a certain postmodern impasse when it comes to both *mythos* and *logos*, but, nonetheless, suggests a way forward by reactivating the millennial tradition of 'foolish wisdom' which is characterised by irony, fantasy and the knowledge that only love can give. Phan makes his case by appealing not only to various biblical and religious traditions, but also makes helpful connections with the negative theology of Nicholas of Cusa and Erasmus' *Praise of Folly*. Whatever the case, a genuine fairy-story will break out of any frame placed upon it. Admittedly, the various components and imaginative dress of the story in regard to actor and incident are artistically conceived; and thus are the product of the imagination. For Tolkien, however, the story itself is not a distortion of reality but a wonderful way of entering more fully into what is routinely regarded as 'the real world' before being creatively re-imagined in the arts of fantasy.

---

3. Brian Swimme and Thomas Berry, *The Universe Story: From the Primordial Flaring Forth to the Ecozoic Era. A Celebration of the Unfolding of the Cosmos* (New York: HarperSanFrancisco, 1992).
4. Peter Phan, 'The Wisdom of Holy Fools in Postmodernity', in *Theological Studies* 62/4 (December 2001): 730–752.

The Origin of the Fair-Story

Tolkien addresses the question of the origin of such stories. In so doing, he touches on deep philosophical and anthropological issues. Investigating the origin of fairy-stories would lead to a consideration of the origin of language and mind itself (21–22). Contrary to Max Müller's judgment that mythology as 'a disease of language', he is more inclined to the view that language is the outcome of mythology, in an anthropological context in which mind, imagination and language are inseparable: 'the incarnate mind, the tongue and the tale are in our world coeval' (25). He thus distinguishes in order to unite, suggesting a more integrated sense of the manner in which mind, speech and narrative expression are inter-related. The Implication of his suggestion is that, while human consciousness is capable of endless differentiations, there is an originating incarnate compactness of existence in which intelligence, speech, imagination, art and feeling coinhere.

Nonetheless, given the variety of fairy-stories, he warns against interpreting them merely as different variations of certain common themes. In the words of Dasent, an authority on Norse mythology: 'We must be satisfied with the soup that is set before us, and not desire to see the bones of the ox out of which it has been boiled' (23). The soup is the particular story as it is served up to us by the narrator. The bones are sources or material if they can be discovered. Still, the soup must not be confused with the bones, nor the story with its ingredients, even if the distinctive tastes of soup of different kinds can be criticised (23). Biblical scholars will be immediately alert to the validity of this point, by recalling the variety of biblical creation stories, or, for that matter, the different literary unities that characterise the four Gospels.

Refining further the notion of origins of fairy-stories, Tolkien now introduces an important notion in their genesis: what he terms 'sub-creation'. It first appears in a passage suggesting the magical power of language:

> When we take green from grass, blue from heaven, and red from blood, we have already an enchanter's power—upon one plane; and the desire to wield that power in the world external to our minds awakes. It does not follow that we shall use that power well upon any plane. We may put a deadly green upon

> a man's face and produce a horror; we may make the rare and terrible blue moon to shine; or we may cause woods to spring with silver leaves and rams to wear fleeces of gold, and put hot fire into the belly of the cold worm. But in such 'fantasy' as it is called, a new form is made; *Faërie* begins; Man becomes a sub-creator (25).

Though the enchanting power of literature, and, more particularly, the fairy-story as it is here understood, the human mind displays itself as a 'sub-creator', a dependent creator within the larger scope of Creation. This is not to say that all human creations are beautiful or wholesome, given their origin in fallen human beings. Still, Tolkien considers that this aspect of sub-creation goes beyond a quasi-theoretical interpretation of symbols of beauties and terrors of the world. He is against any facile understanding such symbols as originally deriving from 'nature myths', or as allegories of the elemental natural experiences of light, darkness, dawn, seasons and so forth. Such an explanation would be all too simple and inhuman, as though natural experience, myth, symbol are all eventually anthropomorphised and localised in epics, legends, sagas, folk-tales, fairy stories—finally to become nursery tales! This view demeans both the mystery of creation—and 'sub-creation'. A narrowly critical mind, dismissive of the place of artful fantasy in the apprehension of the real, might find itself alienated from one of its most precious resources.

As to the higher significance of fairy-stories, and the degree to which they are entangled with some kind of religious experience, Tolkien takes for granted that there a different levels or realms of human meaning. He considers the possibility that the fairy-story works a kind of reintegration of 're-fusion' of what has been sundered in human consciousness. In this regard, he notes the three faces of fairy stories: 'The Mystical toward the Supernatural; the Magical toward Nature; and the Mirror of scorn and pity toward Man' (28). It remains, however, that he views the magical is the essential face of *Faërie*, and that its connection with religious experience or moral responsibility is variable. Though I will suggest here that Tolkien had a theology *of* the fairy-story, there is no theology *in* the stories he produced, nor any evidence of religious activity in their narrative unfolding. Does this kind of literature replace or diminish the possibility of religious faith? Anticipating a little, let me cite Helms' astute remark, 'the poetry of mythic imagination will not, for Tolkien, *replace* religion so much as *make it possible*, putting imaginatively starved modern man back once again into the awed and reverent contact with the living universe'.[5]

Along with the soup, there are 'the cooks', and what they are produce through their culinary art. Tolkien considers that it consists in selecting ingredients in order to produce the what he terms as the 'spell'. This is a richly significant word, connoting both the telling of story (as in *Gospel*) and the effect of some mysterious power on others. The enchantment of such narratives endures into the present, no matter how ancient or gruesome—or many-facetted they appear to be (32). Their magic consists in inviting the reader into 'Other Time'—time experienced in another dimension, even if only for a moment (33). Typically too, such stories lead to the locked door of the 'eternal temptation' confronting human beings, which is to be opened only at their peril (33). The 'other time' and 'the eternal temptation' inherent in stories born of fantasy appear strangely related to the 'Godspell' in its account of what took place *in diebus illis*.

The Present Value of Fairy-Stories

Tolkien moves on to address a third question: What are the values and functions of fairy-stories *now*? (33). He makes the point that they are not essentially children's stories at all. In reality only some children and some adults have a taste for such tales; and in both cases it is something innate (35). To banish this realm of imagination to the domain of the children is to ruin it—either to adapt it to childish purposes—or to adult purposes intent on capturing the 'child market', as we might say in more modern parlance. It is worth asking here whether the recent tendency to expurgate ancient tales according to the demands of political correctness might not result in a form of surgery of the human imagination more likely to produce mutilation than healing. Whilst it is a clear adult duty to protect children from any form of physical and moral violence, it is not clear that much is gained by protecting the imagination of the child from a sense of the enormous cosmic and historical drama in which all human beings are involved.

---

5. Helms, *Tolkien's World*, 24.

In this respect Tolkien strongly opposes the view that fairy-stories are designed to trade on the credulity of children in whom trust and a sense of wonder are still intact. This would imply that such qualities are out of place in the 'real world'. The adult ability of distinguishing between fact and fiction is not incompatible with trust and wonder (36). Furthermore, a properly scientific sense of reality and artistic imagination are not incompatible. The value of the fairy-story has to be sought at a deeper level. For the creator of such stories is one who

> . . . makes a Secondary World which your mind can enter. Inside it, what he relates is 'true': it accords with the laws of that world. You therefore believe it while you are, as it were, inside. The moment disbelief arises, the spell is broken; the magic, or rather, the art has failed. You are then out in the Primary World again, looking at the little abortive Secondary World from the outside (36).

A Coleridgean 'suspension of disbelief' is an attitude properly belonging to the primary world. It is 'a substitute from the genuine thing, a subterfuge we use when condescending to games or make-believe, or when trying, more or less willingly, to find what virtue we can in the work of an art which has for us failed' (37). Here he makes a parallel with cricket, which could be extended into sport generally. Disinterested watching is one thing; participating is another. Still, some obvious questions are left hanging. If the 'secondary world' is that of artistic creation, is the 'primary world' simply that of routine, pragmatic adult common sense? How are the 'truths' of each world related?

Tolkien suggests a range of answers when he returns to the connection of children to fairy-stories. While some, like Lang, suppose that children ask, 'Is it true?', Tolkien considers that the more common question is about the goodness or wickedness of the characters concerned. Thus, fairy-stories are not primarily concerned about what is possible in the primary world, but about what is desirable— that is, about the primordial desires animating human existence' (39): 'if [fairy-stories] awakened *desire*, satisfying it while often whetting it unbearably, they succeeded' (39). In his own experience, a real taste for fairy-stories arose as he began his studies in philology at Oxford, and was 'quickened to full life by war' (40). He was in fact a survivor of the battle of the Somme. Though he has no time for the sniggering over the heads of children (41), he does allow that 'the heart of child' understood in terms of humility and innocence, is necessary for all high adventure, and journeying into kingdoms greater and smaller than *Faërie*. But there is no essential disregard for critical intelligence. Adults should read fairy-stories as a natural branch of literature. In so doing, they are neither playing at being children nor refusing to grow up. The value of the fairy-story lies in its literary art and its ability to carry certain other values with a particular intensity (43), especially that of fantasy (43).

Fantasy

The fairy-story is a particular form of creative image-making (44), and a quite powerful form of art. Works of fantasy are usually characterised by an 'arresting strangeness'. It is disconcerting especially for those who dislike any meddling with their primary world and dismiss fantasy as dreaming, mental illness, delusion or hallucination. True fantasy, however, is difficult to produce, given the difference between the primary and secondary worlds, and our general experience of the merely fanciful or the deliberately delusory. One must expect that this is more so in our age of the electronic entertainment industry, to which is harnessed the power of modern advertising and the professional image-making which is such a part of modern political persuasion.

Of special interest, given the appearance of *The Lord of the Rings* in Peter Jackson's film trilogy, is Tolkien's specific connection of artistic fantasy with the literary (cf 45–49, 67–68). Our master story-teller considers that the story is best left to words (45), for in other arts, for, painting, even stage-drama, are not a vehicle of fantasy in the truest sense, and may even be hostile to it, reducing it at best to a pantomime—which demands no belief of any kind. He finds difficulty even with Shakespeare's *Macbeth* for confusing two modes of art, by introducing the magic of the witches into the historical realism of the story. Drama already has its own magic, and to introduce fantasy into an already achieved secondary world ends up with a kind of tertiary world (47). Actors are not imagined but beheld. The sheer visibility of the dramatic scene distracts from pure story-making, and constrains it to the limitations of stage production. Tolkien does make a passing reference to 'the cinematograph' (67), but says nothing further.

The biblical preference for verbal or literary expression over pictorial image, despite the splendour of religious painting and iconography in general, continues to resonate in Christian consciousness. The religious film or drama is never quite satisfying, because it an artificial objectification of what is intensely personal. In contemporary culture, however, the image is a dominant feature. Tolkien remarks, 'However good in themselves, illustrations do little good to fairy-stories. The radical distinction between all art (including drama) that offers a *visible* presentation and true literature is that it imposes one visible form' (67). The technologically mass-produced image of the cinema or television tends to colonise the imagination, perhaps to atrophy it in some measure. More importantly, in the experience of different stages of faith, some feel called to live beyond images in their surrender to the God 'whom no one has ever seen' (Jn 1:18; 1 Jn 4:12). Even culturally speaking, human equilibrium may well require removing oneself, to some degree at least, from the image-laden bombardment of every moment of waking consciousness. In contrast, there is a special intersubjective creativity proper to literature:

> Literature works from mind to mind and is thus more progenitive. It is at once more universal and more poignantly particular. If it speaks of *bread* or *wine* or *stone* or *tree*, it appeals to the whole of these things, to their ideas; yet each hearer will give them a peculiar personal embodiment in his imagination. Should the story say 'he ate bread', the dramatic producer or painter can only show 'a piece of bread' according to his taste and fancy, but the hearer of the story will think of bread in general and picture it in some form of his own. If a story says 'he climbed a hill and saw a river in the valley below', the illustrator may catch, nor nearly catch, his own vision of such a scene; but every hearer of the words will have his own picture, and it will be made out of all the hills and rivers and dales he has ever seen, but especially out of The Hill, The River, The Valley which were for him the first embodiment of the word (67).

Has Tolkien privileged the word too much? Would he have considered that the film version of *The Lord of the Rings* would defeat its purpose? Whatever the answer to that question, the realm of *Faërie* or fantasy invites a more intimate involvement of the hearer: we are drawn into the secondary world of artistic sub-creation. Though it is difficult to find the right terms for this complete imaginative involvement (48), 'enchantment' perhaps strikes the right note. For it works through the production of 'a secondary world into which both designer and spectator can enter, to the satisfaction of their senses while they are inside; but in its purity it is artistic in desire and purpose' (48). Mere magic, on the other hand, is intent on exercising a power to change the primary world. A magical 'domination of things and wills' contrasts to the enchantment of fantasy. In its purity, this imaginative realm 'does not seek delusion, nor bewitchment and domination; it seeks shared enrichment, partners in making and delight, not slaves' (49). It is a 'spell', therefore, that is intent on releasing and confirming the desires and hopes of the human heart.

Fantasy in this sense is one natural human activity among others. It neither compromises reason nor blunts the appetite for scientific verity (50). In fact, to Tolkien's mind, the clearer the reason, the better the fantasy. The taste for the real, the sense of reality however undifferentiated it may be, saves fantasy from degenerating into morbid delusion.[6] For 'creative fantasy is founded upon the hard recognition that things are so in the world as it appears under the sun; on a recognition of fact, but not a slavery to it' (50). In other words, if you can't distinguish between frogs and human beings, stories about frog-kings would never have arisen! (50). Tolkien concedes that his chosen form of literary art can be misused. It has that in common with all forms of human action when the a corrupted mind or imagination is bent on creating in its own likeness. Nonetheless, it remains that,

> Fantasy is our human right: we make in our measure and in our derivative mode, because we are made: and not only made, but made in the image and likeness of our Maker (50).

In these words Tolkien suggests a deep theology of art, and, of that particular form of his own artistry, the fairy-story. Fantasy is part of our human make-up.[7] Because we are created in the image of the Cre-

---

6. For further discussion, see Helms, *Tolkien's World*, 84–86.
7. See Phan, 'The Wisdom of Holy Fools . . .', 748–749. And specifically on the topic of fantasy, Colin N Manlove, *Christian Fantasy: From 1200 to the Present* (Notre Dame, Ind: University of Notre Dame Press, 1992).

ator, we share, in our human mode, in the activity of creation. This point is made more strongly as we consider some other dimensions of fantasy under the three headings of recovery, escape and consolation.

Three Dimensions of Fantasy

Recovery

The sheer antiquity of stories bred of fantasy, especially when subjected to scholarly analysis, might suggest that nothing new can be expected. It has all be told and done before, to be endlessly retrieved amidst the 'countless foliage of the Tree of Tales with which the Forest of Days is carpeted' (50). For the artist, however, each planting is a new event, the formation of a new and unique pattern. Artists need not despair of drawing because all lines are either straight or curved; nor need they give up on painting, because there are only three primary colours (51). The artist is embarked on a hopeful, ongoing recovery. The originality of artistic retrieval and recuperation contrasts with lapses into grotesque distortion or over-elaboration born of despair over making anything new. The recovery envisaged in fantasy is more like a return and renewal of health. As with every art, it refreshes human experience, helping us to make and see things in their originality. The creativity of the artist works to clean the windows of perception, lest the vision be blurred by interior drabness, triteness, familiarity and possessiveness (52). Thus, it restores the human spirit to a kind of Chestertonian humility in the face of wonder and strangeness of the universe.

All along, fantasy finds its material in the primary world, only to enable one to see those elements 'otherwise': 'it was in fairy-stories that I first divined the potency of the words, and the wonder of things, such as stone, and wood, and iron; tree and grass; house and fire; bread and wine' (52). And so it is that the artistic imagination loves 'nature', but is not her slave.

Escape

The recovery made possible in and through fairy-stories is allied to the aspect of escape. The adjective, 'escapist', is not appropriate in this context since it suggests an attempt to evade the responsibilities inherent in life. Tolkien is trying to clarify the fugitive power of fantasy in quite another sense. For it is freeing and beneficial to those who cling too tightly to the timid dimensions of what the imagine to be 'the world as it is', or who have been too long habituated to the disenchanted domain of 'real life' (53–59). The fugitive power of fantasy is more akin to escaping from a prison—getting out and going home. Literature is, of course, more than talking about jailers and prison walls. Combining a reference to Nazi Germany with a response to critics who would deplore the fugitive aspect of fantasy, Tolkien observes that the escape of the prisoner is not to be confused with the flight of a deserter, just as the acquiescence of the collaborator is not the same as the resistance of the patriot.

For its part, fantasy inspires an escape into dimensions of life that transcends the way things are—even if the *status quo* is marked with great technological achievement. Tolkien is definitely suspicious of a technologically-shaped world. Rather than contributing to the glorification of the 'robot age' of improved means and deteriorating ends, the art of fantasy labours to inspire a new appreciation of nature taken as a whole in its original mystery. The fugitive impulse that marks true fantasy is fuelled by a protest against the ugliness of our works and the evil they have produced in truncating human desire and mutilating imaginative capacities. More positively, fairy-stories nourish the millennial desire to escape-from pain, poverty, sorrow, injustice and death—into a homeland hospitable to the human mind, heart and imagination—in order to be no longer 'out of touch with the life of nature and of human nature as well' (56).

This healthy kind of escape is related to a vivid sense of a rupture in our existence, experienced as a severance from the rest of creation:

> a strange fate and guilt lies on us. Other creatures are like other realms with which Man has broken off relations, and sees now only from the outside at a distance, being at war with them, or on the terms of an uneasy armistice (58).

Tolkien goes on to suggest that the art of fantasy carries the desire for a fuller integrity and an eventual reconciliation in regard to all creation. The fairy-story is a foretaste of a life that does not consist in 'endless serial living' (59), but nourishes 'the oldest and deepest desire: the Great Escape' (59)—from death itself.

Consolation

As the language of desire and fugitive hope, fairy-stories provide their special consolation to the human spirit, endlessly expressed in the motif of 'the happy ending'. In his treatment of this aspect, Tolkien finds it necessary to coin a special word: *eucatastrophe*—the 'good catastrophe' occurring with a sudden and joyous turn at the most desperate juncture in the story. The eucatastrophic tale is the true form of the fairy-story; and the telling of a *eucatastrophe* is it highest function. It tells of 'a sudden and miraculous grace: never to be counted on to recur' (60). It does not deny the evidence of *dyscatastrophe*—of sorrow and failure. Indeed, the experience of temptation, suffering and defeat—the occurrence of catastrophe in the usual sense—is necessary if there is to be the joy of deliverance. The story of the 'good catastrophe' denies, in the face of whatever evidence, the finality of universal defeat. All that the human heart longs and hopes for is not, in the end, under the power of what is worst in our experience of the world. To this degree, the genuine fairy-story is a form of *evangelium*, a fleeting glimpse of joy beyond the walls of the world, striking the human heart with a poignancy as sharp as grief itself (60): 'In a sudden "turn" we come to piercing sense of joy, and the heart's desire . . . rends indeed the very web of the story, and lets a gleam come through' (61).

The peculiar quality of this fairy-tale joy is related to a deeper perception of truth and reality. No artist intends to communicate what is unreal or untrue, but a deeper participation in what is real, in order to express a forgotten or repressed aspect of truth (61). Joy arises from a sudden glimpse of what underlies our being in the world (62). With its realist intent, all art, and the fairy-story in particular, is not concerned to offer illusory consolation in the midst of sorrow, but to answer the question of truth itself. While any art-form has limits inherent in own inner consistency as one form of 'sub-creation', there is an excess implied. The fairy-story as a form of art uniquely expressive of *eucatastrophe*, 'we see in a brief vision that the answer may be greater—it may be a far off gleam or echo of *evangelium* in the real world' (62). In the peculiarity of this form of sub-creation, the storyteller's art bring to expression 'one facet of a truth incalculably rich' (62).

The Gospel Story

The following words are especially significant, and evidently autobiographical, as Tolkien relates the kind of consciousness apparent in the fairy-story with a sense of the Gospel itself:

> I would venture to say that approaching the Christian Story from this direction, it has long been my feeling (a joyous feeling) that God redeemed the corrupt making-creatures, men, in a way fitting to this aspect, as to others, of their strange nature. The Gospel contains a fairy-story, or a story of a larger kind which embraces all the essence of fairy stories. They contain many marvels—peculiarly artistic, beautiful and moving: 'mythical' in their perfect self-contained significance; and among the marvels is the greatest and most complete conceivable eucatastrophe. But this story has entered history and the primary world; the desire and aspiration of sub-creation has been raised to the fulfilment of Creation (62).

On the one hand, there is the traditionally Catholic principle of 'grace building on and perfecting nature'. On the other, nature has its 'strangeness' or peculiarity. Human understanding moves from sense and imagination to what cannot be either sensed or imagined or even understood—save through an imagination and intelligence that has learned to respect what transcends both. More particularly, the truth of the Gospel is a story that embraces the essence of all fairy-stories. It registers the basic desires of the human heart present in all such stories, only to lead them to a fulfilment, reconciliation and recovery. The Gospel story is that of the final 'great escape', as it breathes with the joy that defies the power of evil and death.

In the realm of God's kingdom as the Gospel depicts it, there are many elements similar to the miracles, marvels and sudden turns that make up the realm of *Faërie*—above all the vindication of the crucified Jesus in the glory of the resurrection—the most 'complete conceivable eucatastrophe'. But there is a difference as well: the art of the divine story-teller has entered history and been located in the primary world where the marvels of grace are least expected. Human nature, expressed in the desire and aspiration of the story-teller's art, is raised to the fulfilment that only God can give: it is the glory of God's creation that it includes all the forms of sub-creation as enabled by the creator and redeemer of all. Tolkien adds, a qualification, however: 'the Art is here in the story itself rather than in the telling; for the Author of the story was not the evangelists' (62, n. 2). Note, therefore, the radically theological understanding of the Gospel story that is here presumed. In line with his faith-inspired reading of the Gospel, Tolkien gives a further specification of the reality of the 'good catastrophe' characterising both the Gospel and fairy-stories:

> The birth of Christ is the eucatastrophe of Man's history. The Resurrection is the eucatastrophe of the story of the Incarnation. The story begins and ends in joy. It has pre-eminently the 'inner consistency of reality'. There is no tale ever told which men would rather find was true, and none which so many sceptical men have accepted as true on its own merits. For the art of it has the supremely convincing tone of Primary Art, that is, of Creation. To reject it leads either to sadness or to wrath (62–63).

To interpret Tolkien correctly at this point, it is necessary to give a special weighting to the experience of joy. The sense of joyous fulfilment seems to be the basic criterion for that 'inner consistency of reality' communicated by the Gospel. Tolkien is here rather cryptic, disposed, apparently, to leave the further articulation of his intuition to theologians and philosophers. Why is it that there is 'no tale ever told which men would rather find as true'? Why is it that so many who are natively sceptical and familiar with a critical examination of history have been prepared to accept the Gospel story as true on its own merits? His reason, however briefly, is clearly stated: its art 'has the supremely convincing tone of Primary Art'. Note here that he does not speak of the *primary world*. In Tolkien's vocabulary, that phase is usually employed regarding the routine world of common sense and practical living. He writes of *primary art*, and identifies it immediately with creation, with the activity of the divine artist. For Tolkien, at least, the Gospel instils a sense of reality utterly consonant with the desires of the human heart, and the artistic aspirations that have arisen from it. But it does this, not primarily as a telling, classic form of human art, but as an encounter with the divine imagination—the origin of primary art which is manifested in creation itself, and all the forms of 'sub-creation' it enables and contains.

The implication is that the Word of the divine artist is made flesh in the stories of the world, the sub-creations of human artists. The purpose of the divine Artist is that the world might be drawn into the joy of the divine imagination itself, to find disclosed the ultimately real and primary world. The Gospel story enters history. Such an incarnation does not abrogate the mythical or allegorical significance it has in common with all the stories that have nourished the desires and imagination of the fugitive spirit of humankind. Moreover, it intensifies the joy that is the essential character of such stories. For, in and through the Gospel, 'art has been verified: "God is the Lord, of angels, and of men—and of elves. Legend and History have met and fused"' (63).

At the conclusion of his reflection, Tolkien enunciates a principle that has animated his approach all along. In the Kingdom of God, the presence of the greatest does not depress the small: 'Redeemed Man is still man. Story, fantasy, still go on, and should go on. The Evangelium has not abrogated legends; it has hallowed them, especially the 'happy ending' (63). The coming of the kingdom of God, then, is not bad news for the artist. The grace of that ultimate realm brings an assurance that artistic creativity expressed in fantasy, for example, 'may actually assist in the effoliation and multiple enrichment of creation' (63). Through human sub-creation, the God-intended plenitude of creation unfolds into a manifold enrichment. And yet, there is a certain reserve, expressed in an analogical awareness of similarities and differences:

> All tales may come true; and yet, at the last, redeemed, they may be as like and as unlike the forms we give them as Man, finally redeemed, will be like and unlike the fallen that we know (63).

There is no question of a univocal identification of divine art with the human. What the divine artist is bringing into being in the primary world of creation still exceeds anything the eye has seen or the ear heard, or the heart and imagination conceived. And yet there is an anticipation; and with it a joy made possible through the art of the fairy-story designed to give a unique, fugitive form to the truth of what is to come.

Conclusion

While Tolkien was cooking his imaginative 'soup' of fairy-stories into their final form, an eminent patristic scholar was at work, making similar points. I refer to Hugo Rahner in his *Greek Myths and Christian Mystery*.[8] Even though the book was not published until the later 1950s, it took shape at the same time as Tolkien was writing *The Lord of the Rings*. It is a collection of studies contributed to the Jungian circle that gathered for the Eranos symposia on the shores of Lago Maggiore at Ascona in Southern Switzerland during the dark years leading up to the Second World War. Both writers were inescapably conscious of the darkness that was descending on Europe as the third decade of the twentieth century was ending. Rahner's researches breathe the conviction that the great mythic objectifications of human consciousness were inseparable from what is best in human experience; and thus had a rightful place in the great humanist tradition, then under threat in the perils that had broken on the world. His erudite studies especially document the abiding concern of Christian theology to anchor itself firmly and creatively in the human imagination—to 'Christen' that classical humanist imagination, by preserving it and opening it to a redemptive fulfilment. With that intention, Rahner considered how a number of the myths and symbols of classical antiquity came to be preserved and developed in Christian tradition. He treated, for example, the notion of 'mystery', and its solar and lunar symbolic forms. Likewise he reflected on the symbolism of healing plants and herbs such as the moly and the mandrake, and the special spiritual significance of the willow. His final study is of Odysseus at the mast, transmuted in Christian faith to be a prefiguration of the cross. He shows convincingly that Christian imagination owes much of its fertility to its ability to claim its classical mythical inheritance.

What Rahner and Tolkien have in common is a remarkable sensitivity to the place of the imaginative in human culture, and its necessity for communicating a humane sense of life. In this regard, the work of René Girard is of growing importance.[9] His examination of

---

8. Hugo Rahner, *Greek Myths and Christian Mystery*, translated by Brian Battershaw (London: Burns and Oates, 1963).
9. René Girard, 'Are The Gospels Mythical?', in *First Things* (April 1996): 27–31; *The Girard Reader*, edited by James G William (New York: Crossroad, 1996), especially 9–19, 45–61, 118–141, 145–176; Scott Cowdell, *René Girard and Secular Modernity:Christ, Culture and Crisis* (Notre Dame, IN: University of Notre Dame Press, 2013); René Girard, *I See Satan Fall Like Lightening* (Maryknoll, NY: Orbis, 2001); For a theological evaluation of human-rights discourse from a Girardian point of view, see Peter R Storck, *Human Rights in Crisis: A Cultural Critique* (Saarbruecken: VDM Verlag, 2007).

the myths and literature have led him to a new appreciation of the uniqueness of the Gospel as the God-intended healing for the violence that has marked human history and been expressed in a variety of mythic and literary forms.[10]

Given this wider context, I would understand Tolkien's presentation of the enchanting art of the fairy-story as 'Christening' the imagination in a certain way. Faith may seek understanding in the interests of an intellectual conversion. The same living faith must likewise seek its morally responsible world-forming praxis, if it is to be morally converted, and be the source of ongoing collaboration with all people of good will. But if this faith is to carry out its intellectual and moral responsibilities, it must be alive to the mystery of the Creator and the wonder of creation. It must undergo a kind of conversion in the imagination itself, as it seeks to enter into all the art-forms that characterise our human ability as sub-creators. Arts, visual or dramatic, musical or literary, make up this larger scene. To that degree, an integrated theology must inspire and appreciate a faith seeking its appropriate artistic expression. One aspect of that concern is what I have dared to term, 'faith seeking fantasy'—faith seeking the experience of enchantment, escape, recovery and consolation as described above. In an exposure to this art—as to all arts—a theological faith can find that the windows of perception are cleansed, and its vision, even though the *chiaroscuro* of revealed mystery remains, will not be 'blurred by interior drabness, triteness, familiarity and possessiveness' (52). Faith will lose nothing of its realism if it is more attuned to wonder and strangeness of the universe.

Lonergan's axiom, 'genuine objectivity is the fruit of authentic subjectivity',[11] is instanced even in this context. The authentic self is realised through a self-transcendence, not only in intellectual, moral and religious dimensions, but also on the level of imagination and the its related arts—in this case, fantasy. In other words, the horizon in which our conscious existence unfolds to its full height and

---

10. The larger frame of reference would obviously take in more well-known sources such as the work of Jung on symbolic archetypes and the researches of Eliade on myth and religion. In literary tradition, William Blake especially figures in the background to this kind of exploration, though I am not suggesting that Tolkien was aware of any dependence on him.
11. Bernard Lonergan, *Method in Theology* (London: Darton, Longman and Todd, 1972), 265, 292.

depth is determined by a transformed subjectivity. Through different but related transformations, the way is opened to reach beyond appearances to truth and reality; beyond satisfactions to moral values; beyond the idols of our human projections to the adoration of limitless mystery—and beyond 'drabness, triteness, familiarity and possessiveness' to wonder and enchantment. There is a core of consciousness expressed in imagination, symbol, affect and dramatic experience that can be ignored only so long. To ignore it too long would be at our theological peril, reducing our minds to mere theory-machines, out of touch with the larger stream of consciousness in which the best of our thinking and writing takes place. All this is to say that love for God with a whole heart, soul, mind and strength loses nothing if it also includes the powers of the imagination.

Ron

A quiet day on the coast,
he off for his heart-saving walk,
along the favoured back-beach route.
But that time, only this far --
to the top of the path --
the worst of it over, you'd think-
as the steps lead down.
But there it was; and now nearly the year gone:
tough shrubs cling to the backs of the shifting dunes;
nervous grasses still skitter back
from the deeply shelving beach
to the safety of the reclamation zone;
the Lonsdale lighthouse presides quaintly
over the churning menace of The Rip;
hurrying clouds patch the sea with denim-blue;
the sand yelps beneath the joggers shoes,
and my steps follow his along the beach
widening as the tide goes out.

'Come Holy Spirit, Renew The Face of the Earth!'
Invocation: Holy Space and Crying Need

The vocative mood of this invocation conceals something quite decisive for our theology. The 'word about God', the 'faith seeking understanding' of theology is brought into a larger grammar of Christian existence. It is a prayer arising from the need of the Church in its vocation to intercede for the whole world. The invocation, 'Come, Holy Spirit' is related to the eucharistic epiclesis, 'we humbly implore you: by the same Spirit graciously make holy the gifts we have brought to you for consecration . . .' (Eucharistic Prayer III). There can be no real presence of the Lord to the community and no communion of Christians in Christ unless through the transforming power of the Spirit.

Such an invocation can be felt as a subversive intrusion into theological procedures, privileging as they do, as they must, the precise formulation, the telling propositional expression, the qualified judgement. It would be simple enough to leave out the 'Come!', and proceed to survey the rich results of a theology of the Spirit.[1] But, when theology becomes an invocation of the Spirit, we begin to move into another mood. It is not a matter of praying for a new theology. It suggests rathera new way of letting our theology of the Spirit's presence and energy mean something in shared silence, patience and hope of the here and now. Invoking the Spirit is no mere formality before addressing the real business of the meeting, but an prayer arising from the sense of the absence, waiting and powerlessness that our

---

1. Here one would include notable achievements of those amongst us, of David Coffey, John Thornhill, Dennis Edwards. My own recent contribution appeared as *Trinity of Love: A Theology of the Christian God* (Wilmington, Del: Michael Galzier, 1989).

busy lives try to conceal. Calling on the Spirit deliberately carves into our theological conversations and practical concerns a holy space to allow for the mystery to come in its own terms, in its own time, in its own originality, freedom and surprise. Here, even the best of thinking and action touches its limits.

'Come, Holy Spirit and renew the face of the earth'. Such a prayer invites the Spirit to enter into the resistant particularities of the here and now. We pray for the Spirit to come, not as a nice thought, not even as a good theology or a new system of organisation, but we do ask the renewing Spirit to come into the very way we are experience 'the face of our world', in all its inconclusive, unsettling and demanding reality. Our prayer is an expression of the 'crying need' as it is felt in the particular historical context of who and what we are, in this time, in this place, in this culture, in this actual world.

Invoking the Spirit subverts our usual theological 'mind-set'—a good term in this context. It evokes a certain experience of absence rather than of presence, of surrender rather than control, of urgent particularity rather than of some new coherent synthesis. Invoking the Spirit is, as we will now see, a kind of what the philosophers call, 'deconstruction'.

Invocation as 'Deconstruction'

The recent Deconstructionist turn in literary and philosophical studies[2] aims to bring a healthy irony into a self-sufficient, whole cultural, systematic signification of reality. It thereby criticisess any unexamined conviction of reality being somehow contained and controlled by our systems of thought and action—even in its in our most hallowed formulations and aspirations. Every text must remain open to further reading—to a total context can never be mastered; and in a conversation that can never be closed. The therapeutic purpose of this relativising critique, especially in these times of both incredible

---

2. The Australian poet and literary critic, Kevin Hart, has aligned this whole movement, above all as its represented by Jacques Derrida, with the witness of mysticism and *theologia negativa*, in his outstanding book, *The Trespass of the Sign: Deconstruction, Theology and Philosophy* (Melbourne: Cambridge University Press, Melbourne, 1989).

collapse and novelty, is to make us more patient, more ironic, more attentive, and finally more receptive and responsive to the unspeakable otherness of reality. The deconstructive style of criticism has now occurred as a literary practice because deconstruction has been so massively experienced as an enormous fact. More particularly, deconstructionist scholars of a religious persuasion, tend to claim that the mystic wrapped in the cloud of unknowing really knows more about God than the theologian discoursing on the divine Holy Spirit, more than the philosopher proving or disproving the divine existence. It is too often presupposed that religious ideas about God presents us with a kind of blank cheque that the cultural bank can readily cash at any time or any circumstance. It seems that the bank's reserves are now exhausted.

At this point, let us distinguish a theology of the Holy Spirit from the invocation of the Holy Spirit as the mood in which such a truly discerning theology can be humbly and critically articulated. As we shall stress below, the Spirit is not a presence possessed within the familiarity of a religious system or organisation, something to be administered as a fund, or to be channelled as an energy; nor or someone simply summoned up to support the system. In contrast, the Spirit is invoked as a kind of unspeakable, unsettling otherness, coming in its own originality and calling forth its own unique response, perhaps to appear in a new depth within the familiar, perhaps to surprise all our settled conceptions and policies.

In this sense, both Paul and John, each in his own way, were 'deconstructionists'. For both of them, the mystery of the Spirit demanded a certain kind of receptivity and waiting, coming as it does, as an excess, as a gift, in God's good time. The Spirit thus enters, though we must take that word very figuratively, into theological hermeneutics: the inexpressible things that no theological eye has seen, no theological ear heard, nor even the theological heart conceived, 'God has revealed to us through the Spirit' (1Cor 2:10). This Spirit is given,

> that we might understand the gifts bestowed on us by God. And we impart this in words not taught by human wisdom, but taught by the Spirit, interpreting spiritual truths to those who possess the Spirit (1 Cor 2:8–13).

One cannot but be fascinated by the theological relevance of this text. The context, of course, is far more general than theological concerns, referring as it does to the pervasive need for the Spirit in Christian experience and communication. Such a context is further extended when, in addressing the Romans (Rom 8:18–27), Paul expands his vision with a global sweep of rhetoric: he places the groaning existence of Christians in the midst of the whole creation groaning in its cosmic travail. Though we have the 'first fruits of the Spirit', it remains a matter of waiting, in patience and hope. We cannot master the provisional realities of our existence within any systematic construction, not even that of a good theology, not even a theology of the Holy Spirit: the groaning is not replaced by some clear word of theology. Rather, hope is an openness to the invisible, 'the not seen', to what is not yet. Faced with a future that cannot be seen, 'we do not know how to pray as we ought' (Rom 8:26b). Here the Holy Spirit inspires and supports our hope-filled prayers with his own 'inexpressible groanings'—lest we begin to envisage our future in a way that would foreclose on the radical novelty of what is coming to pass.

What does all this mean for theology? Surely that theology is marked with this groaning if it is to be a critical word of hope, both patient with the limits of our provisional perceptions, and impatient with the congealed forms and sedimentations of those religious forms that have lost the capacity either to wait or venture forth, timidly defending the present against the global travail in which the future is being born.

The question arises likewise in John. For him, though the Spirit is not that field of luminous corporate and cosmic energy as it is for Paul, the hermeneutical importance of the Spirit is perhaps even more radical, more 'deconstructionist', in the Johannine writings, where the paraclete is primarily the Spirit of truth:

> I have yet many things to say to you but you cannot bear them now. When the Spirit of truth comes, he will guide you into all truth; for he will not speak on his own authority, but whatever he hears he will speak, and he will declare to you the things that are to come (Jn 16:12f).

Again a disconcerting emphasis.³ Even in the presence of Christ there is an empty space which only the incalculable, ever-new intervention of the Spirit can fill: words and signs may not change all that much; but there are meanings to come from larger, future contexts which cannot yet be tolerated, ranges of meaning yet to be risked. Once more, the Spirit is not reduced to a consoling element in religious arrangements or theological constructions, but the living deconstruction of such conceptions in the interests of a more inclusive hope. Waiting for the Spirit is to affirm God as mystery, that holy space in which alone the answer to the emptiness and inconclusiveness of our crying need can be found.

These two instances of deconstruction at the heart of our expression of faith in Christ suggest a far more serious appropriation of the invocative or epicletic mode in our theological exploration and its associated discourse. Any theological construction would seem to have its purpose in clearing a space in which the mystery can be revealed. The endemic problem of theology is to be so structured in the indicative mood, so locked into the assumptions of an analytical mode, that, by a methodological reflex, it tries to repress the absence, the emptiness, the generalisation that are its inherent burden. Only by integrating the activity of invocation can theology attain its proper mode of objectivity, as an openness to an inexpressible excess of meaning, to the possibilities of surprise, to an illumination from the inexpressibly particular. To the degree that theology can critically wait on the evidence, in the measure it allows the prayer of invocation, it approximates to a sober poetic art exploring the inexhaustible singularity of the mystery.⁴ Openness to the *data*, the given, and

---

3. Derrida himself has investigated the theme of the invocation of the Spirit, especially as Martin Heidegger has expressed it in his philosophy. Heidegger's naive accommodation of Nazism in this context has made Derrida's deconstructive exploration a most interesting instance of 'the discernment of spirits'. See Jacques Derrida, *Of Spirit. Heidegger and the Question*, translated by G Bennington and R Bowlby (Chicago: University of Chicago Press, Chicago, 1989), 109–113 are of special interest.
4. It would be fascinating to explore theological teaching and writing in terms of the inter-relationship of deconstruction and invocation. By giving both their place, we may discover interesting things about theological communication. Though I am here gliding over enormous questions with this general nod to the therapeutical value of deconstruction, I believe there are ranges of quite classical theological topics that could be brought forward to illustrate the points I have

adoration of the *dator*, the giver of inexhaustible gifts, will not let our thinking shrink from the face of the new.

In a way, all our thinking is left with is our power to invoke, to wait. But today the place of waiting has been hugely changed. We live now at different frontiers. The 'whole of creation' is immeasurably more extensive than the cosmos of the ancient world. The face of the earth now smiles, weeps or frowns with the lineaments of a human face. In the last decade of the last terrible century, we are all somewhat familiar with the human defacement, actively wrought or passively suffered, that has taken place. When Paul spoke of the groaning of the whole creation in travail, his graphic cosmic imagery might have struck commentators of past ages as somewhat exaggerated, at least as peripheral to their experience—for who experiences the wholeness of things? That is not so much the case today. Whether Christians look out, into the world, or into the church, whether we consider the very bio-system of this planet, or the more intimate relationships of family and married life—there is a groaning and a travail of unprecedented proportions. All our constructions have, if not destructed, at least undergone an unrelenting deconstruction. Pending some new construction in the future, our present is a frightening empty space. We may feel forlorn in a dispirited church, survivors in a cultural slum in a suffering and poisoned planet. The two sides are there: a totalising and totalitarian effort to freeze the whole of the human world into any one of the shapes of contending ideologies;

---

been making: I have already mentioned the theology of discernment of spirits. To this we could add the function of the parable, the sacramental enactment of the real presence, the function of the three holy days in the articulation of Christian hope, the one mystery of God's presence and the interplay of threefold trinitarian symbolism; the dynamics of conversion; the theology of the gifts of the Holy Spirit; the experience of the mystical 'dark nights'; the role the Protestant principle in the history of the church; the expansion of Christian consciousness into the world of non-Christian religions—to say nothing of the more familiar deconstruction that Christian faith has been subjected to through the critiques of Marx, Nietzsche, Freud, and in the challenges of a contemporary scientific world view and in the ecological awareness of our day. My general point is that there is an ongoing deconstruction inherent in the vitality of faith which might be far more interesting to secular deconstructionists than the cultural sedimentations of religion or Christianity in the West. Of course, for many of us, the greatest instance of world-wide deconstruction in the reading of our lives is Vatican II itself. But that is a longer matter, yet one of such massively familiarity that it still defies adequate expression.

the other, the tracks of particular histories suddenly converging into a challenging global space in which we now sense that things have to be different.

We invoke the Spirit out of a crying need, in order to clear a holy space. Yet there are conflicts. The first bears on the experience of the self, more on the subjective pole of our experience; the second bears on our experience of the cosmos, more toward the objective polarity of our world—the rough equivalents of the classical notions of 'soul' and 'nature'.

Deconstruction of the Contemporary Self

The experience of the human self has fast become an area of 'crying need' in our time. It is one thing to make the momentous 'turn to the subject', characterising the modern era. The human subject emerged in its vibrant, self-expressive creativity in contrast to the abstract, metaphysical notion of the human soul. But it is quite another matter to find that the great organisations and institutions that once clothed and supported our identity have been undergoing a deep deconstruction.[5] Contemporary culture simply cannot name the human self any more. In some measure, the world can be named and analysed in all its elements, its processes, its intricate structures, even those of the human brain itself. But it remains a risky business to look one another in the eye too long, and ask what mystery is waking is stirring there. Though we can name the Crab Nebula or six kinds of quarks or the structure of the DNA, the singularity of the self is increasingly ineffable.[6] We can define and describe so much of our world—even if the 'I' who does this defining and describing cannot itself be defined or described. Indeed, the great philosophico-religious languages concerning the self are undergoing their own deconstruction from within and from without. Take three classic notions of the self, that of the West, the Sinic (Chinese), and the Indian. Each of them finds itself in a situation of crisis.

---

5. See Walker Percy, *Lost in the Cosmos: The Last Self-Help Book* (New York: Farrar, Straus and Giroux, 1983), for a teasing confirmation of this point.
6. See William Barrett, *Death of the Soul: From Descartes to the Computer* (New York: Doubleday, 1986).

In Western tradition, the true self is always the concrete, historical acting 'I'.[7] Ultimate union with God is not envisaged as a state in which the person will be absorbed, dissolved or annihilated in the divine. Westerners typically sought the salvation of their soul, in liberation from suffering, guilt, and death. This self implied hoped for a fullness of life, beyond time yet achieved in time through ethical action, especially on behalf of other selves, in the love of neighbour. Such a sense of self never contemplates the disappearance of the self, but of the self's union with God, and in the communion of saints, in the company of angels in a transfigured world. But in the contemporary world, this kind of personal consciousness is not without its problems. Darwin has inserted this self into the processes of biological evolution; Marx has dramatically sketched its social structure and conditioning; Freud has pointed to the 'demons' of the unconscious, just as Jung summoned forth the "angels" of our culture's primordial archetypes. Add to such displacements within the western tradition the insistent demand to understand humanity in a more ecologically attuned way, not as transcending nature, but living within and respecting it. And more important than any anthropological analysis is the sheer obsessive driven-ness of the modern technological way of life. The self is little more than a ghost in the world of machines. Hence, the once naively understood ego is now seen to be deeply immersed in a manifold of social, economic, psychological, biological, ecological and technological systems. No wonder the phrase, 'identity crisis', however shop-worn, points to a pervasive cultural phenomenon.

Again, speaking with the utmost generalisation, we can approach Chinese culture with the millennial strands of its tradition as having experienced the reality of the self less in terms of the historical individuality characteristic of the West, but more in terms of the *Tao*, or inherent 'right connectedness' of relationships modulating the whole of existence.[8] The true self results from a harmonious integration into the larger totalities of family, society and people comprising the structured cosmic order. Such is the sacred order of the *Tao* and the pure form of *Li*, in the equilibrium of *Yin* and *Yang*. The self is realised in harmony with all else. Genuine selfhood cannot be understood

---

7. John T Marcus, 'East and West: Phenomenologies of Self and the Existential Bases of Knowledge', in *International Philosophical Quarterly* (March 1971): 5–47.
8. Marcus, 'East and West', 21–26.

outside this realm of 'philharmonic' relatedness and organic connection with all things. Thus, personal consciousness is realised only in sympathetic harmony with the rhythms of the all-encompassing and all-pervading 'right Way'.

With the historical ruptures of Communism, 'the Long March' entered Chinese history. The traditional experience of self has suffered the rigours of Marxist critique and the traumas of social revolution, along with the harsh imperatives of economic survival. The drama of history has intruded as a dissonance into the cosmic harmony. Thus, a new and disturbing element has entered into classically Sinic sense of the self.

In Indian culture, the true self has never been the historical or cosmic self in either the Western or Sinic sense. Rather it is a self realised above and beyond the *maya* of deceptive appearances of the acting or cosmic self.[9] It is a transcendent, quasi-eschatological self, necessarily devoid of historical particulars and personal characteristics. In the language of the Upanishads, the self (*atman*) and the 'I' (*ahman*) and the divine (*Brahman*) are one: as one Indian scholar expresses it,

> In this infinite and true self there is no difference, no diversity, no *meum* and *teum*. It is like and ocean in which all our phenomenal existence will dissolve like salt in water . . . the true self manifests itself in the processes of our phenomenal existences, but ultimately when it retires back into itself, it can no longer be found in them. It is a state of absolute infinitude of pure intelligence, pure being, and pure blessedness.[10]

The illusory self of history and the world must be shed if the true self is to be attained through dissolution into the ultimate. The attainment of unity is the 'supreme goal of every responsible life'.[11] The West cannot but see in this a radical depersonalising of history and a negation of world and destiny. And of course, modern India, has promoted its national and social developments so as to allow for the social imperatives of political democracy and self-determining history, with all

---

9. Marcus, 'East and West', 26–30.
10. Surendranath Dasgupta, *A History of Indian Philosophy*, volume I (Cambridge: Cambridge University Press, 1957), 61.
11. Mircea Eliade, *Yoga: Immortality and Freedom*, translated by WR Task (New York: Pantheon Books, 1958), 124.

the implications of individual and social rights. The transcendent self has returned to history to be contextualized in a social, cultural and national form. Even the 'Untouchables' have a vote! The peculiar transcendence of the classically Indian experience of selfhood is being subject to the another version of self implicit in the realities of political democracy in modern India.

While these brief comments can hardly do justice to the complex realities involved, they do point the radical deconstruction in evidence. This in turn solicits a kind of global conversation on the deepest issues of human identity and the troubled provocative awareness of past limitations. The global present invites into a new sense of planetary identity, by integrating authentic ingredients of our particular and often defensive histories: the Western sense of the dignity of the individual and its historical unfolding; the Sinic sense of cosmic relationship and harmony; the Indian sense of a trans-historical, 'eschatological' unity. Will a new age be capable of subsuming these particular histories of the experience of the self into something consonant with what we are, and must be, together? Though each of the traditional patterns of self-awareness is being subjected to its own deconstruction, each can critically re-possess itself in a compassionate companionship with other selves, so to find what each most needs, and, for that matter, what each has most to contribute. Hope stirs with the possibility that the open global history of the present might produce, out of the wealth of its particular traditional patterns of awareness, a sense of the human self at once individual, relational and ultimately self-transcending? [12]

This brings us to the point of invocation. By reading such 'signs of the times', Christian faith can discern the 'crying need' of dislocation and fragmentation, and the need for a holy space in which the Self in all our selves can be newly invoked and appreciated.[13] The very break-

---

12. There are, of course, many other senses of self, for example, animist, African, Aboriginal Australian. But if what I have suggested about the 'selves' of the classic traditions approximates to the situation of breakdown and confusion, I am afraid it would be more the case for others as well.
13. Elsewhere I tried to see a redemptive point of new integration in a trinitarian notion of self. Understanding the three divine persons as Father, Son and Spirit is not unrelated to the three classic senses of 'self' we have been describing. The Father, the vision of whom consummates the divine self-communication, is, in this context, more assimilable to the Indian experience of the eschatological self. The self-expression of the Word, incarnate in human history, is most easily linked

down of huge cultural and even religious self-expressions certainly creates a terrifying space. Are we to be 'lost in the cosmos' (Walker Percy), as nomadic fragments of consciousness? Or is the time of a new Pentecost, one in which the psychologically scattered peoples of the world can come together in new unity? Never has it been clearer 'that it has not yet appeared what we shall be' (I Jn 3:2). In that experience of absence, the Holy Spirit stirs as the aspiration to a more self-surrendering self-hood, a more relational way of becoming who we are, beyond all frontiers, religious, cultural, national. God's Holy Breath is always the first divine person in our experience, inspiring a new unity, the Self indwelling in the many, so that we can be with, and for, one another in ways that previous isolation or limitation did not allow. Deconstructed former selves inevitably mean cultural loss and grief. And yet we continue to invoke the Holy Spirit as the healing, unifying energy of a new creation. There is a 'crying need' in this unique of our historical moment. In a way that knows no parallel in the past we are being pushed and pulled into a global consciousness as one human community. The co-existence of mutually antagonistic blocs is no longer a tolerable political scheme: solidarity in a global humanity is the commanding value, the political and cultural imperative.[14]

Our past has been marked by two tortured caricatures of human existence, each producing its peculiar hell of human defacement. The first is that of the suicidal isolation of schizoid, materialist individualism, the world of the rootless consumer nomad. This was the unique

---

aligned to the Western experience. And the Spirit, as the subsisting unifying force of love, can be evocatively linked with the Sinic experience of harmony and relationality. As self-giving Love, the Trinity is redemptively present as a model for reconciled, global version of human selfhood. The discovery to be made is that of a more complete humanity 'made in the image and likeness of God'. See my *Trinity of Love*, 228–248.

14. John Paul II is a prophet of this new kind of solidarity. The ambition and scope of this notion is perhaps best summed up in the following words:

The church's social doctrine is not a 'third way' between liberal capitalism and Marxist collectivism or even a possible alternative to other solutions less radically opposed to one another. Rather, it constitutes a character of its own. Nor is it an ideology, but rather the accurate formulation of the results of careful reflection on the complex realities of human existence, in society and in the international order, in the light of faith and of the church's tradition . . . (*Sollicitudo Rei Socialis*, n. 41, par. 7, *Origins* 17/38 (March 3, 1988): 655–6.

product of a capitalism with its naive vision of progress based on an unlimited production and consumption of economic goods. Its cardinal value was a freedom residing in the enlightened and, admittedly, hard-working, individual. Though its industrial accomplishments have been enormous, now the whole bill has to be paid: not readily, for in a world of dwindling resources, with a culture educated in greed, the price is terrifyingly high. Biblical descriptions of idolatry are not foreign to the world as it is. The fathomless banality of consumerist materialism, promoted in modern advertising and made omnipresent in the media, gives a new reality to Marx's originally anti-religious phrase, 'the opium of the people'.

The polar opposite to this libertarian materialist capitalism was the hell of totalitarian collectivism as when the whole of human reality is frozen into an oppressive ideology. As this congealed over every aspect of life, the individual was lost in the collective which became, in turn, the justification of dictatorships of unparalleled ferocity, either bludgeoning the dissident into defeated conformity or simply liquidating the representatives of any actual or possible resistance. All human relationships and freedoms were submerged in the brutal gloom of the Gulag. If the first hell came out of homage to an idol, the second hell, one might suggest, manifested the self-destructiveness of demonic possession.

Now, in the closing years of this century, first the clash, and now the ideological collapse, of both these monstrosities presents us with a choice for a third way. A human community founded on some form of global solidarity has become the historical imperative. We are presented with a choice, economic, ecological and even political. The pressure is not purely external pressure, but arises from what is deeply intrinsic to human aspiration. However rudimentary and precarious the reality, history is revealing a presentiment of what we are called to be, one race in one world.[15]

Though this glimmer of one humanity is still largely a dream, it is a dream after a nightmare. It rises out of consciousness wakening to the excess of suffering and to the real possibilities present in this historical moment. The emergent unity of the human race is not

---

15. This experience of an inner imperative is a large part of the pope's refusal to treat of this new unity in solidarity as an ideology. Founded in an historical moment of human freedom and hope, the values of solidarity do no violence either to the authenticity of human intelligence or aspiration.

merely one more theoretical ideal, let alone one more repressive ideology imposing uniformity and conformism, but a deep historical impulse. We are inspired to explore the new space that has been left by the grotesquely inhuman failures which made us forget our co-humanity on this planet.[16] Even if that space is quickly populated by new problems, one senses it is time to invoke the mystery of a larger, more mysterious belonging. We feel a kind of desperate need for the God of all-inclusive love to be what we have in common, to be the ground, the hope, and the atmosphere of our coexistence. Everything that Christian tradition has told us about the Holy Spirit of unity and love must now form itself into an invocation, that such a Spirit come into what we are becoming. In this context, I find Lonergan's words especially poignant:

> It is as though a room were filled with music though one can have no sure knowledge of its source. There is in the world, as it were, a charged field of love and meaning; here and there it reaches a notable intensity: but it is ever unobtrusive, hidden, inviting us to join. And join we must if we are to perceive it, for our perceiving is through our loving.[17]

To invoke the Spirit is to listen for the music of a new harmony, and to contribute to the polyphony of the great human choir. It means participating in the movement of an ultimate love, so to be open to reaches of our co-humanity that have now become possibilities . . . and necessities.

The Deconstruction of the Contemporary World

The physical and biological world is the objective polarity in our awareness. It too offers evidence 'crying need' and 'holy space'. Characterising this crying need in the environmental world is the awareness of having entered into a new age of scientific knowledge and ecological awareness with a profoundly disturbed, if not mutilated, con-

---

16. R.E, Whitson, *The Coming Convergence of World Religions* (New York: Newman, 1971), 17–18.
17. Lonergan, *Method*, 190.

sciousness. The peculiar human feeling of today is one of alienation, both from the reality of the materialist culture we have produced, and more profoundly, from the world of nature out of which we arose. We are profoundly out of joint with the world we have made, yet feel exiled from the earth from which we have come. There is nothing new in the lament that so much of modern science serves huge military systems. The novel absurdity is that the generalised ecological awareness emerging today is itself becoming the battleground where the well-meaning clash with minds affected by the spent ideologies of the last two centuries, without the realisation that something quite new is being demanded.

Despite the dark side of the what history has called the Enlightenment, our culture now has glimmerings of another or 'second enlightenment'. First, there is a more holistic emphasis in the scientific imagination itself, as step by step, it introduces us into that unimaginably vast, intricate and interwoven process of the universe itself. This, in turn, underpins a new ecological awareness and responsibility with a sense of the interdependence of all living things. Each in its own way envisages a renewal of the face of the earth in which we can be converted, in the most literal sense, to a lost humility—from the Latin, *humus*, literally, 'soil', 'earth', "dirt". For the earth as we now know it has been defaced, on the one hand, by a science methodologically excluding its humanity; and, on the other, by a disenchanted humanity alienated from its earthing in the biological community of the planet.

In the particularity of this crying need, a new space opens in which to invoke the Spirit. The older philosophical-theological tradition had to be content with 'nature' awaiting its transformation in 'grace'. Such venerable notions will always need retrieval, but only in a history apprehended as a phenomenon in the vast generative process that reaches back billions of years to bring forth the interconnected, and now threatened, web of life on this planet. The historical moment for humanity, the geological era of life's emergence, is now part of a story that has to be told in terms of a span of thousands of millions of light years. It posits dimensions of space that includes uncountable trillions of stars in the midst of which our galaxy is one among millions, a mere hundred thousand light years across, our sun a minor radiance, and our earth an infinitesimal tiny planet in the vastness of it all.[18] The emergence of life on this planet turns on a point of wonder–the 13.8 billion year course of the formation of the universe itself when cosmic reality initially bloomed into the particularities of force and structure and elemental combinations that eventually brought us forth.[19]

To Spirit-invoking theology, this overwhelming vision offers its own holy space. It is a clearing formed at the limits of our new knowledge of cosmic expanse and evolutionary time. Christian hope must live, as always, from its receptivity to the ultimate dynamism of God's self-communication to creation. Yet today such hope must be actualised as a spiritual energy within a cosmic field of the gravitational bond uniting all the galaxies, of electromagnetic forces binding molecules into increasingly complex forms, of genetic codes connecting all the generations of living things in the one great tree of life. It remains that the indelible historical marker of the Spirit's activity is the incarnation, death and resurrection of Christ. The divine mystery is irrevocably 'en-worlded' in the cosmos. Through all the measureless dimensions of time and space, the Spirit acts so that the world might become free to receive the Mystery into itself. In this context, Mary represents to Christian faith the beauty of the world blossoming to its maturity through the Spirit's action: let the earth be opened and bud forth the saviour: *aperiatur terra et germinet salvatorem*. It is the singular glory of human existence that it cooperated with the incarnation of the *Logos*, irreversibly now inscribed into the living meaning of what have come to call 'ecology'. The patristic *economia* of the history of salvation is today offered to us as a transcendent *ecologia* in which life is drawn into its ultimate fullness.

The Invocative Space of the Spirit

We have been sketching two interrelated realities, the reality of the self, and the reality of the cosmos in which it is embodied: both of

---

18. A good introduction to the dimensions of our now known world is Isaac Asimov, *Exploring the Earth and the Cosmos* (Harmondsworth: Penguin, 1983).
19. See *Portraits of Creation. Biblical and Scientific Perspectives on the World's Formation*, edited by Howard J Van Till (Grand Rapids, Michigan: Eerdmans, 1990).

these are undergoing radical changes in our apprehension.[20] Both invite us to a new kind of 'holy space', as we feel the 'crying need' for a new inclusive relationship in which the hitherto unnoticed or ignored must now be appreciated as essential to the whole.

How, more specifically, is the Spirit offered to such a 'holy space', in such situations of 'crying need'? First of all, let us note how the biblical symbol of the Spirit breaks the symmetry of any image depicting the reality of God as an enclosed, self-absorbed relatedness, purely in terms of Father and Son. In contrast, the symbol of the Spirit evokes a kind of space within the Godhead to express a dimension of divine communion in which the Father and Son are united in intersubjective communication—in contrast to an undifferentiated, quasi-symbiotic unity. In this sense, the Spirit is always deconstructing the imagination of faith in the interests of a greater sense of the mystery of unity in difference. The Spirit is the giver of a larger communion, so that the open circle of love is a space allowing for the genuinely other—the otherness intrinsic to the trinitarian communion and in God's relationship to creation.

In this regard, the Holy Spirit is the Spirit of otherness in at least four ways.[21] First, and most obviously, the Spirit is given to overcome fixation in the past. To adore the Spirit can never mean establishing our security by privileging the past as the paradigmatic golden age. The 'Lord and giver of life' promises more than repetition of what has been. By breaking the binding power of the past, the Spirit opens the gracious possibilities of the future. But there can be no return to an untroubled existence as if there were no Spirit. If Peter had promised, in the words of Joel, that with the outpouring of the Spirit, the children would prophesy, and the young see visions and the old dream dreams (Acts 2: 1719), he himself would be uncomfortably led to the house of the pagan Cornelius (Acts 11). Moreover, the Spirit surprises the early community with the unsettling gift of the former persecutor, Paul (Acts 9:13ff). The Spirit-Paraclete is the advantage the comes through the departure of the earthly Jesus (Jn 16:7), leading to a knowledge of things that before could not previously be borne (Jn

---

20. The Aristotelian and Thomistic, *anima est quodammodo omnia*, 'the human soul is in some way all things', takes on a new meaning: the *quodammodo* has been dramatically extended!
21. C. Duquoc, *Dieu différent. Essai sur la symbolique trinitaire* (Paris: Cerf, 1977), 105–111.

16:12f). Paul teaches that the Spirit intercedes that we should pray as we ought, in hope for what is radically invisible and unimaginable within our world. All this is to suggest the how the gift of the Spirit works to open the religious imagination to the radically and imaginably new.

The 'holy space' implies a new experience of our own selfhood within an unimaginably mysterious universe. The visions and dreams that we most need must be expressed in new forms of global solidarity, and in fresh forms of cosmic identity and celebration. It would be a terrible judgment on contemporary Christian imagination if the New Age Spiritualities were perceived to be offering more in terms of prophecy, vision and dream that our theology. The one whom we invoke is the Spirit of a transformed humanity, provoking a blossoming of that imagination which Wallace Stevens termed, 'the irrepressible revolutionist'.

Second, the presence of the Spirit counters the pathologies of both legalism and irresponsibility, by inspiring genuine liberty (2 Cor 3:17). Whilst the gift of the Spirit results in a joyous expansion of the human spirit, this is far from licentious self-indulgence. Genuine liberty is manifest in unreserved self-giving and self-sacrifice (Gal 5:16–25). Such a liberty breaks out of the perverse security of legalism yet accepts the social necessity of law for a responsible social existence (I Cor 8:8ff; 10:23ff; 14:26–33). It lets God be God, unrestrained by the idolatry of legalism or the demonic excesses of licentiousness. Once more the symbol of the Spirit creates a space for Christian liberty between the alternatives of an idolisation of law, and of the demonisation of liberty. In modern categories, the Spirit leads beyond the totalitarian oppression of the collective, beyond the isolated self-absorption of the capitalist consumer, into a new form of community and global solidarity. A new human integrity is manifested in a truly relational selfhood. That sense of self offers new capacities to imagine ourselves creatively as celebrants of the wholeness of our co-human and cosmic belonging.

Third, while the Spirit is associated with unity, it is not the unity of some form of undifferentiated infantile symbiosis. In that respect, the 'unity of the Holy Spirit' is not uniformity, for the Spirit stands for, and inspires, a unity in difference, in a community of distinct persons (1 Cor 12:12–30). It allows communication in the different languages of Pentecost (Acts 2:5–12). It leads into a communion which both manifests and depends on a variety of gifts for the achievement of the common good (1 Cor 12:7). The coming of the Spirit forms the Body of Christ with its different members. It abolishes differences in race, sex, religion, and social status only inasmuch such differences cause unredeemed isolation and aggression, but not in their potential as gifts in the one body of believers. In short, the Spirit is the symbol of the gift to be found in the genuinely other. As such it is far from an oppressive uniformity, for the Spirit is invoked as the space in which true unity in difference can be achieved. The Spirit thus moves us to occupy a new space. It brings a new sense of personhood that is inclusive of feminine in a new, less androcentric way. It is as space of meeting for all journeys of other faiths in dialogue, reconciliation and the sharing of ultimate hope. It opens out with a new awareness of the whole living world in a less anthropocentric manner. The Spirit can thus be invoked into the spaces that are calling for all such kinds of new solidarity and relatedness.

Fourth, the symbol of the Spirit counters the pathology of a false spirituality. To a disincarnate spiritual realm of religious individualism it opposes the reality of history, and the living witness of tradition. Above all, it links genuine faith to the dangerous memory of the crucified Jesus: genuine spirituality is not a socially irresponsible religiosity, but a matter of being conformed to the self-sacrificing love of Christ Jesus. Without conformity to Christ, there can be no experience of the Spirit (Rom 8:11; Jn 14:26; 1 Jn 2:22–25). The Spirit comes as the space which allows history to occur, with its fidelity to the past and openness to the future. As the Spirit of Christ, this Spirit overcomes false self-centred spirituality by leading to self-dispossession and self-giving in conformity to the Crucified. It means awakening to the plight of the world's poor in a commitment to a new solidarity in justice and peace and a more compassionate participation in the passion of Christ. Similarly, the Spirit leads into solidarity with the earth itself through a recovery of true humility. Here we must follow the way of incarnation to express in a new context a basic, sacramental earthliness. In such a re-appropriation of Christian existence, the Spirit comes to open our horizons to the Cosmic Christ, in whom, through whom and for whom all things are made, and in whom all creation finds its true form, consistency and coherence.

To sum up, invocation of the Spirit must now occur in the empty spaces of our particular situation. The contemporary context is notably formed by those crises and developments which have affected the very experience of human selfhood on the one hand, and by our vision of the earth, the cosmos and the universe, on the other. The inspired documents of our origins speak of the Spirit as the power of the new, as the inspiration to freedom, as the space of differentiated community, and of more radical conformity to Christ. To that degree our present situation is summoned to welcome the Spirit in order to renew ourselves and, indeed, the face of the earth:

Lava quod est sordidum,
riga quod est aridum,
sana quod est saucium.

Monastique

*How can one of living flesh
not sense that most human joy,
body alive to body's beauty?
Enjoyed, enfleshed, secure delights
Gently eager for the coming nights.
Yet stark in hope, there is a stranger,
this poor monk sleeps alone,
with God alone to say, Goodnight,
and him alone to greet in morning light,
and him alone to hear the groan
should the dark be less than friendly.
He stirs to murmur:
Gently now, my lovely ones,
Waste not your pity here:
I lie stretched cowled between
Vigil and sleep's half-dream,
divining answers about that end
when you too will need a friend;
and you too must sleep alone
to wake to no familiar form.*

Transfiguration

*After the hill-climb,
that exhausted form, that man,
transformed, they said:
meaning broke out --
life just could not abide
the usual limits --
as long seasons hurried
to instant blossoming,
when groping histories surged
into this moment
filled with the future
that could not wait . . .
Eventually, taking their time,
each pulled himself together;
and came down --
to deal with a demented boy.*

Index of Names

A
Aquinas, Thomas, xiii, 5, 6, 24, 25, 51, 58, 59, 78, 88, 121, 127, 128, 129, 131, 134, 135, 136, 141, 149, 190, 210.
Aristotle, 7.
Augustine, 9, 56, 98, 99, 133, 136.

B
Badcock, Gary D, 122, 124.
Badiou, Alain, 28.
Bakken, Peter, 44.
Barbour, Ian, 3, 126.
Barraud, Vincent, 12, 35, 154, 190, 199.
Barrett, William, 253.
Bauckham, Richard, 115.
Berry, Thomas, 138, 228.
Berryman, Philip, 82.
Bevans, Stephen, 82.
Boeve, Lieven, 76.
Bonaventure, Saint, 56, 134.
Bouma-Prediger, Steven, 44.
Bourke, David, 53, 161.
Braithwaite, David, 178.
Brassier, Ray, 28.
Brown, JR, 12.
Bruteau, Beatrice, 138.
Burrell, David, 75, 81, 141.
Byrne, Brendan, xix, 27.

C
Carlson, Thomas A, 35, 154, 190, 199.
Celan, Paul, 125.
Chauvet, Louis-Marie, 11.
Clarke, W Norris, 104.
Clooney, Francis, X, 60, 142.
Coffey, David, 247.
Colledge, Edmund, 59.
Coloe, Mary, L, 15, 165.
Coste, René, 216.
Crossan, Dominic, 18, 27, 45.
Crowe, Frederick, 168.

D
Danaher, William, J, 166.
Dasgupta, Surendranath, 255.
Davies, PCW, 12.
de Chardin, Teilhard, 12, 13, 134.
Derrida, Jacques, 248, 251.
Donceel, J, 56.
Doran, Robert, M, 128, 168.
Dulles, Avery, 56.
Dunn, James, 17.
Duquoc, C, 262.
Durpuis, Jacques, 82, 206.
Durrwell, F-X, 18, 19.

E

Eckhart, Meister, 58, 59.
Edwards, Denis, 247.
Eliade, Mircea, 2243, 255.
Ernst, C, 222.

F

Farley, Edward, 189.
Fessio, Joseph, 54, 201.

G

Gaburro, Sergio, 32.
Gascoigne, Robert, xviii.
Gieben, Servus, 133.
Girard, René, 216, 242.
Godzieba, Anthony J, 11.
Griffith, Bede, 127.
Grosseteste, Robert, 133.

H

Harris, Elizabeth, 146.
Hart, David, B, 115, 201,
Hart, Kevin, xiv, 36, 37, 62, 144, 145, 248.
Haught, John F, 158.
Heidegger, Martin, 57, 58, 61, 154, 190, 199, 251.
Helms, Randel, 227, 230, 231,.
Hill, Edmund, 9.
Hill, William J, 141.
Horner, Robyn, 12, 35, 154, 190, 199.
Hunt, Anne, 51, 59, 137.
Hurtado, Larry W, 27, 90, 115, 143.

J

Janicaud, Dominique, 30.
Jeanrond, Werner, 87.
Jenkins, Philip, 80.

John Paul II, Pope, 11, 202, 209, 257.
Johnstone, Brian V, 20.

K

Kehl, Medard, 36.
Kelly, Anthony J, xi, xii, xvi, xviii, 4, 10, 17, 46, 78, 124, 128, 146, 165, 166, 178, 188, 200, 206, 210, 214.
Koning, Robin, 178.
Kosky, Jeffrey L, 29, 154, 190, 199.
Kruger, Karl-H, 6.
Kühn, Rolf, 11.

L

Lacoste, Jean-Yves, 62, 85, 179, 181, 188.
Lafont, G, 121, 125.
Levinas, Emmanuel, 42.
Löhrer, Dom Magnus, xv.
Lonergan, Bernard, xiii, xix, 45, 52, 53, 55, 56, 58, 143, 158, 165, 166, 168, 178, 182, 192, 193, 243, 259.
Lyons, Irenaeus of, 8.

M

Mackey, James, P, 12.
Macquarrie, John, 4, 127.
Maculloch, Diarmaid, 179.
Marcus, John T, 254, 255.
Marion, Jean-Luc, xiv, 11, 12, 29, 30, 31, 32, 33, 35, 37, 38, 43, 44, 44, 154, 155, 156, 181, 188, 190, 191, 192, 198, 199, 200, 202, 203.
Maximus, the Confessor, 2, 12.
McCambley, C, 160.
McGinn, Bernard, 59.
McGuckin, John, 208.
Moloney, Francis, F, xix, 4, 6, 118, 165, 166, 210, 213.
Morse, Christopher, 148.

N

Neuner, J, 206.
Newman, John Henry, xix, 23.
Nicolas, Jean-Hervé, 131.
Nietzsche, Frederich, 50, 51, 174, 252.
Nyssa, Gregory of, 134, 160.

O

O'Leary, Joseph, 161.
O'Shaughnessy, Arthur, 81.
O'Shea, Kevin, xv.
Ogilvie, Matthew, 166.
Ong, Walter J, 13.
Origen, 41, 56.
Ormerod, Neil, xviii, 178, 192.
Osborne, Kenan, 20.

P

Paul VI, Pope, xv, 208.
Paul, Saint, 19, 20, 25, 26, 27, 28, 37, 43, 44, 45, 102, 106, 107, 116, 117, 144, 145, 152, 157, 190, 197, 203, 207, 211, 217, 249, 250, 252, 263.
Peacocke, Arthur, 3.
Pelikan, Jaroslav, 179.
Percy, Ealker, 253, 257.
Perkins, Pheme, 17.
Phan, Peter, 228, 235.
Pitstick, Alyssa H, 21.
Price, Richard M, 205.
Prusak, Bernard G, 30.
Purcell, Brendan, 89.

R

Rahner, Karl, xviii, xix, 6, 19, 53, 157, 161, 197, 198, 222.
Ratzinger, Joseph, xvii.
Riches, John, 54, 201.
Robinette, Brian D, 33, 192.

Romano, Claude, xiv, xviii, 33, 34, 35.
Rousselot, Pierre, 56.

S

Scheler, Max, 186, 187.
Schroeder, Roger, 82.
Secomb, Meredith, xviii.
Sesboüé, Bernard, 209.
Sheldon, Michael, 42.
Sheldrake, Rupert, 4, 127.
Sittler, Joseph, 44.
Smith, Timothy L, 136.
Smyth, Kevin, 19, 157, 198.
Steinbock, Anthony J, 186, 187, 188, 189.
Steiner, George, 182, 183, 185, 201, 202, 210.
Stewart, Robert B, 18, 45.
Still, Carl, N, 137.
Swimme, Brian, 228.

T

Tallis, Richard, 2.
Tavard, George, 207.
Thompson, William M, 76, 80, 81.
Thornhill, John, 247.
Tolkien, JRR, 225, 226, 227, 230, 231, 232, 233, 235, 237, 238, 239, 240, 242, 243. .
Torrance, TF, 121, 125.
Torrell, Jean-Pierre, 136.
Tracy, David, 181, 183, 184, 193.

U

Untermeyer, Louis, 81.

V

Vale, Carol Jean, 134.
van Tongeren, P, 30, 154.

Vanhoozer, Kevin, J, 9.
Voegelin, Eric, 1, 25, 26, 27, 28, 29.
von Balthasar, Hans Ur, 21, 35, 36, 37, 41, 54, 56, 58, 141, 142, 181, 201.

W
Ward, Graham, 161.
Whitson, RE, 259.

Wimch, Peter, 40.
Wittgenstein, L, 40.
Wright, NT, 18, 27, 45.

Y
Yates, John C, 126.

Index of Biblical References

Genesis

1–3	86
1:26–27	89
2:22	220
2:23	201
2:24	40
3:20	211, 220
4:1–16	211
28:12	72
28:16–17	72
33:19	71
48:22	71

Exodus

3:14	159

Leviticus

18–20	55

Deuteronomy

5:7	55
6:4	101

Joshua

24:32	71

1 Kings

11:17	55
16–18	55
19:12	160

Psalm

33:10	145
36:9	101
42	50
139:13–16	211

Wisdom/Sirach

7:22–25	86
16:26	86
17:19	86
43:27–30	112

Isaiah

29:14	145

Jeremiah

1:4–5	211
31:33	219

Ezekiel

36:25–28	219

Matthew

1:23	214
3:16–18	117
5:48	214
6:24	55
13:47–50	147
13:51–52	147
17:1–8	117
19:6	202
22:32	217
22:34–40	101
25	147
25:31–46	147

Mark

1:9–11	117
4:26–29	147
9:2–8	117
9:7	212, 214
9:23	109
10:8	202
10:27	109
12:29	101
12:31	101
16:8	19
28:19	116

Luke

1:28	215
1:30	215
1:32–35	117
1:35	218
1:37	200, 219
1:38	205, 212, 219
1:40	218
1:45	200, 220
1:48–53	201
1:48	217
1:49	212
1:51–52	216
2:16	214
2:19	200
2:35	212, 215
2:51	200
3:21–23	117
6:27–31	79
6:36	110, 214
6:37–42	147
8:19–21	147
9:28–36	117
9:47	43
10:21–22	117
10:25–28	101
11:17	43
16:1–4	79
22:42–43	152
23:34	215
24:13–35	36
24:44	226
24:50–53	152

John

1:1–3	4
1:1–2	120
1:1	120, 127, 150, 166
1:3–5	5
1:3–4	5, 39, 166

1:3a	5	4:20	71, 98
1:3b–4	6	4:21–26	72
1:4	6	4:21	72, 107
1:5	73	4:22	147, 151
1:10–11	5	4:22a	72
1:11	73, 95	4:22b	72
1:13	149, 218	4:23–24	123, 147
1:14–18	123	4:23	74, 75, 81, 101, 106, 174
1:14	1, 2, 118, 120, 125, 166		
		4:23a	73
1:14b	5	4:23b	73
1:18	100, 101, 106, 120, 148, 149, 150, 151, 234	4:24	73, 101
		4:34	106
		4:42	70
1:23	151	5	169
1:32–34	117	5:17	169, 170
1:38	3, 50, 71, 167	5:18	169
1:41	151	5:18–21	106
1:45	151	5:19	120, 170
1:47–51	167	5:20	170
1:48	43	5:21	120, 170
1:51	72, 73, 76, 123, 125, 148	5:22	120, 170
		5:23	170
2:4–5	171	5:27	120, 167, 170
3:2	151	5:26–28	106
3:8	218	5:26	39, 120, 170
3:9–11	151	5:27	167
3:16	70, 73, 106, 118, 151, 173, 212	5:30	106, 120, 170
		5:36	170
3:32–35	123	3:37b	151
3:34	73	5:43	120
3:35	106	6:35	167
4	79	5:36–37	106
4:7	70	5:36	120
4:9	70, 71, 72	5:37	120
4:11–12	74	6:32–33	106
4:11	71	6:37–40	106
4:12	71	6:44–45	106
4:14	70	6:45	151
4:15	71	6:51	41
4:19	71	6:56	41

6:57	106	15:26	73, 118, 119
6:65	106	16:7	14, 76, 82, 151, 262
7:16–18	123	16:11	215
7:16	106	16:12f	250, 263
7:24	151	16:12–16	119
7:39	123	16:12–15	14
8:12	39, 167	16:12–14	101, 169
8:26–29	123	16:12	31, 76, 82, 122
8:32	73	16:13	119, 122, 123, 132, 147
8:42–43	123		
9:13–39	167	16:13a	123
10:10	171	16:13c	122
10:11	167	16:14	123
10:29	121	16:15	122
10:30	121	16:16–19	123
10:37	121	16:18b	171
11:25	45, 148, 217	16:20	171
11:52	216	16:22	172
12:32	70, 76, 81, 216	16:27	172
12:47–50	123	16:29	169
13:1–11	167	16:33	172
13:3	123	17	118, 120, 148
13:34–35	149	17:3	149
13:34	125, 166	17:4–5	148
14:2–3	149	17:6	172
14:6	73, 123, 148, 151	17:11a	149
14:7	151	17:11b	149
14:8	39	17:12	151
14:9–11	151	17:20–24	172
14:10	39, 123	17:20–21	44, 64, 149
14:16	123	17:21–23	132
14:18	122	17:21–22	64
14:23	123	17:21	39, 118
14:26	119, 264	17:22	102, 116, 121
14:28	118	17:24a	149
14:30	215	17:26b	149
15:1	167	19:24	151
15:4	41	19:25–27	213
15:6	41	19:26–27	199
15:12	149	19:28	70
15:17	149	19:30	151, 220

19:34–35	151	17:28	86, 87
19:34	220	19:23–41	207
19:36	151	19:34	207
19:37	43	20:35	19
19:38	216	25:19	19
20:17	69, 149		
20:19–23	79		
20:21	76, 82	**Romans**	
20:22	220		
20:26	215	6:3–11	44
20:27–29	44	8	40, 117
20:27	213	8:11	264
20:29–31	148	8:15f	107
20:27	215	8:18–27	160, 250
20:28	118	8:22	217
20:31	172	8:26	218
21:25	23, 31	8:28–30	211
		8:31–39	111
		8:24–25	146
		11:33–34	79
Acts		11:33	145
		15:30	116
1:3	144		
1:4–8	116		
1:6	144	**1 Corinthians**	
1:7	144, 186		
1:8	144	1:18–25	156
1:9–11	152	1:19	145
1:14	213	1:20	156
2:5–12	263	1:21	145
2:17–19	262	1:22	146
2:23	116	1:23	20
2:28	116	1:22–25	79
9:13ff	262	1:24	108
9:17	116	1:25	111, 146
10:1–48	75, 81	2:8–13	249
10:34	75, 81	2:9–13	56
10:38	116	2:9–10	56
11	262	2:9	145
11:15–17	116	2:10	249
17:18	20	2:13	145
17:27	102		

8:8ff	263
10:23ff	263
12	117
12:4–8	116
12:7	264
12:12–30	263
12:12	38
12:13	38
12:27	9, 38
13:4–8	217
13:7–8	192
13:8	217
13:12	43, 203
14:26–33	263
15:12–15	217
15:17	19, 45
15:19	26
15:28	87, 127, 200, 206, 222
15:35	145
15:42–58	217
15:42–44	145
16:22	43, 203

2 Corinthians

1:18–20	205
1:20	44
3:17	263
3:18	194
4:6	43, 200, 203
5:17	34, 154, 200, 222
13:14	116

Galatians

3	117
3:11–14	116
4:4	212
4:46	116
5:16	263

Ephesians

1	117
1:3–4	211
1:22–23	38
2:5–6	40
2:14–22	40
3:14–16	106
3:18	83
3:19	83
3:20–21	108
3:20	83, 145
4:6	87, `30
4:25	40, 202
5:25–27	221
5:26	202
5:27	202
5:30	40

Philippians

3:3–6	116
3:4–6	146
3:7–11	146
3:7	146
3:8	146
3:13–14	152

Colossians

1:3–8	116
1:11–14	107
1:11	108
1:15–20	3
1:15–18	44, 45
1:15	64, 203
1:16	65, 90
1:26–27	157, 197
2:9	1

1 Thessalonians

1:1–5	116

2 Thessalonians

2:13	116

1 Timothy

2:3–4	79
2:4	76, 82
6:16	200

2 Timothy

1:9	211

Hebrews

12:1	221

1 Peter

1:8	185

1 John

1:1–3	44
1:1	39, 172
1:2–3	40
1:2	20
1:7	173
1:9	173
1:18	185
2:2	173
2:3	173
2:9	173
2:11	173
2:12–14	173
2:17	173
2:22–25	264
2:23–24	173
2:24	41
2:27	56
3:11	172
3:2	3, 34, 169, 185, 200, 257
3:9	149
3:24	41
3:16	148
3:18	148
4:1–2	148
4:7f	160
4:7–12	139
4:7	149, 170, 210
4:7b	150
4:8	209, 210
4:9	173
4:10	211
4:12	100, 143, 149, 234
4:16	41, 149, 209
4:18	213
4:19	213
4:20	148, 173
5:2–3	170
5:4–5	173
5:8	220
5:11–12	173
5:21	148

2 John

1:10–11	173

3 John

1:5–8	173

Revelation

1:14	43
1:18	43
2:2	43
2:9	43
2:12	43
2:18	43
2:19	43
3:1	43
3:8	43
3:15	43
6:9–11	221
8:3–4	221
12:1–2	221
21:1–3	223
22:20	43, 203

CPSIA information can be obtained
at www.ICGtesting.com
Printed in the USA
FFHW020203080519
52351091-57728FF